THE CELLARS OF MARCELCAVE

Lieutenant Bernard J. Gallagher, M.D.

THE CELLARS OF MARCELCAVE
A YANK DOCTOR IN THE BEF

Christopher J. Gallagher, M.D.

Edited by Mary E. Malloy

Adapted from *A Yank in the B. E. F.*
Battalion Medical Officer in the Great War

Bernard J. Gallagher, M.D.

Edited by William B. Gallagher, M.D.
Margaret Spoo

 BURD STREET PRESS

This Burd Street Press publication
was printed by
Beidel Printing House, Inc.
63 West Burd Street
Shippensburg, PA 17257-0152 USA

In respect for the scholarship contained herein, the acid-free paper used in
this book meets the guidelines for permanence and durability of the Committee
on Production Guidelines for Book Longevity of the Council on Library Resources.

For a complete list of available publications
please write
Burd Street Press
Division of White Mane Publishing Company, Inc.
P.O. Box 152
Shippensburg, PA 17257-0152 USA

Library of Congress Cataloging-in-Publication Data

Gallagher, Bernard J., d. 1962.
    The cellars of Marcelcave : a Yank doctor in the BEF / [revised
by] Christopher J. Gallagher : edited by Mary E. Malloy : adapted
from A Yank in the B.E.F., battalion medical officer in the Great
War, Bernard J. Gallagher, edited by William B. Gallagher, Margaret
Spoo.
        p.   cm.
    The memoir of Bernard J. Gallagher, revised and edited by his
grandson, Christopher J. Gallagher.
    Excerpts have appeared in the June 1965 ed. of American heritage,
under the title: A Yank in the BEF: excerpts appeared also in:
1914–1918 : voices & images of the Great War / Lyn Macdonald. 1988.
    ISBN 1-57249-110-8 (alk. paper)
    1. Gallagher, Bernard J., d. 1962. 2. World War, 1939–1945-
-Medical care--Great Britain. 3. World War, 1939–1945--Personal
narratives, American. 4. Great Britain. Army--Biography.
5. Physicians--United States--Biography. 6. Marcelcave (France)-
-History. I. Gallagher, Christopher J. II. Malloy, Mary E.
III. Title.
D629.G7G35   1998
940.54'7541--dc21   98-2974
                                                                 CIP

DEDICATION

This book is dedicated to

a man who made a decision on a

spring night, long ago,

and lit a candle for

light.

CONTENTS

PROLOGUE

Ashes to Ashes

"Chris! Quit hanging your sister's Barbie doll!"

Four-year-old Chris had fashioned a noose from the drawstring of his hood, and was hanging a Barbie doll by the neck, making choking sounds. Chris' mother was trying to quiet him down—to get him to pay attention to the funeral service.

"This is your own Grandpa's funeral, young man. Now act your age!"

He stopped choking the Barbie for a minute, waited for his mom to look the other way, then started dangling the doll on the end of the string again.

"Aghl, awk, goa-oa-aak."

"Mom. Mo-oo-om! He's doing it again!" Kathy complained. She had the good fortune to own the Barbie doll, the bad fortune to have Chris for a brother.

"Ssshhh! All of you!" Chris' mom swatted at Chris, his aggrieved sister Kathy, then yanked the Barbie doll for good measure. It was still attached to the drawstring going around Chris' hood.

"MOM! Awk, ga-aak!" it was Chris' turn to choke.

The priest looked up from the funeral service and threw a severe stare in the direction of the mother strangling her child.

"Let us pray."

Around the cemetery, stubbled cornfields spread for miles and miles on the flat Minnesota prairie. Long since harvested, the corn stalk stumps lent a somber air to Ben Gallagher's funeral. Seventy-two years old, "Dr. Ben" lay in a mahogany casket, suspended above a steel burial vault by green straps. On one side of the casket stood his family and the priest. On the other, eight men in American Legion hats holding rifles—an honor guard. Funeral workers stood at a respectful distance, they would winch the casket into the vault after the family had left. And a big family it was.

The wind was blowing from the north. Ben Gallagher's five children, and most of his twenty grandchildren, huddled together near his grave. Most heads were bare, but the youngest kids had on Minnesota Viking or Green Bay Packer ski hats. Grandson Chris had settled down, but the other grandchildren were adding a certain amount of chaos to the proceedings. The adults did their best to remain above it all.

Peg Spoo, Ben Gallagher's oldest child, had temporary control of her three charges. She stood next to her brother Bill.

"Ashes to ashes, dust to dust," the priest said, "I am the resurrection and the light."

Leaves stirred and swirled in the wind. Kids started complaining about the cold.

Peg turned to Bill and whispered, "I wonder what Dad would make of all this?"

"He'd say, 'Get inside where it's warm.' That's what Dad would make of this."

On Bill's other side, his wife, Mary Ellen, was trying to hold their own five children in check. Kim—12 years old, Jo Ellen—10, Eileen—8, Kathy—6, and the Barbie-choking Christopher—4 were wiggling, stamping their feet, pointing at the coffin, and deluging their mom with questions.

"Mom, if Grandpa's asleep, when will he wake up?" Eileen asked, her ears protected by great white earmuffs. They'd told her about death in religion class at St. Thomas More grade school, but she didn't buy the bit about "going to sleep, and waking up on Judgement Day."

"Mom, if everybody dies, does that mean I'm going to die?" Kathy asked, one eye on the casket, the other on her Barbie doll.

"Why did Grandpa die?" Eileen again, she wanted some explanations.

"Are you going to die?" Kathy looked right at her mom now. Mom, die? It just couldn't be.

"I have to go to the bathroom," Chris said.

"They don't have bathrooms in graveyards, Chris," Eileen said, rolling her eyes. Chris said the *dumbest* things sometimes. Couldn't he *ever* hold it?

"Why not?" Chris challenged. They had bathrooms in gas stations, in restaurants. Why not a graveyard? Not everyone in a graveyard was dead. Visitors were alive! And they had to go. And I have to go.

"Ssshh!" Mary Ellen said. The children's questions paused for just a second, then ran around her like water flowing around a rock.

"Mom, do we have to play Yahtzee with our cousins? I hate Yahtzee," Eileen asked, hoping the answer would be 'no.' What is it about the grown-ups? They think you always want to play Yahtzee or Monopoly with your cousins. What a bore!

"Mom, are we sleeping at Grandpa's tonight?" Kathy asked, hand tight around the Barbie. Chris was not to be trusted.

"Quiet, Kathy, the priest is talking," Kim tried to force some decorum upon his youngest sister. He had been an altar boy for years; he ought to know about such things.

"Yeah, it's a sin to talk during church," Jo Ellen jumped in. Though no altar boy, she'd been in Catholic grade school for years and she knew all about sins, both mortal (the really serious ones) and venial (less serious). She was pretty sure that Kathy had just committed a venial sin. That *could* land Kathy in hell, or at least purgatory, depending on whether she got to confession soon.

"This isn't church!" Kathy protested. That Jo Ellen! Always knowing the rules! Well, Kathy knows a few things, too, like Jo Ellen was caught passing *notes* to a *boy*. Maybe Mom would like to hear about *that!*

Mary Ellen started tugging arms and putting her fingers to her lips, "Ssshh!" These kids. THESE KIDS! Couldn't the priest get a move on? I need a good book, a cup of tea, and some QUIET!

"It is too like church," Jo Ellen said, sure of herself. It *was* cold, and she *should* be wearing a hat, but Jo Ellen made do with her little veil. It reminded her of First Communion.

Mary Ellen bent over and looked the two girls right in the eyes. "If you don't quiet down, I'm going to drag you both out into the street and spank you bare-bottom."

Kathy and Jo Ellen's mouths fell open.

"But Mom, I'm 10!" Jo Ellen was mortified. Spanking was for LITTLE KIDS!

"Ssshh!"

"*In nomine patris, et filii, et spiritus sancti*, the priest said while making the sign of the cross. "*Ego te absolvo a peccatis tuis*. The ceremony is now ended. *Dominos vobiscum.*"

"*Et cum spiritu tuo,*" the Gallagher family responded, especially Kim. He had all the Latin prayers down pat.

"Ready!"

The American Legion honor guard stiffened, and most of the grandchildren jumped at the command.

"Aim!"

The rifles pointed up to the sky. Even to the youngest child, the angle of the rifles looked pretty irregular, as if they were all pointing at different ducks during a hunt.

"Fire!"

The kids put fingers in their ears, expecting a thunderous, instantaneous volley. Instead they got—pop-pop pop pop-pop-pop and a click, click, click as the last rifle failed to go off.

"Damn!"

The frustrated warrior brought the gun down and was working the chamber of his rifle when the final order was shouted.

"Shoulder ARMS!"

"OK, kids, back to the cars!" Bill held out his hands in a round-'em-up fashion. "Well, Peg, I guess now we can get inside where it's warm."

Bill rustled up the kids, sending some of his own to ride in cousins' cars, and taking some of his nephews and nieces in his car. A last look back at the casket brought a lump to his throat.

Dad was gone. Not that it was unexpected. There had been the stroke, 13 years before, the chronic lung trouble, the heart trouble. Ben Gallagher had lived his three score and ten years, as promised in the Bible, and gotten three more years yet. But now, he was gone.

He'd been a good man, a good doctor, a good dad. His example had pointed the way for Bill to go into medicine. And Dad could spin a yarn, he could. Usually quiet, and given to expressing himself in pithy bits of advice, Ben Gallagher would occasionally let his hair down and tell some great stories. And every once in a while, one of those stories was about the Great War, World War I.

All the children and grandchildren and Ben's widow, Margaret, got into Plymouth station wagons and Ramblers and headed back to Ben's house. Along the way, they passed the emptied cornfields of southern Minnesota, broken only by the occasional farmhouse, silo, or barn. The kids started in with their questions.

"Dad, is Grandpa in heaven?"

"Hey, Dad, do we have to eat the salmon loaf at Grandma's house if we don't like it?"

"Hey, Dad, Kathy took my Barbie and didn't ask me!"

"Mom, it's mine! Dad!"

"Mom!"

"Stop that!" That was *IT!* Bill had enough of that caterwauling.

Bill Gallagher kept his eyes on the road, his fingers clenched on the wheel. Peg sat next to him. Next to Peg sat Mary Ellen. Mary Ellen turned around and faced the children.

"I expect you to be on your best behavior at Grandpa's. I should hate to have to wash any mouths out with soap." The words came out soft, but transfixed the kids. Even cousins froze at the words. Everyone knew that Mary Ellen Gallagher was as good as her word, though no one could recall a time when she actually HAD washed someone's mouth out with soap.

Bill waved a hand in the general direction of the back seat. "That's right, listen to your Mother. Now Kathy, give Eileen her doll, and Chris, you will eat the salmon loaf and you will love it. You got that?"

The back of the station wagon fell silent, for about two minutes, then a low rumble started up again. Mary Ellen turned on the radio and got only static. Turning the knob, she got one farm report, then another, then a disc jockey raving about some new group from Liverpool. She turned the radio off and fished a book out of her purse. As she pulled it out, some tea bags fell out, too. For some reason, Ben Gallagher never had tea in his house, so Mary Ellen always brought along her own.

"Bill, something was gnawing at me a little at the cemetery," Peg said. Mary Ellen had opened an Agatha Christie book and was starting to read.

"What was that?" Bill asked, turning right, going past a sign that said "Welcome to Waseca."

"I was thinking about that journal of Dad's, you know, the journal he wrote after World War I."

Peg, too, had heard her father's stories through the years. Although Ben Gallagher had a black streak in him, a depression that would come and go without warning, he had been a great raconteur. Since Peg was now fully grown and worked as a librarian, she had always wanted to capture those stories of his and catalog them. Maybe get them published, who knows?

The car was going past comfortable one- and two-story homes. Vase-shaped elm trees lined the length of the street. People were raking leaves, burning them, filling the air with that sweet perfume of autumn.

"Oh yeah. Mom had mentioned that." Bill had talked with Peg, on and off, about that pet project of hers—publishing Ben Gallagher's story. But college came along, medical school, World War II, marriage, kids. Where was the time?

There *had* been some talk of a journal, somewhere. Damn! He should have talked with Dad about it. And now it was too late. Maybe Mom knew something.

The station wagon pulled into the driveway of Ben's house. People were walking up to the front door with casserole dishes, cookie jars, cake pans.

"Dad, look! Uncle Mike, Aunt Peri!"

The kids piled out of the car and ran up to the house. Bill and Peg stayed put. Mary Ellen got out, still reading, and walked up to the house, looking down at the book the whole time.

"Did you ever see it, Peg, the journal?" Bill asked, waving through the windshield at an army of nieces and nephews.

"No." Peg waved, too. A couple of the older boys were playing catch with a football.

"Mom swears he wrote one. Never published it or anything."

Bonk! The football bounced off the hood.

"Sorry, Uncle Bill!" A nephew ran past, his hair a flaming orange and face a mass of freckles. Where had that red hair come from? Bill wondered. Most of the Gallagher kids had black or dark brown hair.

"That's OK!" Bill shouted. The wonders of the gene pool, mixing up and recombining. Then poof! A nephew appears with red hair.

"Couldn't get him to talk about it much. No matter how I tried," Bill said. "He'd say stuff like, 'It's too hard to explain,' or 'Unless you were there, you really couldn't understand.'"

"A couple of times I heard him talk to Mom about it, after we'd gone to bed. I'd sneak out to the stairs, poke my head through the banister and listen. He cried sometimes," Peg said.

People kept trooping by the car, occasionally tapping on the window and waving at Bill and Peg.

"Dad cried?" Bill asked, surprised. Dad had been given to long, morose spells, but never to crying spells, that he had seen.

"Oh yes, I heard him cry a long time once. There was something about a cave. I distinctly remember that, a cave. It was hard to hear exactly what he said, because Mom had the radio on, but he said the word 'cave' and he bawled like a baby. It was embarrassing, you know, to hear him cry like that." It *had* been embarrassing, Peg remembered. She had tiptoed back to bed, afraid to let her parents know that she had heard.

They got out of the car and walked toward the light-green, one-story house. The wide front lawn had a huge oak tree. Many of its brown leaves were still hanging on, but the lawn itself was well bedecked with dead leaves. They made a swishing sound as Bill and Peg walked through them. As Bill held open the storm door, he told Peg, "Let's go ask Mom. If there is a journal, she would know where it is." Bill was kicking himself mentally. Why hadn't he taken more time to talk with his dad? He wondered if every child thought this at the death of a parent.

They entered the house. Neighbors packed the kitchen, every inch of every counter was covered with goulash, macaroni and cheese, Rice Krispie treats, corned beef hash, chocolate chip cookies, buttered noodles, pumpkin bread, and salmon loaf. Kids ran everywhere, tugged at their parents' sleeves, fought over toys, yelled, and cried. Grown-ups served dishes, drank beer, smoked cigarettes, cigars, and pipes, and tried to break up fights between the kids.

The newly-widowed Margaret Gallagher sat in a corner, talking with a stream of well-wishers. In the line were colleagues of Ben, neighbors, and former patients. Ben Gallagher had delivered more than one of the people in that line.

Peg walked up to her mom, excusing herself as she broke into the line.

"Mom—Bill and I wanted to talk to you for a minute. Alone, if that is humanly possible in this madhouse." She looked around the house. People were packed like sardines, and cigarette smoke laid down the heaviest fog she'd seen outside of London.

"Sure, Peg." Margaret Gallagher lifted her hand up and waved to get the attention of the people in line. "Excuse me, would you please, for a moment?" She had to raise her voice. Even though most people were speaking in "respectful" tones, the sheer number of voices made for a dull roar.

Everyone nodded and waved their hands in a "go on ahead" gesture. Everyone's hand held a cigarette, a deviled egg, or a triangular, crustless sandwich.

Peg said, "How about downstairs?"

"You don't think the grandkids will be down there, playing hide-and-seek or something?"

Bill shook his head, "No, too many cookies up here. They'll go downstairs later, but only after they're good and full." Already, the dessert trays in the kitchen were emptying fast. No adults were warning their kids "don't spoil your appetite!", so all the kids were going straight for the sweets.

Bill, Peg, and their mother went down the stairs. The basement was finished in plywood, and had plenty of built-in bunk beds for the grandchildren. Sleeping bags, pillows, and toys lay scattered around the floor.

Peg started out, "Mom, how are you holding up?" The funeral and grieving were, after all, for the survivors. Dad was beyond the reach of pain and suffering now. Not so for Mom.

"Oh, not too bad. I mean, your father had been sick for a long time. He was having so much trouble breathing, you remember. Just as well, I guess. He went to sleep, and he just didn't get up. What is it they say, 'Flights of angels whisked him away,' or something like that."

She paused, looking nowhere in particular, her head cocked to the right, a thick shock of gray hair contrasting with her black dress. Beautiful. Beautiful in her September years.

She went on, "And it's not exactly like I'm *alone*. Look at the house. You kids are all here. And your kids. The place is bursting at the seams. And there's enough food up there to feed an army. Did you get a chance to try the salmon loaf yet? I made plenty of that, I know how the grandkids love it."

Bill thought about Chris' comment, the little monster. He'd get Chris to eat that stuff if he had to pinch his nose and shove it down his throat.

"Anyway, Peg, don't worry about me, I'm not alone right now, by any stretch." She sighed, then continued, "But that won't last forever. When the last kid says good-bye and the last casserole dish is returned. I guess that's when I really become a widow."

Widow. The term jolted Peg and Bill both. They'd never thought of their mother as a widow. She was just, Mom. But, that is what you are when your husband dies, you *are* a widow.

"We'll be back to see you, Mom, and L.T.'s right in town here too," Bill said, referring to his brother, L.T., who lived just a mile away. That had to be some comfort to Mom. Especially now that she was a . . . widow.

"Yes, yes. All true, and I appreciate that. But there's no getting around it, kids, I will miss your father. I will miss your father a great deal."

Upstairs, gales of laughter broke out, the timing all wrong. Mom was a widow, a *widow* for God's sake, and people were *laughing* upstairs. Uncle Mike had just cracked a good one and was laughing louder than everyone else. Well, life goes on and all that baloney. Couldn't expect there to be a lot of long faces and subdued tones forever. This was a family of Irish descent, and nearly everyone in it had kissed the Blarney Stone. You could no more stop the Gallaghers from laughing than you could stop the wind at their back.

"Mom," Bill asked, "I don't know if this is a good time, but we were wondering about that journal Dad wrote." Again, he kicked himself. Years, YEARS, he had to talk with Dad about it. But he put it off, put it off. Never again. This was the time to find out about that journal, once and for all.

"The one about the Great War?" Margaret asked, bending down to pick up some of the toys on the floor.

"Yes, is there such a thing, I mean, did he write one? Whenever I asked Dad about it, he pooh-poohed it and said that it was just a few notes, nothing to look at," Bill said. Maybe it had been just a rumor. Maybe there was no story here, after all.

"Did you ever see the journal, Mom?" Peg asked, tiptoeing. Mom had a lot on her mind. This poking around in the past might not be appropriate. It was the very day of Dad's funeral, maybe they should ask about this later.

Margaret had an armful of toys and was looking for someplace to put them. "Well, no, not exactly. Let's see, we got married in 1921, he got back from the war in 1919."

She tossed the toys on a bunk bed. Good a place as any. "He mentioned that he wrote some notes, or added to a diary of his, sometime in 1920, just before he met me. Every now and then he'd scratch down a few pages, but I thought they might just be letters to his old soldier friends." She continued picking up stuff as she talked. "Your father was a great one for writing letters. I recall a few he wrote to me when we were courting." She tossed an armload of dolls onto another bunk bed, then grabbed her skirt and swished it back and forth a few times, a faraway look in her eyes—every inch the moonstruck lover.

Peg and Bill looked at each other, wondering what their father might have written in those "courtship" letters. They hadn't ever really thought of Mom and Dad in that light before.

"Did you every try his footlocker?" Margaret asked. She had climbed off her moonbeam and returned to the basement, and the present.

Bill and Peg looked at their mom.

"His footlocker?" they both said. A footlocker's a pretty big item. How had they not seen his footlocker before?

"Yes, he had a footlocker he brought back from the war. He kept his uniform in there, some mementos, old newspapers, and his medal," she waved her hand dismissively, as if war medals were as common as the toys scattered across the basement floor.

Again, Bill and Peg spoke in unison, "A medal!"

"Oh yes, the distinguished something or other medal. He didn't talk about it much," she was looking at all the sleeping bags now; surely there must be some way to straighten them up.

Bill and Peg were reeling. First, their father is revealed as a kind of Cyrano de Bergerac, writing love letters; then, he is revealed as a hero, complete with medal. All in one minute. This was turning into quite a day of discovery.

"If he has a journal anywhere, it will be in that footlocker," Margaret's hands were on her hips. The sleeping bag situation was hopeless.

"But where would that footlocker be, I mean, how could we have missed it?" Bill asked, looking around. "We've played and hidden all over this house, every nook and cranny, ever since we were kids."

Just then, the furnace started up, with a roar, clicking, and whoosh. Radiators all over the house started pinging and gurgling. Peg, Bill, and Margaret turned toward the furnace room door—a fireproof, metal, black slab, that looked like it guarded the entrance to Dante's Inferno.

"As I recall," their mother said pointing at the door, "you didn't much like hiding in there."

Bill and Peg looked at each other, as if to say, "You're damned right you wouldn't catch us hiding in there. And we don't much like the idea of going in there now, either."

Bill and Peg moved to the door and started to push it open. It was heavy.

"Well, I'm going back upstairs, let me know if you find anything," their mom said, grinning. She had always been able to hide the Christmas presents behind that spooky door. No kid liked going in there, and she suspected that Bill and Peg weren't real keen on going in there now, either.

Bill and Peg watched their mother disappear up the stairs. Bill, a 36-year-old surgeon and Peg, a 38-year-old librarian, would have to go into the furnace room all alone, without their mother. Neither wanted to hesitate, to look "chicken" in front of the other.

The door squealed on its hinges, and the bottom scraped along the cement floor. Bill groped around for a minute then found a dangling chain; pulling it, a 40-watt bare light bulb came on, carving a small island of light in the center of the dark room, and throwing shadows over deep shelving along the wall.

Chess sets, Yahtzee games, and Christmas tree lights came out of the recesses first. Then came musty tarpaulins, boy scout knapsacks, and tents. On the bottommost shelf, under a Mexican blanket, Bill felt something hard, with hinges on the back and a latch on the front.

"Peg, I found something." He slid the footlocker into the small island of light, popped open the latch, and lifted the lid.

Waseca, Minnesota

March 27, 1919

It has been suggested that I write down now, while things are fairly fresh in my memory, some of the events of the past nineteen months which might possibly be of interest to others at some future date when the Great War shall have become a thing of the far distant past. So from memory and from parts of a diary which are at hand I shall attempt to mention at least some of the places I have been and some of the impressions received.

Bernard J. Gallagher

Chapter 1

I WANT YOU

I had seen dead bodies before—in anatomy class as a medical school freshman, in autopsies as a sophomore, even a few during my clinical rotations as a junior. Cancer patients. Heart attack victims. In the emergency ward, I'd gone out to the undertaker's wagon a few times, placing the stethoscope on the still chest, lifting the eyelids to check the unseeing, unblinking eyes, so I could "officially" pronounce the person dead. So I had seen a few dead bodies. But I never talked to one before.

"Ben! Ben!" Abe Haskell, my classmate, tapped me on the shoulder. I was sitting in the Minneapolis City Hospital Medical Library. I had on the short white jacket of the third-year medical student, as did Abe, and my pockets bulged with a reflex hammer, stethoscope, note cards, a 1914 edition of a manual of medical therapeutics, and my lunch. A fountain pen had leaked in my front pocket, leaving a dark blue stain. Abe's pockets were stuffed, too, but his pen hadn't leaked.

"Sssh!" the librarian hissed, waving her hands at us.

"Sorry!" Abe whispered. He went on in a low tone. "Ben, you've got to come down to the emergency ward." At that time, Abe and I were on our surgical rotation, and were on the team that handled all the accidents and injuries that came into Minneapolis City Hospital. "Some kid put a 22 in his *mouth*, and pulled the trigger."

"He's still alive?" I asked, putting away my books and heading out of the library with Abe.

"Yes, he doesn't even look too bad, considering, but Hansen is hovering around him."

Peter Hansen was our resident, he had completed medical school, but not yet completed his surgical training. He was above us in the medical hierarchy, so he served as our teacher.

We got to the emergency ward as quickly as we could. Sitting on a gurney was an 18-year-old kid with dark black curly hair. His mouth looked swollen, and a small trickle of blood came down his lips. Dr. Hansen was standing in the room, looking at a skull film. Small pieces of metal appeared as shiny white spots on the X-ray. The bullet had broken into a hundred pieces and scattered around in the center of the young man's skull.

"Ben, Abe," he nodded to us. "This is Mr. Giancomo. You can see what we're dealing with here," he waved at the X-ray. "Ben, I want you to stay here, keep Mr. Giancomo's head up, make sure he's breathing OK. Abe, you come with me upstairs, we're going to have to explore this man's mouth, and I want you to scrub in with me. You'll join us later, Ben. I just don't want Mr. Giancomo left alone right now. We'll send for you in just a few minutes."

Hansen and Abe stepped out of the room. Giancomo and I were alone.

"It was a girl," his words came out muffled, sounding more like "Ib wav a gibl."

"Oh, yes. I see." I didn't really want him to talk, or move at all, for that matter. It was important for him to stay still. I tried not to let my inexperience show, tried to summon up my best "doctor-like" presence, so when I told him to stay still, he would. If he sensed I was nervous, unsure of myself, he might get agitated and that could lead to trouble. Those bullet fragments could have cut anything and he had to stay calm. "Maybe you should just rest now. There'll be plenty of time after the operation to . . . "

"She left me," coming out more like "Fe weft me."

Then he coughed. A dark clot came out of his mouth, landing right on my jacket, right on the ink stain on my pocket. Bright red blood started pumping out of his mouth, his eyes grew wide and he reached out and grabbed my sleeves.

"Nurse! Nurse! Get Dr. Hansen, get Dr. Hansen in here right away!" I shouted at the top of my lungs.

God Almighty, this man is going to die right in front of me, and I'm supposed to be keeping him alive! I was just supposed to keep him quiet. I shouldn't have let him talk. That was a mistake.

Giancomo stood up, right next to me, blood pouring in a pulsatile jet from his mouth. I tried to lay him back on the cot, but he pushed me back into an instrument cabinet, nearly breaking the glass door. He sucked in, trying to breathe, and there was a sound like "Thuck!" He wasn't getting any air, he'd just breathed in his own blood. His chest sucked in, and abdomen protruded out; his diaphragm was trying to pull in air, but not getting any.

Three nurses came running into the room, two orderlies right behind. With one arm I pushed Giancomo back to the gurney, with the other I pointed to the first orderly.

"You, run upstairs and get Hansen, tell him we need to do a tracheotomy. Go!"

Giancomo's lips and eyelids were getting blue, he thrashed at the nurses, the orderly, me. The blood coming out of his mouth was dark now. He was going to be dead in a minute and it would be my fault. I had to cut a hole in his trachea so he could breathe, but his neck was swelling, obscuring all the normal anatomical landmarks. And there was no time, no time at all. Where was Hansen?

Giancomo was slowing down now, waving his arms less.

"Scalpel! Anything!" My voice was high-pitched, panicky.

A nurse handed me a blade, I aimed in the middle part of his neck, low down, where the trachea should be. The blade went in. If I hit the trachea, there'd be a rush of air.

Nothing. I went deeper. Giancomo didn't move. His face was black. Hansen came in the room.

"Damn! Damn! Damn! Let me take a look, Ben." Hansen's face was grim, his lips stretched taut and thin.

He grabbed Giancomo's neck, moved it back and forth.

"The trachea's deviated, pushed off to the side by the internal bleeding."

Hansen put the blade in to the left, nothing, went a little deeper. There was a crunching sound as he went into the trachea. No rush of air came out, just a jelly-like clot of blood.

Hansen fished out the clot with his finger. Giancomo lay perfectly still. Hansen felt his pulse, not that he really had to. There was no pulse. Giancomo was dead.

Hansen pointed to the X-ray. "Ben, Abe, I think one of those fragments nicked his carotid artery. He must have tamponaded it off with swelling or a blood clot or something. Then, something knocked it loose. Did he cough or something, Ben?" He was looking right at me, but there was no accusation in his eyes, no anger.

"Yes. He started to talk, I told him to be quiet. Maybe I should have told him to be quiet more. I mean, I should have insisted or something. He told me something, then coughed, then . . . this." This. This was a blood-covered, bluish-black dead young man with dark, curly hair, draped across a gurney with his left arm hanging down off the side.

"That must have done it. Well, boys. Nothing we could do. It's a miracle he even made it to the hospital." Hansen looked at his watch. "Ben, you'd better clean up, grand rounds are in an hour." He started out the door then stopped. "Oh, one thing Ben, don't blame yourself. You did what you could. This one was too far gone. Even if we'd gotten him to the operating room, he'd have probably bled to death. People die, Ben. People die." Putting his hand on my shoulder, he gave it a shake. Then he left. Hansen had seen a lot of dead people in his day.

The room cleared out, leaving only the dead young man.

Someone had walked out on him, someone had broken his heart, and he just couldn't stand the pain anymore. So he put a rifle in his mouth, somehow stretched his arm down far enough to press the trigger, and ended his life. More accurately, he caused the injury that eventually ended his life. But he wasn't dead when he was entrusted to me. He was alive. Alive enough to talk to me. Hansen had just assured me there was nothing I could have done, but I didn't know if I believed that. Maybe Hansen was just trying to make me feel better. Quieter, I should have kept him quieter, should have insisted he keep still. Maybe Giancomo could see I was just a medical student, not a "real" doctor. Maybe if I had conveyed more "authority," he would have kept still, he would not have talked and coughed loose that clot. But I hadn't conveyed that authority, hadn't conveyed it one bit. I hadn't kept him quiet. Not only that, I had also failed to place the tracheotomy. So I had made two mistakes, and now Mr. Giancomo was dead. I hadn't carried the demeanor of a doctor and hadn't performed like a doctor. And this young man, this handsome curly-haired young man, lay dead in front of me.

What struck me, looking at him, was that he wasn't breathing. Not that you'd expect a dead man to breathe. But he had just *been* breathing, the chest going up and down, up and down. Like a live person, a live body. But now his chest wasn't moving, wasn't going up and down. Like a dead person, a dead body. He was dead. A dead body. He was another in a string of dead bodies I'd seen—going back to anatomy class cadavers, through autopsy cadavers, and up to the cancer patients and heart attack victims on the wards. But the others, the formaldehyde-soaked specimens, the fileted-open autopsy specimens, the old, debilitated dead patients on the wards—they were all dead, dead bodies. Not so, Mr. Giancomo. He had just been talking to me, telling me about a girl who left him. Giancomo was not a dead, dead body. He was not a cadaver, or a specimen, or an old man whose time had come. He was alive, but he was dead. He was a live, dead body.

As a doctor, I knew there would be more dead, dead bodies. And there would be more live, dead bodies, but that didn't make it any easier.

Walking out of the room to go clean up, I saw some medical students gathered around the nursing desk. A classmate was holding an EXTRA from the *Minneapolis Tribune*.

LUSITANIA SUNK—AMERICANS AMONG DEAD

Beneath the huge block letters of the headline ran the details. A German submarine had torpedoed and sunk a huge English passenger liner, the *Lusitania*, sister ship of the lost *Titanic*. The ship went down just off Queenstown, County Cork, Ireland; it sank in fifteen minutes, taking over a thousand people with her, among them, about a hundred Americans. At the time, the Germans were at war with England, France and Russia, but were not at war with us. Not yet. Sinking the *Lusitania* might change all that.

A thousand people, a THOUSAND PEOPLE, had just vanished to their deaths. Some burned, some blown to pieces, but most of them drowned no doubt. That's how most people die when a ship sinks. I imagined them trying to breathe in, just like Giancomo had tried to breathe in. He breathed in his own blood and drowned. Those thousand people on the *Lusitania* tried to breathe in, but got only sea water in their lungs, and drowned. A thousand people, now dead, and a hundred of them my countrymen. A thousand live, dead bodies were floating in the Atlantic Ocean, or trapped in the wreck of the *Lusitania*, and a German submarine had killed every single one of them.

I got the feeling I'd be seeing more live, dead bodies myself. Would I be called on to keep a few of those bodies alive? We were going to enter this war, sooner or later, and the Army would need a lot of good doctors. Would I ever develop the requisite "presence" and skill to be one of those doctors?

A few days later I sent a letter off to my friend, confidante, and cousin, Sister Marie Francis Barden, a Dominican nun living in a Chicago convent.

Minneapolis
May 10, 1915

Dear Sister Marie Francis,

Hope this letter finds you in good health and spirits, Cousin. With any luck I'll be able to get down to Chicago some time to visit you. Our hospital has a few nuns of your Dominican order working in the anaesthesia department, and I have often told them about you. They remember you in their prayers, as do I.

No doubt you heard the terrible news about the *Lusitania* sinking just a few days ago. It seems like we'll be in the war soon.

Am only a Junior in Medical School, so couldn't enter the "fray" until my training was done, but if my country should need me earlier, then I would go earlier.

Cousin—had a bad experience in the hospital a few days ago. Was in charge of a desperately ill man, who had suffered a terrible wound to his mouth. He died right in front of me, and can't help but feel that my actions may have contributed to his death. The thought keeps me awake at night, keeps me reliving the scene in my memory. Suppose that every doctor must go through this at some time or another. Just a shock, that's all, just a shock right now. Guess that up until now, I had led a kind of hot house plant existence—study hard in high school, study hard in college and in medical school, but now this. A real patient with a real life-threatening wound, and myself, I just wasn't up to snuff. Makes me wonder if I can cut it. In a few years I will be a doctor, and that responsibility weighs on me.

And now this talk of war. Am a bit of a worry wart, to be sure, and tend to pull tomorrow's clouds over today's sunshine, but I can't help but wonder if I could do the job in the military setting. If I couldn't take care of this one fellow, what to do if there's three or four wounded fellows, all at once, as can happen in war time.

Sister Marie Francis, you have remembered me in your prayers before, could you include me in your next Novena? Confidence a bit shaken, and a little help from the Almighty couldn't hurt about now. Always need your prayers, Cousin, but right now, need them more than usual.

Sincerely,
Cousin Ben

For some reason, we did not go to war against Germany after the sinking of the *Lusitania*. Germany scaled back their submarine attacks and diplomatic efforts resulted in a kind of uneasy peace. But it still seemed that we would go to war with them sooner or later.

My cousin's prayers worked, and I was able to carry on for the rest of third and fourth-year medical school, graduating in 1916. During my clinical rotations, I did as much hands-on work as I could, knowing that experience was a better teacher than any book. One of my interns during my senior year summed it all up.

A few of us were washing up after a long operation to relieve a bowel obstruction. It was 3:00 A.M. and we all looked unshaven and haggard. The patient had not yet woken up from the anaesthetic. The intern shook the water off his hands and grabbed a towel.

"The only way to get good is by experience. And the only way to get experience is by being bad. Try to do all your bad stuff during your training, when there's someone around who can pull your chestnuts out of the fire." He tossed the towel in a laundry bag. "Keep that in mind. Meet me on the fourth floor ward in fifteen minutes. It's time to start morning rounds."

Taking the words to heart, I worked as hard as possible my senior year, but I still felt "inadequate to the task," both in my doctor "presence" and in my ability to do procedures with my own two hands. When the dean of the medical school handed me my diploma at our graduation and called me "Dr. Gallagher," I felt guilty.

Minneapolis City Hospital provided my surgical internship (the first year of training after medical school). Though most of our time was spent in treating patients, all of us at the hospital followed the progress of the Great War, raging in Europe since 1914.

The newspapers were full of accounts of the massive battles in Europe, where Belgium and France, with Britain at their side, struggled with German invaders.

The "Western Front" (a line about 500 miles long running roughly northwest to southeast through Belgium and eastern France) pitted Allied forces (Belgium, France, and England) against the German Army in an unbroken series of trenches. These trenches started at the North Sea and ended at the Swiss border. This was the area where the largest battles occurred, and both sides lost huge numbers of men. Fighting was also going on in Eastern Europe (Germany and Austria fighting Russia) and Italy (Austria fighting Italy) as well as more far flung places such as Turkey and Africa. These other areas seemed more remote. Everyone knew that the Great War would be lost or won on the Western Front. The Germans had almost captured Paris in 1914, in the first few weeks of the war, but the French had sent reinforcements to the Front in the nick of time and saved Paris. They called it a "taxicab" army, because the army had borrowed Paris' taxis to move their men up to the battle lines.

In spite of the fact that my grandparents all came from Ireland, and had no great love for the English, my folks and I identified with the Allies and their cause. Most of the people I knew at the university or back home in Waseca also backed the Allies. The Germans started the war with a brutal invasion of neutral Belgium, and had occupied the tiny country with an iron fist. The Germans were no kinder to that part of France they occupied, and stories of murdered civilians filled the newspapers. The Kaiser's arrogance and all the trappings of Prussian militarism—with no trace of democracy—repelled us.

There were many German immigrants in Minnesota, and many Scandinavians whose homelands were neutral. But people sympathized with the Allies.

An old German in Waseca told me, "Dat's why I left Germany. De Prussians wanted me for deir army. Dey got my brudder."

In 1917, the Germans opened unrestricted submarine warfare on our ships going to England. As the Germans sank more and more of our ships, anti-German feeling rose to a fever pitch. The uneasy peace was about to fall apart.

Then came the news that the Germans were stirring up the Mexicans to fight against us. German Foreign Minister Arthur Zimmerman actually offered to see that Mexico got Texas, New Mexico, and Arizona back, if they would declare war on us! What colossal Teutonic gall.

That did it.

I was on the third floor of Minneapolis City Hospital on a rainy April 2. It was nearing the end of my internship. Crouched over a pillow in front of me was one Olaf Gundersen, farmer. He had tuberculosis in the left upper lobe of his lung, and I was going to drop that lung, gradually, I hoped, but drop it, none the less. That is, I would poke a hole in it with a needle so it would slowly deflate, like a balloon leaking air slowly deflates.

"Okay, Mr. Gundersen, you know what we have to do here, don't you?" My white jacket was on, but the sleeves were rolled up, and I had rubber gloves on.

"*Jah, jah!*" Gundersen was thin as a rake, his individual ribs easy to make out as he leaned forward.

"You understand me, don't you?" You never knew. The Norwegians tended to say "*Jah*" to you no matter what.

"*Jah, jah,* go ahead doctor. I know you got to be stickin' me with the needle, sure."

Like most other Norwegians I'd treated, Mr. Gundersen was stoic. He kept milking the cows and mowing the hay until the coughing, night sweats, and weight loss drove him to the doctor. Hard to get him to see us, but once in the hospital, whatever we had to do was fine, *Jah*, sure.

"Okay now, I'm going to wash off your back here. The solution will be a little cold." The stuff must have felt like ice water on his back, but he didn't flinch.

Nurse Sark stood to my left, all starch and high nursing cap, holding the tray of instruments—swabs, bandages, antiseptic solution, and a thick needle.

"*Jah, jah.*"

The left side of his back was all brown from the antiseptic solution.

"Hold still now." I introduced the needle below his eighth rib on the left side. Gundersen jumped, but just a little, and a whooshing sound escaped through the needle. Gundersen's breathing became a little more labored. "That's it, all done Mr. Gundersen."

He wheezed a thanks. I had just caused a pneumothorax, a deliberate popping and collapsing of the left lung, the lung affected by the tuberculosis. The lung itself was sticky from the infection, so it wouldn't collapse right away. But slowly, it would shrink down. The medical reasoning was—since the tubercle bacillus needed oxygen to grow, by collapsing the lung, depriving it of oxygen, we'd stop its growth.

"Okay, Nurse Sark, take Mr. Gundersen to the X-ray department, he'll need a chest plate to document the pneumothorax, but first place a bandage on this and . . . "

The big door at the end of the ward flung open with a bang; Abe Haskell, my old crony and fellow intern, was running toward me. His white intern's jacket was unbuttoned, his face flushed red. He looked like an excited fan at a football game.

"Ben, Ben! Did you see?" Abe was clutching something in his right hand, waving it above his head.

Nurse Sark frowned. She shushed him.

Haskell ignored her, "It's war, Ben! We're in, we're finally in!"

He held the paper up in front of me. In huge block letters, the *Minneapolis Tribune* shouted:

U.S. DECLARES WAR

Beneath it was the text of President Wilson's speech to Congress, including the unforgettable phrase: ". . . to make the world safe for democracy."

So this was it, after all. Uncle Sam had finally had it. We were going into the fight, and heading over there—to Europe, to fight the Germans.

Nurse Sark interrupted my reverie.

"Dr. Gallagher, may I put the bandage on Mr. Gundersen now?" Acid dripped off her words. She did not like disturbances in wards, did not like them one little bit.

I folded the paper in half.

"Oh, yes, certainly." War. We are at war. The last time we'd been at war was 1898, against Spain. I'd only been nine years old at the time. And that war was over in a few months.

Mr. Gundersen was working harder at his breathing. Part of his lung power had just been taken away. I took out my stethoscope and listened to this chest. Full expansion and breath sounds on the right. Poor expansion and softer breath sounds on the left. A successful procedure, his left lung was slowly collapsing.

"Let me know when that chest plate is done, Miss Sark." I was doing all the right things, making sure Mr. Gundersen was well cared for. But the notion of WAR was eclipsing everything else.

Sark nodded curtly. War or no war, these interns should behave themselves. This is a *hospital,* not some bawdy house.

Abe and I walked down the hall to the staff quarters.

"So Ben, what do you say? Are you in?" Abe's eyes were wide open, he had the eagerness of a puppy.

Was I in? Here I was, born and raised in the heart of the world's greatest democracy, the *WORLD'S* greatest country. The best Constitution ever written guaranteed my freedom, the best schools in the world educated me. This was the country that accepted my Irish grandparents, fleeing the potato famine, and let them carve a living out of the Minnesota prairie. This was the country that nourished me from childhood, and had let me, a farmer's son, become a doctor. And now my country wanted something back. My country wanted me to go make the world "safe for democracy." My sister Rosella couldn't go. My three brothers, Frank, Henry, and Bob couldn't go. They were already married, and the army didn't draft married men. But I wasn't married, and if my country needed me, they had me.

"I'm in Abe, you?" No need to ask him, really, his excitement told me that he wouldn't miss this war for all the tea in China.

"Well Ben, if you go, I suppose I'll go, too. I'd hate to have you go over there, win the war single-handedly, come back with a bushel basket full of medals, and sweep all the girls off their feet. There'd be no one left for me!" Abe had jet-black hair, dark eyes, and a ready smile. He had the sharp features of the motion picture actors. He was rarely at a loss for girlfriends.

And so, the decision came that fast. We were going off to war. Me, to bring American style democracy to the world, to turn Europe into a vast replica of Minnesota, and Abe Haskell, to gather glory unto himself, and use that glory to make a good impression on some pretty girl. It all seemed like a kind of a lark. Off we'd go to war! It was like we were going off to some vacation resort.

About twenty of us were living as interns at Minneapolis City Hospital. All of us were draft age, but we chose to volunteer. We all joined the Medical Officers Reserve Corps and got commissions as first lieutenants.

Abe Haskell took off some time from his amorous adventures and joined another classmate of mine, C.W. Paulsen and me. We went to the University of Minnesota to try to talk to somebody about going into service right away.

The University of Minnesota was beautiful, hugging high bluffs overlooking the Mississippi River. Even this far north, the Mississippi was an impressive expanse, swollen with spring runoff.

The campus itself was festooned with flags, posters of Uncle Sam saying "I Want You!", Army, Navy, and Marine recruiting posters, and banners saying "Remember Belgium." Back in 1914, Germany had violated Belgium's neutrality and marched its armies right through the little country. Belgium's tiny army had put up a heroic resistance, and its citizens had sniped at the Germans as they passed by. The Germans countered by rounding up hundreds of hostages—men, women, and children—and shooting them. In 1914, the British had rallied to the call "Remember Belgium." Now, in 1917, we were, somewhat belatedly, "Remembering Belgium." We had been contributing to food packages for the Belgians for years. (Mr. Herbert Hoover had been in charge of this Belgian Relief and reportedly had done a good job seeing to it that the Belgians, and occupied French actually got the food parcels.)

After a little wandering around, we made our way to a Major Corbett. He was in charge of the medical officers. We found him sitting at a table in the university gymnasium. Long lines of college age kids were formed in front of tables. Everyone was filling out a yellow piece of paper. For some reason there was no one in front of Corbett's table.

"Major Corbett?" we asked.

He looked up. He had a thin, clean-shaven face, hair already graying at the temples. Haskell and Paulsen saluted, and I immediately followed suit, even though we had no uniforms. Saluting seems like the kind of thing you do to majors.

Corbett returned our salutes with his fountain pen.

"Hey boys, what can I do for you today?" His face was that of any civilian, but those brass buttons, the things on his shoulders—*this* was a soldier.

Haskell took over, informally electing himself our spokesman.

"Sir, Major. We are interested in active duty, sir, as soon as possible. We would like to join the Medical Corps, sir. So, you see, basic training, shooting practice, and taking apart Springfields is not really necessary, so to speak, for us. If we can, we'd just as soon go over right now." Haskell was still saluting the whole time, then thought better of it and put his arm down.

Major Corbett smiled. "That's what we like to hear, fellows. Let me get your names."

A grammaphone in the gymnasium started playing a song I'd never heard before. But the noise of many people talking and the acoustics in the cavernous gym made it impossible to hear the words.

Corbett filled out Haskell's name, then Paulsen's. As he began to fill out my name the fountain pen splotched all over the paper. Corbett was none too happy.

"Great God Almighty, we can make a train go 60-miles-per-hour, we can fly in the air with a machine, but the United States of America has not yet made a pen that will write." Corbett set the offending instrument down and took out a handkerchief to wipe off his hand.

Haskell, Paulsen, and I maintained a grim silence: we'd just had our first taste of action. We were no *strangers* to action, of course, as we had all read Guy Espy's *Over the Top*, the account of an American volunteer serving with the British Army. It was exciting to think that I, too, was going to enter this great conflict. But a nagging doubt worried me. How good of a doctor would I make?

Much to our surprise and delight, the blotchy list with our names made it to somebody, because on August 8, Haskell and I got telegrams ordering us to report to Washington, D.C. at once.

Back at Minneapolis City Hospital, they threw a going away party for us. Haskell and I were to be the first interns to go into active service.

At this party, the nurses hung flags and banners, and served up a ripping good cake, all red, white and blue. Haskell took three or four of the nurses aside, individually mind you, and gave them each a tearful good-bye.

Someone had gotten hold of a grammaphone, and I heard the song that had been playing in the gymnasium, "Over There" by Mr. George M. Cohan.

> 'Cause the Yanks are coming.
> The Yanks are coming,

The tune was catchy, and I would whistle it a lot in the months to come. The words were stirring.

> So beware. Say a prayer.
> Send the word, send the word Over There.

The Germans had a hell of an army, and a hell of a good navy, too. And their pilots weren't half bad either. Germany had fought France and England to a standstill, and had Russia on the ropes. Their submarines scoured the seven seas, and their battleships had fought the mighty British fleet to a draw the year before at Jutland. Their flying aces, especially someone named Richtofen, had swatted the British and French out of the skies for years.

The American army was tiny by comparison. The papers mentioned that we had fewer men under arms than tiny Portugal. Our last "big" war was the Civil War, and then we were fighting ourselves! The only thing our army had done lately was chase Pancho Villa around in Mexico, and he had gotten away. Some army!

So the Germans were probably not losing much sleep over our arrival in the war. We had to create our army from scratch, find enough ships to get them over to Europe, dodging torpedoes all the way, then go into action against the most seasoned army in the world.

But we would do it. We would do it. You could see it in the faces of those nurses and doctors at that party. You could see it in the faces of the orderlies, the janitors, the visitors, the clergymen. You could see it in the faces of the patients, lying in their beds. When we all started singing that song, marching around that ward, the Germans should have packed their bags and gone back to Berlin. If ever a song could win a war, this song could.

> So beware, say a prayer.
> Send the word, send the word, over there.
> That the Yanks are coming, the Yanks are coming.
> The drums drum drumming everywhere.
> Send the word, send the word, over there.
> That the Yanks are coming, the Yanks are coming
> And we won't come back 'til it's over, Over There.

Over There. It might take a while for Uncle Sam to get over there, and you may give him a bloody nose once he gets over there. But you Germans had pushed Uncle Sam far enough, and you would soon feel his wrath. And you would feel it over there. Steal Texas, New Mexico, and Arizona away from us, indeed! Remember the *Lusitania*! Uncle Sam is on the way.

Abe and I said our farewells at the hospital, I leaving fewer broken hearts behind, in fact, none that I knew of. The following day, August 9, I went home to Waseca, a town of 4,000 souls nestled between two lakes in the southern Minnesota corn belt. The next night I left for Chicago on the Northwestern Railway. The tears in the eyes of my family and friends called attention to the seriousness of this journey. After all, I was not heading off to medical school, or a vacation at the beach along Lake Minnetonka. I was going to war. My parents, my brothers, Henry, Frank, and Bob, my aunts and uncles saw me off. My sister Rosella, especially, gave me a "last fond look" expression.

"Hey sis, come on. This melodramatic look, I feel like I'm reading a penny dreadful novel." I was standing on the step of the train, the whistle had blown, and the conductor hollered, "'Board!"

"Well, Ben, take care of yourself!" Rosella said. Again I got the "last fond look." Rosella was full-grown, had children of her own, but that look she gave me! She could have been a character in a Charles Dickens novel.

The train started to pull away. Climbing in, I sat down next to an older man who was sound asleep. Clickety-clack, clickety-clack, the train picked up speed. Cornfields swept past, brown tassels showed it was about harvest time. My impression was that, once in the army, I'd be given three or four months instruction at the Army Medical College, and then possibly be sent to foreign service. My sister's tears and looks seemed overly solicitous, given the fact I wouldn't be in harm's way for many, many months, if at all. How dangerous is it to be a doctor? (The next few months would prove how much nearer right she was than I.)

On August 11 the train pulled into Chicago's Union Station. Haskell was waiting for me on the crowded platform. The entire world had decided to go through Chicago this day, or so it seemed, for there were thousands and thousands of people jostling each other on the platforms.

"Abe! Abe! Over here!" I shouted across red-capped porters, men in uniform, and a jumble of people in business suits.

Abe heard me and waved.

"Ben!" He waved frantically at his pocket watch. "Ben!" He bumped his way through the crowd. "Ben, look, it's 8:30 now, and we've got a 9:30 train to catch for Washington!"

"9:30? But, I was hoping we'd leave this evening. I was hoping to see my cousin while we were here."

Someone bumped into me hard. Reaching for my back pocket, I made sure my wallet was still there. Pickpockets and big cities go hand in hand.

"Your cousin?" Abe asked. "A female cousin, perhaps?"

"Abe, this cousin of mine is a NUN! Sister Marie Francis Barden." Abe's face drained to the white of steam escaping the engines.

"Oh, yes, Sister Marie, of course. Well, holy orders aside, Ben, *our* holy orders say to get to Washington as soon as possible. And these are *orders* Ben, not requests. So, we'd better shake a leg. Ring your cousin up on the telephone, and tell her you'll see her when your training is done. A month or two from now. There's all sorts of trains back to Chicago from Washington, D.C. You can visit her anytime." Abe was agitated. The crowds, the need to catch that train were pressing him.

I mulled it over. He was right, we were under *orders*, not requests, but *orders* from the commander in chief, to get to Washington.

"Right again, Abe. I'll telephone her. Do you want to get the . . . "

He held up two tickets. "Already got them Ben, sleeping arrangements, everything. You just leave it up to me."

Abe was the business end of our partnership; he would have been a great carnival huckster, all he needed was the striped suit, straw boater, and cane.

"Sister Marie Francis?" The phone line crackled a little, so I put my mouth up close to the speaker mouthpiece. I plugged my non-listening ear with my finger to muffle out the noise of crowds and trains.

"Ben? Is that you? What time are you coming out to the convent, I can't wait to see you. I've told the other sisters all about you, they'd love to hear about your . . . "

"Pardon me, sister. Pardon the interruption, but I'm afraid I won't be able to make it out to see you. I've got to catch the next train to Washington." She would be so disappointed. No matter what, I'd catch a train back here and visit her soon.

"No. Oh, Ben. It's been so long. And I've remembered you in my prayers every day. Especially since that, difficult time, a few years ago, when that young man died."

Giancomo again. He still haunted me.

"And believe me, sister, I appreciate your efforts. I truly do." I did. She was my guardian angel, always on the job, praying for me every day.

Holding the listening piece of the phone to my ear, my mouth pointing at the speaker, I started to nod to Sister Marie, then thought how foolish that was. She was talking to me on the *telephone*, she couldn't *see* me.

Abe waved at me and banged on the door of the telephone booth. He pointed at his watch and waved the tickets.

"I'm afraid time is short, Sister Marie Francis, but I promise I'll find my way back here and we'll have a nice visit. I want to thank you in person for the great vote of confidence you sent me in your prayers. Here I am, all graduated from medical school, done with my internship, and now I'm off to the army. Your prayers were no small part of that." No one with Irish blood minds a prayer or two said on their behalf. And a prayer from a nun, a nun who is your *cousin*, now that's a fine thing indeed.

"God's will be done. You've come a long way, Ben, I can just tell you're growing in the medical arts. Just make sure you continue to grow spiritually." Sister Marie kept me on a tight rein in all matters, ecclesiastic. Woe to me if I should miss church, war or no war.

"Yes, Sister Marie Francis." That was the other side of the coin with Sister Marie. She would serve up the prayers, but you had better toe the line when it came to receiving the Sacraments.

"Promise me you'll get to Communion, once a week, at least."

"Yes, Sister." Forget trying to escape the long arm of the law. Sister Marie wielded the long arm of GOD.

"And don't neglect confession. Once a month. Promise me, Ben."

"Yes, Sister." That was a promise to a nun. I would break that promise at great peril.

Abe banged again on the telephone booth.

"Sister, I'm afraid I must go. I'll write you as soon as I can. Don't worry about me, but do keep me in your prayers. My biggest worry is still my level of training. I've only got an internship under my belt. I don't know if that's enough, Sister."

Bang, bang, bang!

"Ben, come on, come on!" No smile on Abe's face now, we had to get going.

"OK, Abe! I've got to run, Sister. *Dominos vobiscum!*" God be with you, cousin, and let's hope God is with me.

"*Et cum spiritu tuo.* Oh, Ben! About your level of training. Trust me. It will be enough. God will guide your hands and heart." This was Sister Marie at her best. She could get on that high horse about going to church, and nag me to go to confession, but what I really needed from her was a vote of confidence, a signal that she believed in me. And she gave me that signal.

"Thank you, Sister Marie."

"God be with you, Ben."

Abe hustled us into the sleeping car and pointed out he had saved us half the normal price by getting, not two berths, but one, and an upper one at that. Abe had little experience in traveling, and I not much more, yet I knew enough to climb into that sleeping berth first. I slept fairly well, while poor Abe hardly slept a wink. Being on the outside, he had to cling to the edge and stay awake, lest he fall out as the train twisted and rolled through the mountains of Pennsylvania.

We arrived at Union Station in Washington on the morning of August 12, and had our first look at the nation's Capitol—I through well-rested eyes, Abe through bleary ones. In spite of Abe's admonitions that we "had to get to Washington right away, orders you know," our haste was in waste, for it was a Sunday and everything was closed. War or no war, we weren't able to report to the Army Medical School until it opened on Monday, so we checked into the Willard Hotel. The place was full of senators and representatives, with prices to match. Since we were lowly first lieutenants, and had not yet drawn any pay, we checked out after staying only one day, and took up residence at a dusty, modest apartment. We ate our meals at a dairy lunch on Pennsylvania Avenue.

The next morning Abe and I showed up at the Army Medical School and reported to a Major Jones. We assumed we'd be getting some training, and then move around the United States for a while. That thought quickly got derailed.

About two hundred of us were sitting in a large room, the sun streaming in through large bay windows, providing a great view of the Potomac. A Major Jones entered the back of the room, and some sergeant-at-arms or something, it was all pretty new to me, shouted, "Ten 'SHUN!"

Half of the men stood up straight at attention, the other half just sat up straight in their chairs, then thought better of it and stood. Major Jones made his way to the front of the room.

"Okay, doctors, sit on down. As you were."

He sat down on the edge of a table and took in the room. His uniform was spotless, adorned with colored ribbons and medals. They must have been medals from the Philippine insurrection, or possibly the Pancho Villa campaign. Smiling at us, he looked more like a Scout leader than a major. When he finally spoke his words hung in the air.

"Congratulations, men. You've just joined the British Army."

Chapter 2

U-BOAT ALLEY

Everyone looked around the room. The British Army?

"Here's the story, fellows," Major Jones got off the desk and walked to the window. Outside, a few leaves were starting to change into fall colors, but most were still green. "The British keep their doctors right up front, sometimes even in the front lines, so they've lost a lot of them since 1914."

Someone in the front row raised his hand. Jones turned to him.

"Put your hand down, son. This is the army, not medical school. Let me finish, then you can ask all the questions you want." His scowl was that of a schoolmaster, but more than a schoolmaster—this was the *army*.

"So in the person of Mr. Arthur Balfour, their former prime minister, the British have asked us to send over a bunch of doctors to help theirs out." He let that sink in for a minute. "You'll go over to England, put in some work there, then go over to France, to get assigned to the RAMC, the Royal Army Medical Corps, at the Front. They'll put you where they need you. That could be a Rear Area Hospital, a Field Ambulance Company, a Dressing Station, a Casualty Clearing Station, or a front-line Aid Post." The faces on most of the fellows looked a little confused. They didn't know the difference between a "Dressing Station" and a "Casualty Clearing Station" any more than I did.

The same hand went up.

"Yes." Major Jones' patience was wearing thin.

"Sir, I joined the American Army. I'm not sure I really want to join the British Army." The man's face was all innocence, as if he'd been assigned to the wrong baseball squad.

Major Jones took that in, nodded with tightly pursed lips, then let him have it.

"Well, son. We're not really interested in what you want and don't want. We are ordering you to volunteer. And we thank you." Jones had walked over to the man with the question and was standing two inches in front of him when he shouted "we thank you." The poor fellow was pulling his head back into his shoulders, like a turtle trying to disappear inside his shell.

The sergeant-at-arms hollered, "Ten 'SHUN!"

This time, everyone stood bolt upright, a few chairs fell over backwards. Major Jones walked towards the back of the room. "That will be all, Sergeant." The man who asked the question looked ashen.

"Yes, sir!" the sergeant-at-arms snapped. He now strode to the front of the room, clearly in charge.

None of us moved. We continued to stand at, what we perceived to be, attention. The sergeant walked around us, inspecting—what? We had no rifles, no packs, nothing. All I had was a pen, and it didn't work very well. Surely he wouldn't ask me to "present pens" or something.

"Dismissed!"

He shouted so loud we nearly jumped out of our skin. Then he strolled away, rolling his eyes, muttering, "Maybe I don't want to join the British Army, maybe I don't want to join the British Army."

Washington, D.C.
August 18, 1917

Dear Sister Marie Francis,

Felt quite sure when I left Waseca that I would be in Chicago from morning until evening and would be able to see you, but after meeting the other fellow who was to make the trip with me we decided it would be best to come right on. I was very glad at least to be able to talk with you for a few moments and only wish that it had been a day or two earlier so I might have talked with you in person. I heard your mother and father were there, too, wish I could have seen them. I suppose the best we can do is to look forward to a future day which I hope is not too far distant.

Oh, Marie, forgot to tell you. I made A.O.A. (Alpha Omega Alpha) when I graduated from Medical School. It's a national honorary medical fraternity. Some people think it's pretty important, but myself, I think it's just a bunch of baloney.

As always, I will need your prayers, Sister Marie Francis, pray that I learned enough in my internship to get me through this upcoming trial.

Sincerely,
Cousin Ben

Washington was a very interesting place. Shortly after I wrote Sister Marie, I made a boat trip down the Potomac to Washington's old home at Mount Vernon. All along the river were many places of great historic interest in Revolutionary and Civil War times. Arlington Cemetery, with its long rows of headstones, was particularly moving. So many young men were buried there, a lot of them in their teens, even. Among them were a lot of names from Minnesota—some killed at Gettysburg, some at Fredericksburg, Chancellorsville, Cold Harbor, Petersburg. The headstones were a roll call of the great battles of the Civil War.

I was standing underneath an oak tree, looking at one particular headstone.

Patrick Moriarty
Born 1849 Ireland
Died 1864 Spotsylvania
20th Maine Vol. Inf'y

Fifteen years old, he was, just 15. Must have lied about his age to get into the army. If he lived in Maine, he was probably a lumberjack or a fisherman, so he must have looked husky enough to pass for older. And to think he was born in Ireland, so it wasn't really his fight. Maybe he said, "When my country goes to war, then I go to war, too." And off he went, only to die at Spotsylvania battlefield. Was he a good soldier? A brave man? Did he die in an instant, shot down during an assault? Or did he linger and die in a hospital after the battle?

No answers to these questions were on the gravestone. It just said an Irish immigrant boy fought and died to preserve the Union. And now he rested beneath an oak tree in Arlington cemetery. He died at 15 and would remain 15 forever.

After a few weeks in Washington, D.C. (spent mostly filling out paperwork and doing sightseeing), the army sent us up to New York, to await transport to Europe.

New York
September 7, 1917

Dear Sister Marie Francis,

Received your very welcome letter at Washington. Was sent up here to New York on the last day of August. The little badge of Saint Christopher which you sent is very nice and just what I, a true traveler, needed. Sister Richard sent me a little medal also, so with rosary and all I should be fairly well equipped.

New York is quite an extensive city to say the least and though only a "boob for the burdock patch" I have gotten around and seen quite a bit. The cathedral windows in the Brooklyn Bridge are quite striking, and at night, the Statue of Liberty's torch is lit up. Quite a sight.

She continues to "lift her lamp beside the golden door," as she lit it for our own ancestors from Ireland some sixty years ago.

Soon I will be sailing past that torch and heading over to quite an adventure, of sorts. I will do my part to keep that torch lit, Sister Marie Francis. The Germans want to put that light out, but I will not let them, and we will not let them.

Say a prayer for me, Sister Marie Francis. Say a prayer for me tonight. Pray that Lady Liberty will keep that torch lit for all the world to see. And say one more prayer, if you would. If God in his infinite mercy sees fit, pray that Lady Liberty will keep that torch lit for me, too.

Lovingly,
Your cousin,
Ben

The next day, September 8, 1917, at 2:40 P.M., our arms aching from smallpox, typhoid, and paratyphoid vaccinations, Abe Haskell and I boarded the troopship *Orduna* in New York harbor. It was still warm—Indian Summer weather, but there was a stiff wind, raising whitecaps in the water. The second we were on the deck, Abe spoke up.

"U-boat Alley." His voice had an air of foreboding. Abe's face was grim. His comment left me in the dark.

"What's a U-boat?"

"*Untersee Boot*—a submarine, you dummy! You're the one's supposed to know German so well! We're now officially in U-boat Alley." Abe seemed exasperated. We were in deadly peril, and I just wasn't getting it.

I looked around New York harbor, taking in the Battery, Ellis Island, the Statue of Liberty. Whitecaps appeared and disappeared, appeared and disappeared. The warm breeze felt nice.

"Abe, I don't see a lot of German periscopes out there." There were a few tugboats, and a ferry going to Staten Island. Pretty harmless stuff.

"Do you think you would? How easy do you think it is to see a dark periscope in dark water, Ben?" Abe's face was glowering, reprimanding. He spoke like a veteran of a thousand sea battles, who was addressing a hopeless landlubber—me.

He had a point. One of the whitecaps seemed to take a long time breaking. Maybe it was the wake of a periscope. That would look just like a whitecap, wouldn't it? Or would it? We were told to go below, but I looked long and hard at that suspicious whitecap before I did. Maybe I should have told one of the crewmen about it.

A sailor directed us down a long, narrow corridor, our bags kept catching on valves, pipes and doorways. The vaccination spots on my arms hurt like blazes as I kept lifting my bag again and again.

"Well, Abe. What you say about the U-boats is true, but, I mean, we're in American waters, I don't think U-boats can come all the way over here, can they?" That whitecap . . . I kept seeing that damn whitecap. Or maybe it was a periscope, a German periscope, right here in NEW YORK HARBOR.

Abe hit his head on a low hatchway.

"Ow!" The great sea warrior had gotten his first wound.

"Watch your head, sir!" the sailor shouted, a little after the fact.

"Thanks." Abe rubbed his forehead, a little knot was already appearing right in the middle. "I don't know, Ben, maybe they can, maybe U-boats can reach us, maybe they can't. I guess we'll find out."

We'll find out? That wasn't too reassuring. (Probably that whitecap was nothing. Besides, it *was* pretty far away. There were so *many* whitecaps, it *wasn't* a periscope. Surely, it was *not* a *periscope,* just my imagination.

"Say, just how far can those German submarines go? Have they sunk ships all the way over here?" My voice didn't reveal any nervousness, I hoped. Nonchalance, that's what I was trying to convey, nonchalance—both to the sailor and to Abe.

The sailor continued forward, without looking back, and said, "Oh, they get around. Keep your eyes open, and keep your life jacket handy. Here you go." He showed Abe to one cabin and me to another, right next door. Then the sailor disappeared down a labyrinth of hallways and pipes. *He* had certainly conveyed nonchalance. There must not be *too many* U-boats in New York harbor.

"What does that mean, 'they get around, keep your life jacket handy'?" I asked. Surely Abe, the now-wounded warrior would know what the sailor meant.

Abe turned the handle on his cabin door, "I think it means that we're in U-boat Alley." He was trying to look stern and foreboding, but the goose egg on his forehead reduced me to laughter. It's hard to look grim and ridiculous at the same time.

Stowing my stuff in the cabin, I wondered how quickly I could make it back up on deck if we *were* torpedoed. Trapped below decks, with water filling up the long, twisting corridors—that was the nightmare. No matter what, if we got hit, I had to get up, up to the open spaces of the upper deck. Maybe I'd get in a lifeboat, maybe I'd have to jump overboard. Anything was better than getting stuck down below, with the water rising all around me. God help me, I did not want to drown like a rat in the belly of a ship.

Someone else had put his things in the cabin, too, but he was not around. A note on the inside of the door said, "Please stay inside your cabin until we are out of the harbor. This is a security precaution." My cabin mate sure wasn't staying in the cabin. Maybe he saw a periscope and was staying up on the upper decks, ready to jump overboard at the sound of an explosion.

A copy of the *Cunard Bulletin—Orduna* lay on my bunk. (Cunard was the name of the company that owned the *Orduna*.) Apparently the crew put together some kind of newspaper.

WELCOME, COUSINS

The captain and crew of the *Orduna* welcome our American cousins aboard. We hope to have an enjoyable and safe journey together, please observe the following precautions.

There followed a long list of do's and don't's, mainly linked to submarine safety. No cigarettes on deck after dark, no uncovered portholes. We were to be as invisible as possible to an enemy that was also invisible.

The paper gave a quick "introduction" to the war for us. Of course, the paper presented the British side of things, and emphasized the good while minimizing the bad, but everyone knew the war was stalemated and there was no explaining that away. Settling on my bed, I put my feet up on the gray cover blanket, but didn't take my shoes off. (If I had to run, I didn't want to be stubbing my bare toes on all those pipes and hatchways.)

- June 28, 1914. A Serbian nationalist assassinates Archduke Ferdinand of Austria and his wife in Sarajevo. Austria declares war on Serbia.
- A series of treaties pull different countries into the war: Austria, Germany, Bulgaria, and Turkey, against Serbia, Russia, Italy, France, Belgium, and England. All of the English dominion countries (Australia, New Zealand, Canada, South Africa, and India) also contribute troops. Numerous other countries get involved, and soon the war is a global conflict, with fighting going on from Pacific Islands to Turkey, Africa, Syria, and Italy. But the main fight is in Europe, on the Western Front.
- England enters the war after Germany violates Belgian neutrality. The German armies commit atrocities against Belgian civilians, shooting hostages every time their troops are fired upon. The world is outraged by Germany's behavior.
- The British blockade Germany. The Germans have a "counter-blockade" of submarines trying to prevent ships from getting to England.
- In initial "open" warfare, the Germans threaten Paris but are held off by combined British, French, and Belgian resistance. After about a month, both sides dig in and form an unbroken line of trenches that goes from the North Sea, through Belgium and France, down to the Swiss border. From 1914 to the present, September 1917, the lines hardly move at all.
- Barbed wire; machine guns; rapid, accurate artillery, all favor the defense, and neither German, nor French, nor British assaults can achieve a decisive "breakthrough." Casualties are enormous. (On one

day alone, for example, the British lose 60,000 men in an unsuccessful assault on the German lines near the Somme River.)

- Techniques to "outwit" each other have failed. The British send an expedition to Gallipoli (Turkey) and use a lot of Australian and New Zealand troops to try to defeat Turkey, but the assault founders in a repeat of a trench war stalemate.
- Aeroplanes, observation balloons, flamethrowers, poison gas, more and more machine guns, more and more artillery, all fail to "break" the other side. The slaughter at the Front goes on and on. Tanks have gone into action, but only in small numbers and only in a few places.
- On the Eastern Front (Germany and Austria versus Russia) the Germans achieve success, and the Russians are teetering. Revolution has broken out and Russia will likely leave the war soon. (You had to read between the lines to get that, but I had read it in the American newspapers.) Germany is dictating crushing peace terms to Russia.
- The Southern Front (Italy versus Austria) was also a stalemate, with both armies stuck in high mountain trench lines.

The *Cunard Bulletin* finished on a high note, pointing out that the blockade was choking off Germany, the Allies were wearing down the Germans, and it was only a matter of time before the Hun was defeated. (The Germans were called a number of different things: Hun, as in Attila the Hun; Boche, which was a French word meaning swine; Jerry; or simply Fritz.) General Haig, the British commander in France, announced that the Third Battle of Ypres (which American papers described as another costly failure) was a great success, and the Germans were "close to cracking." I took this bit of information with a grain of salt.

Setting the paper down on the bunk, I crossed my hands behind my head. No matter what was going on in other areas of the war, one thing was clear—the Allies had to beat Germany on the Western Front.

And that's where I was going.

With a clanking and clunking, which I took to be torpedo hits, the ship pulled out from the dock. Almost immediately, the ship started a slight, gradual roll from side to side. My porthole looked right out at the Statue of Liberty.

Photographs and paintings did her no justice, one had to see the Statue of Liberty in person to appreciate her. Atop an enormous pedestal, she held a tablet in one arm, and a huge golden lamp in the other. Words, too, fail to describe the Statue of Liberty, the symbol of our country. The only description worthy of her was a poem written in her honor. That poem ended, "I lift my lamp beside the golden door."

As we passed by the Statue of Liberty, as we passed through the golden door, I hoped that Sister Marie Francis' prayer would work. Keep that lamp lit for all the world, Lady Liberty, and, if you can, keep it lit for me, too.

On board the *Orduna* were some 450 Reserve Corps officers, and 600 enlisted men, all bound for Halifax, Nova Scotia. We would wait there until travel by convoy was readied.

The ship's crew made us keep out of sight until the ship was well out of the harbor, presumably so German spies would not know a troop ship was departing. All this security seemed rather superfluous, since everyone in the world seemed to know when we were leaving. At a dinner in New York a few days earlier our host had said, "Oh, I heard you are sailing out on the 8th."

Once out of the harbor we were allowed to stroll around on deck, but at night the portholes were covered, and you weren't allowed to smoke a cigarette on deck, as noted in the last *Cunard Bulletin*. One sailor said we didn't want any of "King Willie's fish" to find us (a reference to Kaiser Wilhelm's torpedoes). En route to Halifax we did not zigzag and make rapid changes in course to throw off a submarine's aim, but rather we steamed straight ahead. Presumably, the danger of submarines on this side of the Atlantic was pretty small, regardless of Abe's dire predictions, and my phantom periscope sighting in New York harbor. The danger would increase steadily as we neared Europe, however. As I looked out over the vast ocean, I wondered how anyone could ever see a tiny periscope in all that water.

On our left, or port side (we all started using the sailor terms, fancying ourselves old salts after just a few days at sea), we could just barely make out land as we sailed north. Long Island, the New England states, and Canada all looked like a thin line on the horizon. The air got crisper as we got farther north.

A few times we hit waves big enough to throw a little spray of water on us. That water was *cold*. One couldn't help but think of all those sailors in all those sinking ships during this war. What an awful thing to have to jump into that icy water. God help us if we got hit.

Monday afternoon, September 10, at about 4:00 P.M. we steamed slowly into the harbor at Halifax. The harbor is shaped like a basin, almost entirely land-locked, and entered by a long, narrow channel crossed in a couple of places by submarine nets—gates which could be opened in the day time and closed at night. It is a beautiful harbor, said to be one of the best in the world. It was much colder at Halifax than at New York, and the air was so clear one could see for long distances. The stunted trees and vegetation on the hillsides gave the country round about a frigid aspect.

We were not allowed to get off the ship to go ashore and the time dragged heavily, but we did our best to occupy ourselves. Boxing and wrestling matches were arranged for every day, we had certain hours for physical exercises, classes in French were organized, and the ship's library had a good supply of books. Guy Espy's *Over the Top* was always checked out. (The book about an American volunteer serving with the British Army.) By the time one fellow got it, the book was almost in tatters. Needless to say, many larger and smaller games of poker were played in various parts of the lounge and saloon. On the decks below especially, the enlisted men "rolled the bones" (played craps) at a lively rate.

Eight ships formed into our convoy, and at 5 P.M. on September 12, we set out for England. We were going to enter U-boat Alley, all right, the real thing.

Abe and I were standing at the stern of the *Orduna* as we moved slowly out of the mouth of the harbor.

"Are those British ships, Ben?"

Abe pointed at two gray cruisers on either side of us. On the stern of their ships stood a line of musicians in immaculate white uniforms. An officer with a baton stood rigidly at attention, saluting in our direction. How very odd they should be lining up at attention like that and saluting *us*.

"I think so, Abe, that's the Union Jack at their masthead. I wonder what . . . "

On both sides of us, the officers with the batons spun around and started conducting the bands. Behind the band members, a chorus started singing a familiar song in English accents.

> "Oh say can you see? By the dawn's early light
> What so proudly we hailed, at the twilight's last gleaming!
> Whose broad stripes and bright stars . . . "

Great God Almighty! They were saluting *us,* the Americans. The British were saluting their American cousins, coming to fight alongside them in the Great War. They were singing our national anthem, which was written while *we* were fighting *them.*

Behind us, the sun was sinking like a ball of fire over Halifax harbor. I thought of Fort McHenry in Baltimore harbor, and the dawn's early light. The swells of the open Atlantic started to lift and drop the boat. As we moved out into the gathering darkness, the "Star Spangled Banner" fading behind us, Abe spoke up, "Ben, if you never wanted to fight before, this sight made you want to now."

At night we traveled in darkness, save one tiny twinkler on the troopship *Adriatic* at the center of the convoy. The other ships looked like low clouds on the horizon. The two English cruisers which had serenaded us in Halifax did not accompany us on our journey, so our only "punch" was one armed freighter. Not much of a punch. Our ship could actually travel much faster than it did, but we had to go as slow as the slowest freighter, so we seemed to be crawling. Every mile brought us closer to the safety of England, and also brought us closer to German submarine territory. As of February 1, 1917, the Germans announced they would sink any and all ships on their way to Britain and France. This was the German "counterblockade" and it was one of the reasons President Wilson had asked Congress for a Declaration of War.

I shared a stateroom with another medical officer, Lieutenant Enbanks of Little Rock, Arkansas, who snored so loudly I feared he'd either choke to death or else tip off our location to a submarine. Enbanks had missed few meals in his day, and I regretted giving him the upper bunk. Each night, as he lumbered into the bunk above me, I watched with growing terror as the bunk slats creaked and sagged towards me. If those slats should break and I should die beneath his bulk, would I still merit a hero's burial?

The crew of the *Orduna* was English, and this voyage gave us our first chance to meet our "adopted" countrymen. An episode at breakfast introduced me to the gulf between the English and the American way of thinking.

"Another rasher of bacon, sir?" the English steward asked me at breakfast one morning.

"Rasher?" Rasher? What was he talking about?

"Rasher." He looked at me with even eyes, no condescension, no anger, no judgement. Nothing.

"Piece, he means, Ben," Abe helped out. "Rasher is a piece, it's the word for piece that goes with bacon. How should I know, I'm Jewish and don't eat the stuff? But I know."

"Oh, sure," I said, reaching up to take a piece.

"Please sir, allow me." He blocked my reach and tried to hand me the piece himself.

"No, I can get it myself." I was trying to reach around him.

"Please sir, please," the steward placed a piece, a rasher, on my plate. He had won.

A reserve officer from New Jersey jumped in the discussion and tried to melt the English steward a little.

"Say, Jeeves, I should rah-thuh like a rah-tion of bacon rah-shers, if you please." He exaggerated the voice and manners a little, but didn't go overboard.

Chuckles all around the table, but not so much as a hint of a smile from the steward.

"Come now, Jeeves, I hope you don't find us American cousins such hopeless bumpkins as all that. Eh what, cheerio and all that rot!" Now he was going a little too far.

More chuckles now. Other tables were looking on and getting a feel for the fun.

"Yes, sir. As you wish, sir," the steward said, straight as a pin, then he returned to the galley to get more bacon. Never a smile.

The New Jersey fellow hooked a thumb in the direction of the galley. "Boy, I was making a little joke. You'd think I stamped on his foot, the way he looked at me."

"I guess that's just the way it is, over there in England," Lieutenant Enbanks, my roommate, said. "My aunt is English, and she says it's pretty cut and dried over there." He spoke as one who knows. Why shouldn't he? We certainly knew little about England and its ways.

Enbanks was making short shrift of a huge breakfast. Maybe I could get some more slats to support his bunk.

He went on, "There's the upper class, the blue bloods, and there's the lower class, the servants. And ne'er the twain shall meet, if you know what I mean. You just won't catch a steward comfortable with the idea of hobnobbing with us officers. We're not in his class, so the door between us is closed." His voice had a southern accent, but not as strong as I would have thought for Arkansas.

"Crazy system," the New Jersey officer said. "Wonder if that's what the Revolutionary War was all about."

The steward returned with a big platter of eggs and bacon. We Americans all exchanged some embarrassed looks around the tables. This class system and its associated deferential treatment made us all a little uncomfortable.

"Say, I'll take some more of those!" Enbanks said.

Besides the odd behavior of the English stewards, another curiosity of shipboard life was the availability of booze. Whereas in America, liquor could not be sold to a man in uniform, here, on board this ship, we could have all the whisky we wanted. Some of the fellows were happy to take full advantage of this.

Myself and another fellow were assigned the duty of holding a sick call in the ship's dispensary every day. We attended to a lot of seasickness, a few bruises from boxing matches, and the ill effects of John Barleycorn.

I was examining an infantry lieutenant from Michigan one day. He was leaning forward, his head in his hands, groaning.

"Lieutenant, uh, Dendel, what seems to be bothering you?" I asked, sitting on a metal stool, my stethoscope draped around my neck. Dendel looked like death would be a welcome release.

"I don't feel so good." The words came out in a croak, his tongue sticking to the roof of his mouth.

Just outside the dispensary, a sailor dropped a wrench with a resounding crash!

"Sorry, gov'nor," the sailor apologized through the open door.

"Ooooh!" Dendel moaned. The crash was echoing around inside his skull, that was apparent.

My clinical acumen had just narrowed down the differential diagnosis to one thing.

"Too much to drink last night, Lieutenant?" I tried to sound clinical and impassive, without a note of judgement in my voice.

"Oooh, you could say that again." Dendel had passed far beyond *my* powers to judge. He must have felt like it was THE Judgement Day.

"And what did you have for breakfast this morning?" Suspicion. He must have heard the suspicion in my voice.

"Well, Doc, I sort of, hesitate to say." He lifted his eyes up to me, but sunshine through the porthole caught him right in the eye. God was meting out stern justice this Judgement Day.

"Let me guess. You woke up with Vulcan forging a hammer in your head, Satan burning brimstone in your mouth, and you thought you'd treat yourself with that old home remedy that your grandpappy taught you." A hundred times I'd seen this, a thousand times.

Dendel lifted his head, turning it to avoid the wrathful sunbeam, and held two fingers sideways, indicating the depth of the whisky he had poured himself that morning.

"Two fingers of whisky, neat. The 'hair of the dog' that bit you. Daddy told me it never fails," Dendel said, still croaking the words out of a tortured mouth.

His head sank back into his hands.

"Guess it fails sometimes, huh, Doc."

One fellow who showed up on sick call happened to be the son of a former neighbor of mine in Waseca. It is indeed a small world. He was of German descent—headed to fight the Kaiser.

The sea calmed down about a week into the voyage, and the sky became crystal clear. Good news for those with seasickness, and good news for the German submariners, too. Whereas large waves and bad weather *obscure* the view from a periscope, flat seas and good weather *clear* the view from a periscope. And a good view through a periscope meant a good shot, a good shot at us. For days on end any prowling German would have had a good view of our eight ships slowly zigzagging across the North Atlantic. Sitting ducks. We were ordered to keep our lifebelts with us at all times, even in our bunks. Everyone, including me, tried to keep up a bravado spirit, but I would often wake up at night with a start. If a heavy wave hit the ship, or the engines made an extra roaring sound, I'd think that a sub had just fired upon us. My heart would pound for a few minutes, then I'd try to go back to sleep. Lieutenant Enbanks's labored snoring didn't help, since it sounded like he'd been torpedoed himself and was drowning in the bunk above me. And every night his bed sagged lower and lower.

Lying in that bed at night, after some sound or another had awakened me, gave me time to think. Time to think about this trip, what it meant, why we were doing it, the part I would play in this upcoming drama. It struck me that 150 years ago, British forces were traversing these waters to put down the American

Revolution. And they brought German allies, the Hessians, to help them. Now, we were going the other way to help the British fight against the Germans. History does tend to turn things around.

American history got batted around a little bit, too, particularly at the dinner table. Our second week at sea, Abe and I sat down at a table with three other medical officers. The dining room was spacious, taking up most of a deck, it seemed. White walls and portholes gave it a wide open feeling, but the ceiling was low, only about seven feet high.

"OK if we sit here, gentlemen?" I asked. There was an atmosphere of a restaurant about the place, a restaurant where you could meet new people every day.

"Please, *suh*." The southern drawl in the pronunciation of "sir" was unmistakable. All three looked friendly enough. The one who said "*suh*" looked smooth, like someone who might try to sell you insurance.

The English stewards served up our soup, in grim silence, as usual.

"Y'all from Minnesota, ya say?" asked one of the other officers. Apparently all three of them were from south of the Mason Dixon Line.

"That's right, and you?" I said.

"Well, I'm from Richmond, Jim La Fleur here is from Macon, and Will Beauregard hails from New Orleans. (It sounded like *Naw lins*.) I am Robert Lee, at your service."

It sounded like he said *suhvis*. Lee was the insurance salesman. The other two, La Fleur and Beauregard, looked as American as apple pie, in spite of the French names. We were a nation of immigrants.

Abe ventured out onto thin ice. "Robert Lee, that wouldn't be, I mean, would your full name be . . .?" Abe was gesturing with his hand, making little circles, as if to "draw out" the obvious conclusion.

"Yes. My full name is Robert E. Lee. My father had great respect for the man." Lee was getting expansive, placing his hands wide apart on the table, leaning back and throwing his chin out as he spoke—a salesman, a politician. "It was an accident that my last name is Lee, but it was no accident when my father gave me Robert E." He gave a long, slow nod. This was not the first time he had told the story of his name.

Jim La Fleur spoke up. "My grandpappy was with Lee. Right from the beginning. Took a Yankee bullet in the Wilderness. Lost his right arm, right here." He pointed at his elbow. Whereas Lee had given a long, slow delivery, La Fleur blurted out his story in a rush, then he seemed to run out of "story" too soon.

Beauregard was itching to get his two cents' worth in, "Say, it ain't so. Y'all oughta hear my granddaddy's stories. Rode with Nathan Bedford Forrest, he did. Ooowee, did they make those Yankees run!" He hit his fist on the table, rattling the soup dishes and silverware. Beauregard didn't look like he'd ever run out of "story." His face and eyes were flushed with excitement.

Abe and I started to redden a little. Abe was a native of South Dakota, and I from Minnesota. Our allegiances ran to the northern side of the Mason-Dixon Line, when it came to a discussion of the Civil War.

"Ran circles around 'em," Beauregard went on. "Didn't know if he was comin' or goin'. I swanny, don't make no never mind who they sent after him, or how many, he'd whup 'em, time and time again." Beauregard could have gone on forever if I hadn't stepped in. And what did "swanny" mean?

"I've always had quite an interest in the Civil War myself," I said, trying to be pleasant, but conceding nothing on the relative merits of Nathan Bedford Forrest. My favorite generals had been Ulysses Grant, William Sherman, and Phil Sheridan.

The only sound was the clink of dishes at the other tables and steady thrumming of the ship's engines. The three Southerners looked upset. La Fleur and Beauregard in a hot huff, Lee being more cool and calculating about it. Had they read my mind? All I had said was, "I had an *interest* in the Civil War." Nothing derogatory about the South.

Dr. Lee steepled his fingers together then spoke as if tiptoeing on eggshells, "I believe you are referring to the War for Southern Independence, or perhaps more accurately the War of Northern Aggression?" No longer the salesman, now he was the professor. The three Southerners had taken exception to me saying "Civil War."

Abe stood up so fast he nearly tipped the table over, "What the hell do you mean 'Northern Aggression'?" Abe had taken a little exception himself. Men at the other tables heard the commotion and were all looking at us. The low ceiling in the room seemed to sink lower, and I was getting uncomfortable.

Lee leaned back with the satisfied smile of the winning debater, "I hope the irony of your words is not lost upon you, sir. As you can see, none of us Southern gentlemen are ready to settle this argument with fisticuffs, as you Northern, uh, gentlemen seem so ready to do."

Abe sat back down, looking at his soup. It was steaming. So was he.

Lee, ever the diplomat, went on. "Perhaps, we wax a bit eloquent about Confederate exploits." He looked around the room, noticing all the stares. The situation needed defusing, and Lee was up to the task. "I do ask your pardon if we have overstepped the bounds of good taste, gentlemen. But surely we are all now fighting in a common cause. This war against the Germans, which we will win with the help of you fine men from the North, should help us bury the Bloody Shirt that has so long separated us."

Never in my life had I heard such eloquence delivered off-the-cuff like that. Lee must have spent some time on the stage, (just like John Wilkes Booth). La Fleur, in contrast to Lee, lacked such polish and tact.

"Well you know, the German march through Belgium ain't no different than Sherman's March to the Sea, in my book. As I recall Sherman had some fine men from Minnesota along with him, too." His voice came out just loud enough to keep the entire dining room focused on the unfolding drama at our table. The men on board this ship craved entertainment, and we were providing it.

Though Abe was not native to Minnesota soil, he had done his schooling there, so he prepared to defend the state's honor. My hand kept him from bolting up again. At the same time, Lee leaned toward La Fleur and whispered something. Tension was simmering, but Lee was trying to mollify all parties. Beauregard changed the subject.

Beauregard turned to Abe, "Did you have any family in the, uh, Unpleasantry Between the States, Dr. Haskell?" Unpleasantry Between the States? Where did they come up with *that* one?

"I don't know." Abe shrugged his shoulders, still looking down. He was not enjoying this dinner too much.

His comment drew a stunned look from the Southern contingent.

"You don't know?" Beauregard asked, unbelieving. In the South, everyone knew everything about every family member that served in THE war.

"No. My grandparents ran a feed store, I think. On my mom's side, I don't think they'd even gotten to America yet. They were still in Russia, I think. Dad never mentioned anybody going off to join the army." Abe was loosening up a little.

The stewards came in with the main course—Yorkshire pudding, creamed peas with mashed potatoes, and bangers (sausages).

"And you," Lee asked me, "anyone you know of involved in the kind of heroics that Will Beauregard and Jim La Fleur described?" Smooth as silk, Lee was, trying to patch up the rift at our table. Most of the other tables went back to their own dinners and conversations. Silverware started clinking again.

"No heroics that I know of. My mother had an uncle, though, John Barden, an Irish immigrant. A farmer by trade." Mom had told me the story many times. She recited it as if she knew the man personally, but that couldn't be. She had been only three years old when he went to war. Three years old—still in the forgetful years. Mom could have no living memory of Uncle John.

Tension left the table. The Southerners settled back in their chairs, even Abe relaxed.

"His friends told him not to go, that it wasn't his fight. Why should an Irishman get involved in a fight between Americans?" As an Irishman and a Catholic, he'd probably seen plenty of fighting and dying already. And most of that fighting would have been against the English.

Everyone started eating, but kept their eyes on me. So hypnotizing is a tale of long ago.

"But he said, 'I'm an American now, and when my country goes to war, so do I. Besides, I don't hold no truck with slavery.'" The Southerners winced, they didn't want to talk about slavery. "'And I'm sick of this farmwork.' And with that, he joined the 5th Minnesota Volunteer Infantry, enlisting at Fort Snelling, not far from the present University of Minnesota where I myself enlisted. He got down south by October of 1862. His first action, as nearly as we can tell, was at Corinth, Mississippi."

The engines made their thrum-thrum-thrum sound, the table rolled slightly with the ship's movements. Clink, clink, rattle, and the low hum of conversation from the other tables.

"And?" It was Beauregard, his voice softer now. He wanted to know what happened to my great uncle John Barden, no matter that his uniform was blue.

"The regimental record says only 'Killed in action. Was a good and faithful soldier.'"

Thrum, thrum, thrum. Beauregard, La Fleur, and Lee all nodded, stopped chewing for a second. Then Lee swallowed his food, put down his fork, and raised his glass.

Clearing his throat first, Lee said, "Gentlemen, here's to us, North and South, in the hope that we, too, will be good and faithful soldiers." No longer the snake oil salesman, the politician, or Southerner with a chip on his shoulder, Lee raised the toast as an American, pure and simple.

"Here' here," everyone said, and all five glasses clinked together.

About halfway through the voyage, Abe and I were standing on deck, leaning against the railing. A steady whoosh-whoosh came from the side of the ship as it pushed through the water. What a vast amount of steel went into this ship, this floating city! The sides of the ship alone were big enough to cover a city block. Then add the pipes, the fittings, the bulkheads, the boilers. Cabins, galleys, smokestacks. A whole mountain of steel, and yet with all this weight, it still floated!

"I wonder if it was like this on the *Titanic*?" Abe asked. He had a habit, Abe did, of coming up with the most unsettling comments.

"Little early in the season for icebergs, Abe."

We scanned the horizon, visibility was perfect. A few puffy clouds danced around in a clear blue sky. Though it was September, the clouds had the carefree look of a spring day. No icebergs, that we could see.

Five years before, on a spring night, the *Titanic* had gone down, taking over a thousand people with her. It was in all the papers. Abe and I had been in college at the time, just about ready to graduate. Some of the wealthiest people in the world had been on that ship—Astors and Vanderbilts, as I recalled. And there had been some poor people, too. Immigrants. Irish immigrants. Down below, in the steerage compartment, deep in the inner reaches of the ship. Far from the upper deck.

"At least we've got enough lifeboats," Abe said, reading my mind. The *Titanic* had not had enough lifeboats.

"Imagine the panic on deck, Abe, when they saw there weren't any lifeboats left."

Abe shook his head and looked down.

"You know, Ben, there were a lot of Irish immigrants on the *Titanic*. A lot of them. Down in the steerage compartment. Not many of them survived."

He was right. Most of the survivors had come from the first-class section.

Abe went on, "The English crewmen didn't seem in a big hurry to help the Irish passengers."

We'd been aboard the ship long enough to tour its confusing labyrinth of gangways and corridors reaching deep into the bowels of the ship. One could imagine being trapped deep within the ship, far from the open spaces of the upper deck, as ice-cold water filled up these same corridors. That was how it had been on the *Titanic*. Then you arrive at the end of one corridor and there's a locked gate. Behind you, hundreds of panic-stricken passengers push you forward, but the gate won't give, then you feel the water around your feet, and the lights go out. By now everyone's screaming. And no English crewman bothers to come down and open the gate. After all, you're only steerage compartment passengers, you're only Irish.

"Tea?"

I jumped up off the deck as if electrified by a great shock. Both my hands went straight up in the air and a great "Aaaaa!" escaped my throat.

An English steward holding a tray of tea took a step back and gave me a stare most curious. Abe, too, looked at me with raised eyebrows.

My breath came fast and I must have looked a fright. That daydream of being trapped in the *Titanic* had worked me up, and the steward had surprised the living hell out of me.

"Sure, yes, um, yes, tea would be . . . uh . . . you want some tea, Abe?" I got over my initial shock, then took a good long look at this steward, this English crewman. Would *he* bother to rescue us if the ship started to sink? After all, we were only Americans.

"Sure, Ben, you OK?" Abe must have thought me some kind of lunatic.

"Just a little jumpy, I suppose." I was still concentrating on that steward. Maybe he had been on the *Titanic* himself? Maybe he had kept those Irishmen locked up below decks. No. Ridiculous. Five years ago, this steward would have only been about twelve years old himself.

I declared the steward "not guilty" in my mind. It would be a mistake to keep thinking bad things about the English; to rekindle the Irish-English hatreds that had burned over the centuries. American I was born. American I was raised. And America was sending me to fight alongside the English, not against them.

"Good, I thought you'd seen a torpedo when you jumped like that," Abe said.

We took the tea. My hand didn't shake, thank goodness, it would have been embarrassing if the cup had rattled. Silly me, getting all worked up about an iceberg, then turning my anger towards my English allies. Why should I give a second thought to the *Titanic*, or an iceberg? For that matter, why should I worry what the English had done to the Irish? The English weren't the enemy, the Germans were. And the Germans had the man-made, year-round equivalent of an iceberg to worry about—a torpedo.

On September 20, a spooky, additional precaution was taken. The lifeboats were actually lowered down the sides and provisions were placed into them. Should the ship get hit by a torpedo, we might have only a few minutes to get off, so the lifeboats were ready to go at a moment's notice. And still our only protection was that one armed freighter chugging slowly in the middle of the convoy. That vision of the Irish passengers on the *Titanic*, trapped behind a locked gate, kept coming back to me, no matter how much I tried to shake it. God, to think of it.

"Jesus! Open the gate, open the gate for Christ's sake!"

Hands on the gate, shaking it, rattling the metal bars, hands clawing at the padlock. Bloody hands, fingernails torn off in the effort.

"Sorry, first class area, you're not allowed here, Mick."

And the English crewman disappears as he heads up to the upper deck, to the open upper decks, the place where there were still lifeboats.

"No, Christ Almighty! Get us out of here! We're sinking, there's no other way out! Help us, help us. Jesus, Mary, Joseph, help us! There are babies in here, babies! Take them at least! Take the babies!"

And the water comes up the corridor, inch by inch.

That very evening some additional protection arrived, much to our relief. At 7:10, a few specks could be seen on the Eastern horizon. In a few minutes, there were on us—8 torpedo boat destroyers. They looked Lilliputian compared to the freighters, and they skittered around us like nervous greyhounds. But, they bristled with guns, and their sterns held racks of depth charge canisters, so they were a welcome sight. We had our escort for the last, most dangerous part of the journey.

It struck one as marvelous that two fleets starting at opposite ends of the Atlantic could meet in mid-ocean with pinpoint accuracy. The wonders of modern wireless communication, and the skills of the sailors—it was not surprising Britannia ruled the waves.

A wild gale blew up our first night with the torpedo boat destroyers. Huge waves raised up and dropped us. Still we continued zigzagging with lights blacked out. At this point I worried more about a collision than a torpedo. If we were to sink in this storm, how could we even get the lifeboats off? Still, drowning in a gale, in the open sea, would be better than being locked up, trapped like those Irishmen on the *Titanic*. (That scene kept playing in my head, over and over again. "Open the gate, open the gate!")

By morning the gale was gone and we saw our first landfall—Scottish islands to port, and the north coast of Ireland to starboard. The sun shone on Ireland, so we had a glimpse of "a little bit of heaven dropped from out the sky." It was just after harvest time, and the small farms, all green and yellow, looked charming. At a distance it gave the impression of a great toy farm. The small villages, like a picture from a fairy tale they were.

That day at noon, the slower ships in our convoy separated from us and went off to Glasgow. That left us with three troop transports and three escort destroyers to cross the Irish Sea—a short distance, but in the heart of the danger zone. German submarines had sunk plenty of ships in this area.

With no slow freighters to hold us back, we tore through the Irish Sea in a sickening zigzagging course. No one even bothered to go to the dining room, for we couldn't have kept anything down if we tried. About dark we made it safely into the Mersey River, which leads to Liverpool. On Saturday, September 22, we anchored safe at last behind submarine nets and free of the unending roar of the engines. No bumps in the night, no strange engine noises, no waking up with pounding heart. No more visions of the trapped Irishmen on the *Titanic*. We had made it through U-boat Alley. None of King Willie's fish had found us, and Enbanks's bunk had not collapsed on top of me. Sister Marie, my guardian angel, must be on the job.

From Liverpool, a gloomy looking place which we were glad to leave, we took a train to London. We traveled across the heart of England and pretty country it was, too, in post harvest time. Vegetation was abundant everywhere, with hedges along the railroads and around nearly every house. Stations were much closer together than in America and the road was double-tracked all the way. The little engines and coaches with first-, second-, and third-class compartments seemed queer at first. In typical American tourist fashion we laughed at their size and quaintness.

In the large, open railway cars in America, "all men are created equal." Not so in England. A rich Englishman wants his privacy, and his first-class compartment. He does *not* want to rub elbows with any third-class passenger, thank you.

Our first night in London, it was bombed by the Germans. The night had started out tamely enough. A few of us went to the London Hippodrome to see a show called "Zig-Zag," which featured my favorite song, "Over There." (Abe was not with us. He had met a pretty ticket taker on a double-decker bus and was nowhere to be found.) Before the show the manager came out and said an air raid was imminent, and anyone who wanted to could leave the building. An air raid was on the way? I looked around me, it was a theater like any number of theaters I'd sat in through the years—rows of seats, heavy curtains on the stage, exits, carpeting on the floor. An air raid was coming, here? A plane would load up with fuel and bombs, and fly over from a German aerodrome, to drop bombs on me? Here? Sitting in this comfortable seat looking at thick, plush red curtains? It struck me what a ridiculous enterprise this thing they called war really was. Why would some German, a complete stranger, want to kill me in a London theater? We just sat there not quite knowing what one does in such a case. After a few minutes passed, the manager came out again and told us the air raid was over. What? Over already? The air raid hadn't even *begun*, that I could tell. But, apparently, that was it. The air raid started and ended without so much as a "Boo!" My first encounter with the enemy had come and gone and all I had done was sit in this theater. No aeroplanes, no bombs did I hear. And then, the curtain went up, and I watched the variety show. So much for my "baptism by fire."

We were pleased as punch when they started the second act with a rousing rendition of "Over There." They had a peculiar name for it—"The Sammies' Marching Song." Apparently, the tune had caught on in England, too, and was the newest show stopper. Of course, now that I was in England, I was now technically "over there" myself, so the song held special significance. After the show, we stepped outside and saw several big searchlights shooting up to the sky, but still we heard nothing.

The searchlights were certainly impressive, a white dagger cutting through the night. They must strike great fear in the enemy pilots. What a helpless feeling to be caught in that brilliant beam, like a butterfly pinned in a collection.

We learned later that many bombs had been dropped and that one of our very own, Dr. La Fleur, the Southerner, had gotten a severe laceration in his arm. It was sobering to think that our little group was already suffering casualties, and we had just arrived. Fine welcome. And that laceration to Dr. La Fleur didn't have to be in his arm. It could have happened in his throat, or belly, or chest, or spinal cord. He could have died. Furthermore, that bomb could just as easily have landed on me. Words like "fate" or "chance" or "luck" started to dance around in my head.

The next night I shook off those gloomy thoughts and went to His Majesty's Theater to see another light-hearted variety show called "Chu Chin Chow." Again, the orchestra played "Over There." Another air raid occurred, this one much closer. The band stopped playing in mid-show and everyone went outside to watch "the other show."

I could hear the engines of the Gotha bombers overhead, and their bombs lighting in various parts of the city. Whoomp. Whoomp. WHOOMP! Whoomp.

WHOOMP! WHOOMP! This raid seemed real to me, unlike the raid on the previous night. Whoomp. WHOOMP! Searchlights cut swaths through the blackness. Where were those bombers? Where were they? Back and forth the lights went, catching nothing but black sky. Wait! What was that? Out of the corner of my eye I thought I saw a movement, an edge of a wing caught by the spotlight. By the time I turned my head, the corner of wing was gone. Maybe it was my imagination. (The periscope in New York harbor.) Then, it happened again—a speck of dark in the brilliant white light, but this time the searchlight swung back and caught the German bomber full on. High above London, high above me, a black, gull-winged biplane was framed in light. The butterfly was pinned.

Other searchlights, sensing the kill, swung around, and soon four or five had fastened onto the bomber. All the time, Whoomp! WHOOMP! Whoomp! Anti-aircraft fire started reaching up to the target, the illuminated Gotha bomber. Colored bursts and trails of glowing bullets reached up, trying to hit the plane. Whoomp! WHOMP! He seemed to be twisting left and right, trying to get out of the light beams, but they stayed fastened to him. The anti-aircraft fire kept hitting below him, and the streams of glowing bullets petered out before they got to his altitude, and arced back towards the ground. Still, the lights stayed on him.

Poof! He disappeared, just like that. All the searchlights were illuminating a big cloud, making it look as white and fluffy as daytime. The German bomber had ducked into a cloud and vanished.

No more whoomps! No more colored shell bursts, no more streams of bullets, shooting into the sky. No more engine roar. The "other show" was over. I wonder what the crew of that German bomber were thinking.

The all-clear signal was given; we went back into the theater and watched the rest of "Chu Chin Chow." It *was* a good show, but, after the drama of the bomber and the searchlights, it seemed a little trivial.

The English people seemed little disturbed, and the raids served only to firm up their resolve to defeat Germany. Most Londoners made wisecracks and jokes about the air raids. No one seemed in any way panic-stricken or demoralized. This was my introduction to the tough, gritty aspect of the British character. If the Germans expected to break the morale of the English by air raids, they were sadly mistaken. The English might seem overly polite and even "prissy" by American standards, but they were defending their island home now, and they were proving themselves resilient in adversity. Bravo to the brave Englishman.

But London wasn't always under attack, so I took in the sights. Though large, London was still a walkable city, so I walked along the Victoria Embankment beside the Thames River, and past the Egyptian obelisk called Cleopatra's Needle. Damage from the air raid lay scattered about. Workmen were cleaning up, smoking cigarettes and cracking jokes all the while. They tipped their hats to me as I walked past. Many bridges spanned the Thames, including London

Bridge of nursery rhyme fame. While walking past it, I ran into a young lieutenant. His left arm was in a sling.

Pointing to the bridge, I asked, "Excuse me, is this *the* London Bridge, as in 'London Bridge is falling down, falling down' London Bridge?" I had sung the "London Bridge is falling down, falling down" part, so ingrained is the song from childhood.

"That it is, Yank."

His accent was harder to fathom than other British accents, kind of musical, and I must have leaned forward a little, and wrinkled my eyebrows.

The ruddy fellow, short, but with great broad shoulders, picked up my quizzical look.

"There is Welsh, it is. That's why you're having a hard time of it. Even the regular English English have a hard time making out what I say." He spoke in a lilting sing-song. "Of course, these Saxons tried to take this island away from us."

We both laughed at that. Wales, in the western part of the United Kingdom, had fought England for many years, and had finally been "annexed" into England (in a way of speaking). This Welshman was trying, in a humorous way, to distance himself from his Saxon conquerors, i.e., the English. As an American, and as a descendant of Irish blood, I could immediately make common cause with this man. And to think, we were both now in the British Army! What a tangled web we weave.

"There is medical, you are?" he asked. What a curious way to talking he had.

"Yes, come from America. They haven't assigned me much to do yet, though, so I'm just taking in the sights. What happened to your arm?" I pointed to his sling.

We started walking along the Thames together, the Houses of Parliament and Big Ben ahead of us.

"Oh that, well. Jerry put a mortar on top of us. Not the nicest thing he'd ever done for me, nor the worst either. It is true the Red Indians in—North Dakota I believe it is—speak Welsh?"

I allowed as I had never heard such a thing.

"That must have been terrible! The mortar, I mean." Sounding like a child, I went on, pushing the words together. "You see, I guess I'll be going out there, sometime, and, well, I've read about it, but here you are, and you've been there. I guess I'm just dying . . . maybe that's the wrong word, well, I'm awfully curious." Did every "newcomer" to a war ask such foolishly phrased questions to every veteran? I had promised myself not to do that, but I just couldn't help it. What was it like "out there"?

He nodded. "I know, I know, I was the same way before I went out in '16. You want to know everything, but you can't really know anything until you get there, and round and round you go." Nice person, this Welshman, and his accent was nothing short of charming.

"Yes, that's it. I know I can't know 'til I go there, but I can't help but ask, I want to, well, know what it's like." Slow down! Why was I acting like such a ninny? I took a deep breath, tried to collect myself.

"Well, look you, my American friend, let's have a little tea and a bit talk and we'll go from there. Are there more of you coming over, then?"

The Welshman asked me the question as he might have asked about the weather. "Are there more of you coming over then?" No desperation in his voice, no pleading, just simple curiosity. But he asked because he wanted to know, and he wanted to know, because he needed us. That sling would come off his shoulder soon, and this brave Welshman would return to the Front, perhaps to get wounded again, or killed. He and his British brothers had been getting wounded, patched up, and sent back into the line for years now. And the same went for the French and Belgians. There was a limit to what flesh could endure. America had to get into this war, and soon.

"Yes, my friend. There are more of us coming. Can you hold off Jerry for a little longer?"

"There is a good man." He clapped me on the back with his good hand. "I can hold off Jerry, as long as you buy the first pint."

We had arrived in front of a pub, "Llewelyn's Ale House." A crowd of khaki-clad soldiers was within.

"Llewelyn, there is a Welsh name it is. They'll not be watering the bitters in here." That accent of his! He would slay the girls in Minnesota with that accent, might even provide some competition for Abe Haskell.

Pushing our way through the crowd, we happened on an empty table by sheer luck. Someone was playing on the piano, a soft song, a sad song. A few soldiers leaned against the piano and sang.

He ordered a pint of bitters for himself, the same for me, and then he tossed me out a few useful pointers. At last! News from the Front. And straight from the horse's mouth. I hung on his every word, often leaning forward to hear his voice better over the noise of the pub.

"The Hun keeps his aim low, so when you're crawling in the open, really crawl in the ground, don't be pointing your bottom up into the air, like a small baby does, or you'll get shot in the arse. I ought to know, it happened to me on the Somme." Standing up, he pointed to his left buttock, his pants hung slack there. Clearly, he had lost a lot of tissue in that left buttock. Then he retook his seat, putting most of his weight on the right, the intact buttock.

"Sleep whenever you can. And get your socks off, too. I swear we lose more men to wet feet than we do to hot lead." He pointed down to his feet.

Trench foot, a combination of frostbite, infection, and poor circulation, brought on by prolonged immersion in cold water or wet boots, had caused thousands of casualties. Some soldiers had toes or even feet amputated. Others had died from it, the infection having spread up their legs and into their bloodstream. Just *living* in a trench could kill you.

But I wasn't interested in talking about trench foot. What was it like to go into action? That's what I wanted to hear.

"What is it like when you go 'over the top'? I read in the papers the terrible accounts of the Somme and other battles. But reading about it only tells you so much. Just what is it like? I cannot picture it, or how you could build up the nerve to leave the cover of the trenches and head right at the Germans." That was the acid question. How had the British, or anyone for that matter, built up the nerve to fight these tremendous battles over the last three years? What went through a man's mind as he walked into the Valley of Death?

The Welshman had to think about that for a while. With his good arm, he pointed forward, as if at the German lines. In the background, the piano continued playing sad songs: songs about saying good-bye, songs about lost loves.

"Believe it or not, you're usually pretty bucked up to get out of the trench and have a go at the Hun. You stay cooped up in those dugouts so long, you want to get out, push Jerry back a bit, try to finish this war up before we all get too old to shoot any more." He was still pointing forward, "seeing" the Hun's lines.

"And each time you think it will be different than the last time. I remember out on the Somme, we shelled the Hun for a week, a *whole week*, we thought sure his wire would be blown apart. And then, of course, all the other fellows are getting ready, gearing up, checking maps. You'd hate to hold back, tell the boys you have another engagement, and you just can't make it."

His tone was so matter-of-fact. No drama or pathos in his voice.

"So you are so busy with the workaday business that the time just flies. Then the whistle blows, you stumble up the ladder as best you can, and then you just hope for the best. You only see the few fellows to your right and left, and there's usually enough smoke around to make it hard to see too terribly much." He wasn't looking at me now, wasn't looking at anything. But what he must be seeing!

"You hope your number isn't up, and when you pass a friend, curled up on the ground, or see him hanging on the wire, you think it's bad luck for him, and hope you don't have the same bad luck. You don't really miss them right then, that comes later.

Now his voice did drop a notch, his gaze went down to his beer, he swirled it around a little.

"When the machine guns open up, then you know the attack's not going too well. You always hope you'll get in their trenches before they get to those machine guns, but that doesn't happen too often, maybe in a quick night raid, but not in the big shows. Certainly not that day on the Somme.

He was seeing Death, looking it right in the eyes.

"Jerry fires those machine guns right through his own wire, so you start to see a lot of sparks, red, yellow, sometimes blue sparks. And a ping-ping, pinging as the bullets go through the wire. And a thunking sound when it hits the fellow at your side.

His focus came back to me, he had left Death behind, this time.

"Not a pleasant thing, going over the top. But that's what we have to do. Just have to carry on as best we can, my friend, just have to carry on. But enough about me and my old stories." He reached up with his good arm to signal the waiter for the bill.

"One last thing, my friend, one piece of advice that may serve you well."

The piano started playing the song, "Dixie," which struck me as odd.

"There will come a time when you've got to run. When that time comes," he paused to empty his glass, "Dixie" playing in the background, "do run with dispatch."

Later that day the Welshman and I were passing Buckingham Palace and the royal carriage drove out with the queen in it. The Welshman stood at attention and saluted and so did I. The queen nodded and smiled very graciously.

Queer to think we had fought a revolution to rid ourselves of kings, queens, and the trappings of royalty, yet there was something still magical about actually seeing a queen.

Chapter 3

MEETING A TRAIN

September 28 – November 19, 1917

George Bernard Shaw wrote, "The English and Americans are two people separated by a common language." I was to discover the depth of this separation at my first official assignment, Graylingwell War Hospital at Chichester, about 60 miles southwest of London, near the south coast.

Chichester was a quaint, old English town of about 7,000 souls in one of the most picturesque parts of England—Sussex. It's said to have been the first Roman settlement in England and was called by the Romans "Regnum." Parts of an old Roman wall, several feet thick and several feet high, were still about a part of the city. The buildings and streets were mostly of an old English type, many of them several hundred years old. In the center of town was an old Market Cross. Chichester was still a great market town.

There was a cathedral in town, built in the eleventh century. Saint Richard was once Bishop of Chichester.

The hills of Sussex, known as the South Downs, were all around, and in the changing colors of autumn afforded a walk of great scenic beauty. On the peak of a hill a few miles out of town lay the remains of an old fortification, thought to date back to the time of the Romans, or perhaps even earlier to the Britons. A deep ditch or moat several hundred yards in circumference circled the peak of the hill, and inside the moat the earth was thrown up in a low wall. Centuries of rain and weather had served to partially wash the wall and fill the moat, and while hundreds of sheep now grazed on the grassy hillsides, but in imagination one could see "the knights of old in their armor bold" as they dashed madly in and out over the draw bridge. On a clear day, you could see the Isle of Wight from this hill.

The Duke of Richmond owned an estate, known as "Goodwood," about two miles from Chichester in the direction of the ancient fortification. It contained a fine hunting preserve, a golf course, and one of the finest race courses in England. At that race course, every August, the king, queen, and nobility assembled as guests of the Duke of Richmond for a week of horse racing. After that, the whole party went to Portsmouth for a review of the grand fleet. The races were on at Goodwood, I believe, in the summer of 1914, when the war clouds began to gather over Europe, and the sports were abruptly ended. England and the world took up a more deadly game a few weeks later in the fields of France and Belgium. Injured players from that game came to us at Graylingwell War Hospital.

The British Medical Service ordered four Americans, including Abe and me, to go there on September 28. The Graylingwell's medical staff had dinner with us that first night, but we started wearing out our welcome mat pretty quickly. Several older English doctors, civilians who had been helping the military doctors there, had been summarily dismissed to make room for us "greenhorns" from America. Those civilian doctors *must* have resented us, but they were perfectly gracious at this, their going-away dinner. Unfortunately, we were not gracious in the least.

One of our doctors, a Dr. George from Chicago, took it upon himself to compare England and America. He spoke to no one in particular and everyone in general, and he spoke good and loud.

"Say, fellas, couldn't help noticing how *short* London was."

George had just addressed a roomful of doctors, our hosts, as "fellas."

"Short?" one of our hosts asked. The dining room was paneled with some kind of dark, rich wood, maybe cherry wood. Inlaid bookshelves and wainscoting, I think they called it, made it look like a library. The library of an earl or duke or something.

"Well, yes, short. You ought to come to Chicago. Now there's a city. Skyscrapers everywhere. Twenty stories high, some of 'em. Why, the biggest thing you've got here is just shrimpy." Hand gestures punctuated the greatness of our buildings, the insignificance of theirs.

The English doctors looked at each other, said nothing.

George went on, uninvited. "And those trains of yours, with those little dinky compartments." He held his two fingers close together. "A man can hardly stretch his legs but that he hits the fellow across from him. Or, maybe the lady." All four of us Americans broke out in laughter, too loud.

"Oh, that's rich, George," Abe said, "bump into the lady. That's rich!" Abe nudged the people on both sides of him with his elbows. On the bookshelves around us, there were some busts—Homer, Shakespeare, Milton. They seemed to be frowning at us.

More loud laughter from us. Nothing from the English. A Dr. Haigh from New York picked up where George left off, just in case the English weren't feeling bad enough about their country.

England had stood for over a thousand years, had given us our language, our rules of law. England, the land of the Magna Carta, of Shakespeare, of parliamentary procedure. England's empire stretched across the globe, from India to Africa, from Hong Kong to Australia to the Falkland Islands. Union Jacks flew on ships in all the seven seas. But our Dr. Haigh, from New York, chose to complain about the heating in England.

"Now I'm not one to complain, and I think all your castles and such are great, but, you sure you couldn't put a little central heating in some of them? I mean, it's cold in these rooms. Get yourself a good old boiler down in the basement, like we have in New York, run a few radiators here and there. Make it nice and cozy. You ought to come over sometime, we'll show you how to make a room nice and toasty." Haigh looked quite satisfied with that. He knew what was best for the British Empire—radiators.

"Yeah," Abe chimed in, "I've seen that big fireplace you've got in my room. No thanks! I don't mind dying a hero's death at the Front, but I sure don't want to get burned up while sound asleep at an English hospital."

That brought down the house, at least among the Americans. The English doctors remained as unmoved as the frowning busts of Homer, Shakespeare, and Milton. The dark, ornate walls absorbed our laughter, trying to muffle it, drown it, shut us up.

For some reason unknown to me, Dr. George just couldn't stop going on and on about the great things in America. A blind man could see the English doctors were bored to tears by the conversation, and even we other three Americans were losing interest in all this "American grandeur."

"Mammoth Caves. There's a sight. A sight to behold, believe you me. Why, you could fit Stonehenge, the Tower of London, Big Ben, and all that other stuff in the *entrance* to the place. It's enormous!" Mammoth Caves? Where did George come up with that? Of all the things to brag about. Statue of Liberty, maybe, or even the Grand Canyon, I could see that. But Mammoth Caves?

He shoveled a big forkful of creamed peas into his mouth.

"Where *did* you learn to cook, fellas? Now, I'm not one to complain either, but you could use a little home style American cooking around here, too. Now, where was I?" He was in the middle of the god damned Mammoth Caves is where he was.

I found myself starting to side with the English doctors, strange to say. In my mind's eye, I saw George getting tossed head first into the deepest chasm of Mammoth Caves, and after him, one of Haigh's radiators getting thrown in for good measure.

By now George was talking with his mouth full, waving his fork around in the air. None of us wanted to prompt him, to get him talking again, but one of the English surgeons, perhaps out of dutiful politeness, answered George's question.

"You were mentioning how nothing in England could compare to your Mammoth Cave structure in Chicago." He spoke with his eyebrows lifted, the best "feigning interest" expression I'd ever seen.

"Chicago? No, *I'm* from Chicago, Mammoth Cave is in Kentucky, mister, Kentucky! Don't they teach you anything about geography over here?"

The eyebrows went down and the rest of his face sank, too. Why bother feigning interest with this boor?

"Apparently our schools are *also* rather second-rate, Dr. George," the surgeon said.

By now, even Haigh, of radiator fame, was getting embarrassed.

"Yeah, well, let's not get into that. I'd hate to come across as some kind of ingrate, after all."

The Englishmen looked at each other as if to say, "Yes, how on earth could we ever draw that conclusion?"

George forged ahead, blind to the Englishmen, blind to the Americans' growing unease; as blind as a Mammoth Cave bat.

"So anyway," another big forkful of peas, this time some of them rolling down his chin. He caught them with a finger and slid them back into his mouth, "Mammoth Caves, boy oh boy. And at the bottom of it, in this huge chamber, there are these . . . these . . . "

Waving his hands and fork around, he was trying to "draw" a conical shape.

Over the centuries, dripping water, laden with minerals, had laid down enormous stalactites (conical stones hanging from the ceilings) and stalagmites (conical pillars rising from the floors) in Mammoth Caves. Our self-appointed "expert" on all things Mammoth Cavernal had apparently forgotten the terms "stalactite" and "stalagmite." George was hanging, hanging himself with his own tongue.

At last the English doctors were interested. Their braggart American cousin had painted himself into a corner. They seemed to lean in, to say, "Well, yes, tell us what was at the bottom of these all-important Mammoth Caves of yours. We're dying to know."

George kept drawing a triangle in the air, the best approximation of a cone-shaped stalagmite that he could muster.

"These . . . these . . .," still spinning his wheels.

Farther in the Englishmen leaned. The walls themselves, the cherry wood, the bookshelves, the wainscoting, everything was inching inwards with bated breath, waiting for the next word out of George's mouth. Homer, Shakespeare, Milton seemed to inch forward, threatening to topple off the shelves. These men, authors of *The Odyssey*, *Macbeth*, and *Paradise Lost* were breathless in anticipation. What the hell was at the bottom of Mammoth Caves?

I jumped in, couldn't help myself.

"Fish," I said.

Pandemonium. The normally grim and staid English doctors all broke out in huge, guffawing laughter. A steward (famous for their icy reserve, as demonstrated on the *Orduna*) threw his head back so hard that he hit a bookshelf with a resounding "thunk!", toppling Shakespeare's bust down onto a lamp, which fell to the ground and broke. Another steward smacked his knees (an exclusively American gesture, I had thought) and ran through the swinging doors leading to the kitchen, shouting, "Oh Lord, I'm going to pee, I'm going to pee!"

George looked at me like I was Benedict Arnold. Haigh kept saying, "What's so funny, what's so funny!" Abe laughed and laughed.

It was the only time that I saw Englishmen laugh to tears. They could not stop laughing all night. In the days that followed, the English would often bring up the famous fish of Mammoth Caves. The menu at the hospital even jumped on the comedic bandwagon:

Menu for Tuesday, Sept. 30

Creamed Peas
Mashed Potatoes
Fried Cod á la Mammoth
Tea

But in spite of my little joke, the damage was done. Our critical ways and boorish behavior at the first dinner had insulted the English. From that first night on, social contact between the Americans and English was pretty much nil.

We sat at different tables at dinnertime, and after meals, we went to different rooms to smoke and chat. Their room was always quiet, subdued, and closed to us. They played bridge. We kept our door open, and laughed and shouted, making no attempt to disguise our ridiculous attempts to imitate an English accent. When it came to cards, we preferred poker over the more straight-laced "English" game of bridge.

No doubt they felt slighted by our oafish humor. We were *so far* from home, so nervous, so unsure of our roles, so uncertain of our skills, so *outnumbered*, that we overdid our American-ness. Braggadocio and bluff did a poor job at covering up our insecurity. As for the English, they made no real attempt to make us feel welcome, nor, for that matter, did they seem thankful that America had entered the war. Just one word of "thanks" or "Glad you're here," would have gone a long way toward healing this English-American rift. But they wouldn't say it, and we couldn't have pried a "thanks" out of them with a crowbar. The English acted put-upon, as if we were no more than a nuisance, an uninvited country cousin who appeared on their doorstep. As time passed, we found the English getting more and more standoffish. In response, we just became more raucous and insulting.

So this was our first contact with the English. Neither of us understood nor tried to understand the other. It seemed a shame. A pox on both our houses.

At times, we would go to the pubs in town. The English seemed standoffish there, too, but for some reason were crazy about the song "Dixie," which they played and sang over and over again. Few Englishmen even knew what the Mason and Dixon Line *was*, but they loved that song.

The one bright spot in Chichester was my chief of staff, a Dr. Maxwell, "Old Maxwell" as he was called by the younger English doctors. He had been a missionary doctor in Formosa for years, and his long separation from England had done some good, opening his eyes to other ways and other peoples. Gray-haired, spare, and tall, he was more open to us, more accepting of our differences. All in all, he was less "English." And he loved to teach.

Walking down the wards the first day, he spoke up, talking straight at us, not down to us.

"In Formosa, they had a saying, 'I see, and I forget. I do, and I remember.'" He even recited it for us in Chinese. Somehow, he expressed that whole sentence in only four syllables. Chinese must be a compact language. "Doctors, on this service you are not going to *see* me do operations, then *forget* what you saw. You will DO the operations, then *remember* what you DID. Got it?"

"Yes, sir." Boy did we ever get it.

Nodding at us, he took an elaborately carved scrimshaw pipe out of his pocket. Dragons and Chinese characters covered it. He clamped it in his teeth and lit up.

"All right, boys, let's get to work." His accent was pure English; his attitude, pure American.

Sister Marie Francis' prayers were working. This was just the kind of experience I needed—lots of work with a mentor nearby. Soon, at the Front, I would have a lot of work, but there would be *no* mentor nearby. God help me when that day arrived. More accurately, God help my patients when that day arrived.

If an assignment put me in harm's way, and a bullet or shell found me, that would not be my fault. It would be the luck of the draw, the fate that can befall any soldier. No shame in that. But if I failed my *patients*; if I fell apart when men needed a *skilled, confident* doctor; if men *died* who might otherwise have *lived* (Giancomo), then it would be my fault. There *would* be shame in that. *My* shame. I stuck close to Maxwell, as close as his shadow, and kept my eyes and ears open. He kept my hands moving.

I see and I forget. I do, and I remember. So I did, and did, and kept doing. Maxwell helped build up my confidence. Someday, men's lives would depend on me, ME, so I took to the clinical work with deadly earnest. Each clinic visit, each dressing change, each operation, each discussion with Maxwell might teach me *the* clinical lesson that might save a man's leg, his arm, his sight, or his life. (I had studied seriously in medical school, and had paid close attention to all my clinical work as an intern, back in America, but the fact that I would be so *alone* at the Front, and the fact that so many casualties might come under my direct care, put the fear of God in me.) No teacher has ever had such an avid student as I was under Maxwell.

I see, and I forget. I do, and I remember. Roll up your sleeves, Ben Gallagher, get in there and do something.

We operated. We operated and operated—set and splinted fractured arms and legs, debrided necrotic tissue from head, feet, groins, everywhere, and irrigated, irrigated, irrigated. The wounds from France were all dirty, and often infected, so we irrigated them with Dakin's solution, a weak hypochlorite mixture that washed out germs and—we hoped—cured the infection. (This method was developed by Drs. Carrell and Dakin, and represented a real advance in the treatment of dirty wounds.) One frequent problem we encountered was getting the irrigating solution into and out of a plaster cast, without dissolving the cast itself into a sticky paste. Many a time I headed back to my room encrusted with plaster and Dakin's solution.

One day in the operating room Dr. Maxwell let me remove an eye. There is something terribly human about an eye and taking it out was grisly business. But war is grisly business, too, and at the Front, I'd have to treat whatever came my way. So up went my sleeves, out came the eye.

All of the patients got tetanus antitoxin. (This was a relatively recent development, first used in 1915. It was not perfect, and some patients had allergic reactions to it, but overall it prevented tetanus in most cases. Tetanus antitoxin was a real lifesaver.) Most patients had received one or several doses in France at the Dressing Stations. Luckily, none of our patients in Chichester developed a full-blown case of tetanus. (When full-blown tetanus did happen, the patient would first complain of stiffness in his jaw, then within a few hours his muscles would tighten up, twisting his face into an awful grimace, called, in Latin, "*rhisus sardonicus*," meaning sarcastic smile. The back muscles would then seize up so tight that the patient would arch, stiff as a board, with only his heels and head touching the ground. Death came from respiratory failure, the muscles tightening up so much that the patient could not breathe.) Such deaths had occurred during my training in Minnesota. Usually, a farmer injured himself, got dirt or manure in the wound, and the tetanus set in. It was an awful death to witness. Wherever I finally got to in France, I would always make sure to have a reserve supply of tetanus antitoxin on me. No tetanus deaths on my watch.

"Dr. Gallagher, Dr. Haskell. When you're over there, in France, get those wounds clean as quick as you can, and get that tetanus antitoxin into them. I saw a lot of tetanus deaths over in Formosa, and it's not a pretty sight," Maxwell told us, his pipe clamped in his teeth. He was a treasure trove of clinical "pearls," (short, useful medical lessons) and could find something instructive with nearly every patient.

"Don't take forever getting a bone perfectly straight. Line it up pretty good, get a cast on it, then move along."

"Soldiers have one thing going for them. They're young. If they can get better, they will."

"When you're sure, absolutely sure, that the wound is completely clean, irrigate it *again*."

"You'll be playing tug-of-war with the Grim Reaper. Sometimes he has a better grip on the rope than you do. People die, boys, people die. Don't worry about it. Go save the next one."

Maxwell was a teacher.

My confidence started to build, body part by body part.

—The leg. A tourniquet can stop the bleeding. Clamp the spouting arteries. Watch for compartment syndrome (swelling in the lower leg that can cut off the blood supply). If that happens, incise the leg to relieve the pressure. If the entire leg is too badly damaged—amputate. A leg wound means a stretcher evacuation, most often.

—The arm. Again, a tourniquet can always stop the bleeding (though you can't leave a tourniquet on forever—that will cut off *all* blood supply and assure that the limb will be lost). Check for compartment syndrome in the forearm (the equivalent of compartment syndrome in the lower leg). A sling can handle a host of evils, can buy you time, and allow the man to evacuate *himself*, a real plus when the number of casualties are enormous. An arm is a *little* better at fighting off infection than a leg (an arm has better circulation), so, if it came down to the *very last* battle of irrigating fluid, irrigate the leg wound before the arm wound.

As I treated the patients at Chichester, I would keep mentally testing myself, "How would I do this in the field? How would I do this if Maxwell weren't here? How would I do this if 25 other men needed help at the same time?" Maxwell did the same thing, saying things like, "See that dark, purplish color in the man's fingers? In a dugout, during a bombardment, you'd make one incision, lengthwise, put in one piece of gauze, and move on. Of course, here, in a hospital setting, we take a little more time. Time is one commodity you won't have 'out there'."

"Out there." Soon, I'd be "out there," and I had to be ready.

Body parts. Know the important things to do with each part, and that should keep the men alive.

—Abdomen. A wound in the large blood vessels is untreatable, let that man go. A wound that spills intestinal contents into the abdomen will eventually kill the man with overwhelming infection, but drainage, irrigation, and an operation at a Rear Area Hospital *may* save his life. *Don't* let that man go. Irrigate the hell out of the wound, restore some semblance of integrity to the abdominal wall (binding it with a huge gauze pad, if necessary) and evacuate him FIRST.

—Chest. Once again, a wound in the heart or one of the great blood vessels is untreatable (it's unlikely such a man would ever make it to the Aid Post). Rib fractures—bind with gauze to relieve the pain of breathing. Pneumothorax (like I had done on purpose to Mr. Gundersen to treat his tuberculosis), treat by slapping a bandage on the wound and securing with tape, to prevent further entry of air. *BUT,* if the pneumothorax is so big that the patient can't breathe at *all* (a so-called tension pneumothorax), then put a needle in the chest and *allow* air to escape. Treating chest wounds would be quite difficult. Such a patient needed evacuation right away.

—Head and neck. (Giancomo's ghost came back to haunt me on this body part, for he had injured his head and neck, and died under my care.) Scalp wounds bleed like stink, but they don't tend to get infected. Sew them up one, two, three. Though no wound should go uncleaned, a scalp laceration would be more "forgiving" if I ran out of irrigating solution during a battle. Skull open, brain exposed? That needed irrigation. Then cover with gauze and evacuate. Don't panic and give up on such a patient. Some amazing things were being done to save such people—some returning to normal lives. Neck wound? Keep the airway open. Keep the airway open. Keep the airway open. If that meant a tracheotomy—DO IT RIGHT AWAY!

Head and neck, chest, abdomen, arms, legs. A stick-man appeared in my head, the kind you would draw in a game of hangman. At the Front, out there, when I would be all alone, and men's lives would depend on me, I would draw that stick man in my head. The I'd go down the parts, starting at the top, working my way down, fixing what I could fix, then moving on.

I was getting ready.

The hospital held up to 1,100 patients, all soldiers from France, though not all were surgical cases. As the patients came in, they carried a card around their neck that had clinical information on it. These cards were labeled "W" (wounded—this included gas cases) or "S" (sick—this included "shell shock"). Trench fever, trench foot, pyrexia of unknown origin (fevers we couldn't figure out), heart trouble, shell shock, nephritis (kidney infections), and poison gas rounded out the cases at Graylingwell. By this point in the war, the Germans had developed several kinds of poison gas; the most feared was mustard gas. This burned not only the lungs and eyes, but also any exposed skin.

The poison gas victims looked frightening. Eyes swollen shut, faces burned—they hardly looked human. Their lungs were seared so they coughed day and night, making it hard to sleep—both for them, and those in the ward around them. They always had to sleep propped up on a lot of pillows, to ease their labored breathing. Awful as these cases seemed, they usually got better by themselves, even the victims of the terrible mustard gas.

Trench fever patients complained of terrible pains in the bones, especially the shin bones. At night, these men would tear their blankets and sheets off, convinced the weight of the bedclothes was breaking their bones. The primary treatment for them was rest, time, and delousing their clothes. (All men from the trenches were infested with body lice.) The lice were thought to transmit this typhus-like "trench fever." (Typhus is a blood-born infection characterized by high fevers, musculoskeletal aches, and a prolonged, slowly resolving course. In all respects, we could have called "trench fever"—"trench typhus.")

Most of the shell shock patients looked perfectly healthy by the time they got to Graylingwell, though I saw three who continued to shake and tremble for several days. Loud noises, like a ward door slamming, or a dinner plate falling on the floor, would make them nearly jump out of their skin. Luckily, rest and quiet brought them around in a few days, though talk of going back to France, back to the trenches, brought on many a relapse.

Maxwell, my kindly mentor, and I often discussed the nature of shell shock. Neither of us had any training in the realm of diseases of the mind. In medical school I'd heard a little about Mesmer's work with hypnosis, and a few students had been interested in Sigmund Freud's work on dream interpretation. But the closest I'd come to an understanding of the mind was neurology and neuroanatomy—an understanding of the wiring of the mind, not an understanding of the mind itself. Maxwell and I were treading into terra incognita with our conversations on shell shock.

We knew some men were malingering. "Slinging the lead" the English called it. These soldiers were terrified of getting wounded, dying, or being buried alive in a dugout which, if you think about it, is a very normal thing to be terrified of. From what I saw, though, both in England and at the Front later, shell shock struck me as a kind of nerve exhaustion. Each individual had a certain amount of reserve nerve power, just as each individual had a certain amount of reserve muscular power. So, just as Hercules could do great muscular feats before wearing out, so could some men endure great nervous feats before wearing out. How many long bombardments, "over-the-top" advances, and blown up friends could a man endure before he reached his limit? Assessing that limit, and differentiating it from malingering was beyond modern medicine's ken. The Royal Army Medical Corps had recently ordered that "shell shock" not be used as a diagnosis. The medical officers were ordered to write NDNYD (nervous disorder not yet diagnosed). Giving it a different name struck me as ridiculous, because everyone knew that NDNYD just meant "shell shock."

One fellow, a private named John Leeds, was admitted to Chichester with NDNYD. He always wanted to talk with me about his experiences. It seemed he wanted to "justify" his admission to the hospital; to "prove" that he really should be out of the line. It made me feel somewhat uncomfortable, for who was I to "judge" him. He had been "out there." I had not.

One rainy evening, he caught me tiptoeing past his bed.

"Mister Gallagher?" Leeds asked (the English called their surgeons "mister," rather than "doctor").

"Yes, John." (Damn, I had so wanted to go back to my room and get some sleep.)

"Mister Gallagher, do *you* think I'm 'slinging the lead'?" Here we go again. He was asking me to judge whether he was a coward or not.

"Well, John, no, I don't think . . . " What would Maxwell say? He was pretty diplomatic.

"The other ones do. The other fellows here," he motioned around the ward. Most of the men were sleeping. At the far end of the ward, two men sat propped up, coughing every now and then. Weighted pulleys and ropes held several men in traction. The air was pungent with antiseptic smells.

"The fellows with holes in their bellies, with broken legs. They think I'm 'slinging the lead' all right."

I had almost fallen asleep off the chair, but caught myself.

"Look, John, could we talk about this in the . . . " Morpheus, the god of sleep, was pulling me into his arms.

"It was when I killed that Jerry with the flamethrower, that's what did me in," he tapped his head, "that's what did me in up here. That's why I just can't go back." Leeds had on white cotton hospital pajamas, his face pitted with old acne scars, his eyes bloodshot and sleepless. A hunted animal look.

"What happened, John?" He had never gone into the details of what had occurred. This piqued my interest. Morpheus would have to wait, for I was always eager to hear a story about the Front.

"The lines was all mixed up. We'd taken their line, and we ran a communication trench across the old No Man's Land. Then they took our line, and ran out their own communication trench. And each of us had pinched some of each other's lines on either flank, so it was all balled up. A real mess.

A patient with both legs in traction tried to roll over in his sleep a few beds down from us. The traction pulleys squeaked in protest, the man let out a moan, then fell back to sleep.

"So Jerry gets a stunt up. And it's raining and getting dark, and before you know it, I don't know where I am. Then, down the trench a ways, I see something dark, big and dark, and going away from me. So I run up to him, hoping it's one of me mates, but it's not. It's Jerry with one of those big dark flamethrower oil tanks on his back. He must be lost, too, 'cause they always have an infantryman or two with them, to protect them, you see."

A sergeant with a belly wound, I had operated on, let out a long, noisy fart in the adjacent bed. Good sign! His bowels were working again.

"Well, he tries to turn around and shoot me, with that bloody flaming nozzle, but he's right at an angle in the trench—they zigzag, Mister Gallagher, the trenches do, they aren't in straight lines—so this Jerry gets stuck. I don't want to shoot him, of course, for fear the oil in his tank will blow up, so I pull out my bayonet." He pantomimed pulling a bayonet out of a scabbard. "I guess I could have captured him, but I don't know but that some other Jerry's going to appear in a minute and do me."

Two more tiny farts popped out in the next bed. It was difficult to maintain my professional aplomb.

"Just what did you do, John?"

"There he is, stuck, at this angle in the trench, but I can't stab his back, the oil tanks are there, and his helmet covered the back of his neck and head, even his arms I can't get at, they're on the other side of the angle in the trench."

Picturing this was difficult.

"So all I could get at was his underside, his arse, excusing the expression, and the back of his legs. The whole time I'm thinking—if he gets loose and turns around, he'll burn me up, so it's him or me. I'd killed some Jerries before, even close up in a trench raid, but they were fighting back, they weren't so helpless as this one."

"Go on." What had that German been thinking?

A poison gas patient at the end of the ward started a terrible coughing fit. My first impulse was to shush him, to tell him to quiet down so I could hear the end of this story. Leeds waited until it was quiet again.

"So I swung it up, underneath him, burying it to the hilt, down below, by his arse. It was the only place I could get at him. Oh God, you should have heard him scream. '*Hilfe! Hilfe!*' he's yelling, '*Mutter! Mutter!*' it was awful. And the damn bayonet got stuck, must have been buried in the hip bones or something. I couldn't pull it out, and the poor bloody bastard wouldn't die. I picked up my rifle and tried to bash it on his skull, to put him out of his misery, but that damned angle in the trench, I just couldn't bash him good enough to finish him off. I tried to get my rifle low, to try to shoot up into him, but some oil was leaking from those tanks, and I was afraid a spark would set it off. And all the time, '*Hilfe! Mutter! Lieber Gott! Hilfe!*'" The German had been crying out, "Help, Mother, dear God, help!"

"Did you find a way to kill him?" A bayonet right up the rectum. I shifted in my seat, almost a reflex, as I pictured the agony.

"Never did, I started hearing other Jerries talking out in front of that trench—there's no mistaking the sounds of German—so I made may way back down the other way, happened across a trench that was going the right direction, and stumbled into some mates of mine about twenty minutes later. They weren't even in the same division as mine, that's how lost I got." There were lots of accounts of men getting lost in the "fog of battle." Fear, gun smoke, the featureless landscape of No Man's Land, the overcast sky of France, could disorient anyone.

"And the whole time I was getting away from that place, I kept hearing '*Hilfe! Mutter! Hilfe! Mutter!*' as if he were still right next to me. That night I heard it when I tried to sleep. And I keep hearing it, over and over again, sometimes I wake up shouting, '*Hilfe! Mutter!*' myself." Leeds was staring at me with those bloodshot eyes. He needed help. He needed to shut off that voice. I had no idea what to do or what to tell him.

It was quiet on the ward now, no coughing, no squeaking.

"You were doing your duty, John, you have nothing to be ashamed of." It was all I could think to say. Not much use.

"I know that, but the thought of going back there," he shook his head. "'*Hilfe! Mutter!*' I don't think I'll ever get that out of my head, Mister Gallagher, not 'til the day I die." He laid back in bed, continuing to stare, hardly blinking, those eyes red, red, red.

Once, after evening rounds, I found myself alone with Dr. Maxwell in front of the hospital. He pulled his faithful pipe out of his pocket and lit up.

"You know, Ben, all right if I call you Ben?"Maxwell was far less formal than the other English doctors.

"Sure, Dr. Maxwell." I wasn't about to call him by his first name. Come to think of it, I didn't *know* his first name.

"This hospital, Graylingwell, it used to be an insane asylum. Did you notice how thick the walls are, how small the windows?"

I hadn't, but, now that he mentioned it, the windows *were* pretty small. They must have prevented insane patients from escaping.

"Now, it's *not* a hospital for the insane," Maxwell went on. "It's a hospital for men who leave their homes, crawl into muddy trenches, and get bombed, shelled, machine gunned, buried alive, and poison gassed. And they do the same thing to a group of complete strangers who left their own homes and also live in muddy trenches. Sound sane to you, Ben?"

Madness. That's what it sounded like to me. And I was about to enter that madness. I didn't say anything.

"There's something else you should know, Ben. You, Abe, and the other fellows, too. You've done some good work here, real doctoring. We've got an operating room here, X-ray machines, anaesthetists, laboratories—all the trappings of modern medicine. And with all these trappings, you can be a modern doctor. When you come *back* from France, you'll go back to the Mayo Clinic, or the Minneapolis Hospital, and you'll again take up modern medicine."

We continued walking around the grounds, Goodwood was visible in the distance.

"You're pretty well read, Ben, aren't you?"

It was hard to say. I'd read a few things along the way.

"Ever read *The Inferno*, by Dante?" Maxwell asked.

"Parts of it," I said. It was such a long poem. I'd never gotten all the way through it, but I knew *about* it.

"It's an old story, really, the kind of story that recurs in different societies, in different times. On Formosa, they had an epic story along the lines of *The Inferno*. Anyway, where am I going with all this, you're probably asking," Maxwell said.

I was, but I didn't.

"Dante descends. Descends into hell," he said.

There was that one line above the entrance to hell, which read, "Abandon all hope, ye who enter here," it was the one thing I remembered from *The Inferno*.

Maxwell said, "Dante leaves his modern world, enters a barbaric realm, and comes out again, back to his modern world. You follow me, Ben?"

"I follow you, Dr. Maxwell."

"Up at the Front, Ben, in some dugout, you won't have an operating room, X-rays, anaesthetists, and laboratories. You will not have the trappings of modern medicine. You will descend into a barbaric realm, Ben, you will step backward in time."

"Up at the Front, Ben, you're going to take a little intermission from modern medicine. And it will frustrate you no end. The army has been criticized, and rightly so, for putting doctors so far forward. Up there, in some little Aid Post, with nothing but bandages and splints, you'll be little better than an orderly. Bandage, splint, evacuate, Bandage, splint, evacuate."

He took a few puffs, the curling smoke looking like the curling dragons carved on his scrimshaw pipe.

"But you're more than an orderly, and the men up there know that. It does their hearts good to know, when they go over the top, that there's a doctor right up there with them. A doctor who will set them right if Jerry does them wrong." Maxwell could turn a phrase.

"Don't forget that, Ben. You are more than a bandage-placer to those men, more than an orderly, putting on splints. You are hope. You are hope to those men." Maxwell looked at me, studied me. "How does all that sit with you?"

Mulling it over for a while, I said, "Dr. Maxwell, if I had my druthers, I'd keep on doing real doctoring, rather than be a front-line placer of splints."

Maxwell took another puff. "I can understand that, Ben." The sun had gone down behind the nearby hills. Colorful autumn foliage was yielding to the gray and black of night. The old Roman fortress on the hill was going to sleep.

"But I wasn't sent here to do what I wanted, I was sent here to go where I'm needed," I said.

"You're needed at the Front, Ben."

"Then that settles it." Not that I had much say in the matter. The army would send me anywhere they wanted.

We walked along for a while, our feet swishing through fallen leaves. There was something else I wanted to talk about with Maxwell, something I hadn't brought up before. The episode with Giancomo.

"Dr. Maxwell, I lost a patient when I was just a junior in medical school. I can't tell you how much it shook me up. I still think about it. Sometimes it wakes me up at night."

I recounted the whole story, the loss of the airway, his death struggle, the guilt afterwards.

"What scares me, Dr. Maxwell, is that I was *alone* with Giancomo, just for a few minutes, and I *lost* him. Up at some Aid Post, I'll be *alone*."

Alone. The only doctor. Dozens of lives, hundreds of lives, could depend on me. And I would be alone, like I was with Giancomo.

"I just don't feel like I'm *there* yet, Dr. Maxwell. I'm *getting* there, but . . . well." At that moment, I did not feel like Dr. Maxwell's star pupil.

"I've been at this for 27 years, Ben Gallagher, and I feel like I'm just getting there myself," he said, pipe clamped far back on the right side of his mouth, his right hand holding the bowl.

"You mean that, Dr. Maxwell?" Maxwell, the mentor, the experienced one, the world traveler, suffered from doubts himself?

"I mean it, Ben. Any doctor who feels he has it down pat is a danger to his patients. We're *all* still learning. Keep this in mind: Medicine is a humbling profession. It humbled you. It's humbled me. And it's going to humble us again. Again and again. That fellow you lost, when you were a junior in medical school, he's not the only patient you're going to lose. You'll lose plenty." *That* was a sobering thought. "But you'll save plenty more. Remember those ones." He unclamped the pipe and pointed the stem at me. "Remember the ones you save."

We stopped walking.

"Dr. Maxwell, am I ready to go over to France?" I was not fishing for compliments. I wanted to know what he thought.

His pipe had gone out. He banged it a few times and replaced the tobacco. By now, the darkness was almost complete. Wind was making the leaves chatter. From the windows of the hospital, you could here coughing, coughing, coughing.

"*Hilfe! Mutter!*" came out of one window.

Maxwell motioned his head toward the window.

"I heard you were talking to John Leeds the other night, Ben."

Maxwell lit up, the orange glow of the tobacco reflecting off his face.

"You're ready, Ben."

That night, I was assigned to go to the station, to meet a train of incoming wounded. It made a deep impression on me.

Standing on the platform with me was the station master, an older man with slouched shoulders, thick glasses, a blue cap, and a sad face. Hooded lights provided the faintest illumination in and around the station.

"The blackout, you know, Leftenant. Can't be 'avin' too many lights on. Jerry might see the lights and bomb us. At night, they might not see the red crosses on the hospital train, not that that would stop 'em." Germans had sunk hospital ships, why not bomb hospital trains?

Pulling my jacket close around me, I looked up at the station clock.

"9:45. Should be soon, don't you think?" England was cold, a damp cold that worked its way into your very bones.

"They're usually just a bit late, Leftenant, they slow it down well before they get 'ere, to keep the cars from lurching too much when they stop." He looked as old as the hills, this station master. Even in the poor lighting of the blacked-out station, the million wrinkles on his face were visible.

A long, shrill whistle down the line announced the train's arrival. Then the whistle blew three more times.

"That means there's wounded aboard, Leftenant, those three short ones. Toot-toot-toot, wounded it is." The station master had no teeth, and his upper and lower lips caved into his mouth. He kept working his gums, making smacking noises.

The train crept in, slowing ever so gradually. When it finally stopped, a few cars still lurched a little, and steam came hissing out of its belly. Then a lower sound started up—moaning.

The station master went up to the first car and slid open a door. Lying on a stretcher was a man with a dark shadow covering his face.

"A little light over here, please."

An orderly from the train held a lamp over the man. It wasn't a shadow covering his face, the man on the stretcher had no face. No eyes, no nose, no upper lip. Just a huge gap with bubbles coming out.

"OK, let's see his tag." The urge to vomit was overpowering. I swallowed hard and fought it off.

Attached to the patient's shirt button was a tag with his name, date and kind of injury, and—most importantly—dates and doses of his tetanus antitoxin. At the bottom was a signature of the doctor who initially took care of the patient. I was surprised to see the name of the doctor was Theodore Sweetser. He was a medical school classmate of mine.

Here I had been plagued with doubts about whether I could handle the work out in France. (I was still a little embarrassed about my "confession" to Dr. Maxwell.) And here was proof, living proof, that a *classmate* of mine could handle it. That served to reassure me quite a bit. If Ted Sweetser could be a doctor at the Front, then Ben Gallagher could, too. Dr. Maxwell was right, I was ready.

"OK, ambulance number one with him. Make sure he gets another 750 units of tetanus antitoxin as soon as he arrives at Graylingwell." I wrote that down on the patient's card.

The train held one hundred seventy men in all. Every tag was labeled W (wounded) or S (sick), as was the usual practice. Wounds of every description went by—legs, arms, and eyes gone, bodies peppered with shrapnel. Men quaking with fear. The air was thick with the stench of pus, unwashed bodies, dying tissue, dying limbs, dying men, dying hope. And to think, this mournful procession had been going on now for three years.

The last patient was packed off at midnight, straight up.

"Leftenant, you look like you could use a spot o' tea and biscuit about now." My friend the station master was working his gums into a kind of smile.

"Kind sir, you are right on both accounts," I said. His smile broadened, and the million wrinkles on his face all seemed to turn upwards, and smile, too.

He took me into his little office, brewed up some strong tea, and produced a real rarity—a cookie with some jam on top. (Sugar was hard to come by in wartime England.) There was hardly room to sit, and his desk was covered with timetables and other paperwork.

"You are a lifesaver, Mr. uh?" I asked. Hours I'd worked with the station master, and I'd forgotten to ask his name.

"Keith." He laid a little red and white checked tablecloth across his cluttered desk, turned his million-smile face to me, and winked. "I pinched it, the tablecloth. Pinched it from an Italian restaurant. That'll be our little secret, Leftenant."

Why, the little thief!

"I'll go to the grave on it, Mr. Keith. Your secret is safe with me."

"You know, Leftenant, uh?" He hadn't bothered to ask my name, either, out there on the station platform. But now we were partners in crime. The stolen tablecloth made us brothers.

"Gallagher."

"Leftenant Gallagher." His face changed, the smiles going flat, the mirth leaving his voice. No longer the nimble-fingered tablecloth thief, he was back to being a station master. A station master who had just unloaded a trainload of wrecked humanity. "You know, early in the war, the coming of this 'ospital train," he pointed at the train with his cup, "this convoy of wounded, meant the turning out of the 'ole town. But now," he sipped his tea, "now the people of Chichester 'ardly turn their 'eads." The station master looked so old. His upper and lower lips caved into his mouth. He worked his gums, making smacking noises. A million wrinkles creased his face and they all pointed down.

I wrote a letter to my brother Frank.

To: Mr. Frank Gallagher   Graylingwell War Hospital
Waseca, Minnesota   Chichester, England
U.S.A.   Nov. 18, 1917

Dear Frank,

Expect to be leaving here in a day or two for France. Thought I might be here a little longer but it has been ruled otherwise and it don't make much difference because war is war and wherever they say to go is where you go. Am writing the folks too for there is no use of trying to keep it from them. I will write from "over there" (they love that song here, I do, too) as soon as I get located. Everything will be all right I'm sure and I'll be glad to live like a man for awhile instead of like a hot house flower like I've always done before.

        Love to all,   Ben

P.S. Frank, do me a favor, would you? It's a little odd. Stop by Waseca High School and find whoever's teaching French there now. Find out how you'd translate "Over there" into French. Best I can come up with is *"Lá,"* or *"Lá bas,"* or *"Pour lá,"* or *"Sur lá,"* but that doesn't seem to really capture the flavor of it.

Opened by Censor:
    Approved

From: Lt. Bernard J. Gallagher
       RAMC   Chichester, Sussex

Chapter 4

TO THE FRONT

November 1917

WAR OFFICE
19 NOV 1917
TO: 1ST LTNT B GALLAGHER
ENTRAIN IMMEDIATELY FOR PORT OF FOLKESTONE VIA
WATERLOO STATION STOP
EMBARK TO BOULOGNE FRANCE STOP

I bid a warm farewell to Maxwell and headed up to London. There, I met up with many old friends from the *Orduna*. They, too, had worked at various English hospitals and we all swapped stories. My "Mammoth Caves' fish" story brought down the house, but I was careful not to let Dr. George hear me tell it. As we left London for Folkestone the church bells were ringing—and in every town along the way. There had been some big British victory in France, but we didn't hear the details.

The two-hour cross channel trip was choppy and many men aboard the ferry had the pasty complexion of seasickness. Abe Haskell was one of them.

"Ben, I shouldn't have had that big lunch," Abe said. We were sitting on a long bench on the enclosed upper deck of the ferry. A gray sky dripped down into a gray-green sea. Abe's face had the identical gray-green color.

"Oh, shake it off, Abe, we should be there pretty soon. How about a drink of water?" Back and forth we pitched, then a roll, then we hung up, seeming to stop at a steep left tilt, then we heaved back to the right. The *Orduna* hadn't been this bad.

"Oh God, Ben. Nothing. Nothing more for my stomach." He was eyeing the door, ready to go outside and join the others hanging over the railing.

"Well, how about if I mix up some mustard in lukewarm water, and maybe toss in a cigarette butt or two?" I said.

Abe grabbed his mouth and headed for the door, joining the parade of misery at the railing. It had been for his own good, what I'd done. Cruel, yes, but necessary. Like any good doctor, I'd seen that my patient needed to empty his stomach. So, I merely helped him. Abe should be thankful to me.

Also on board the ship were about twenty other American doctors, and several hundred glum English officers returning from leave. The Englishmen looked none too happy to be going back to the Front.

Abe returned, wiping his mouth and smelling to high heaven.

"Ben Gallagher, I will get you back for that one." He was livid, bright red. Good! My therapeutic procedure had worked. His color had returned. A cure.

"I was just trying to help." Innocence shone from my face; sincerity rang in my voice, but to no avail. Abe would get me back, no doubt of that.

"Well, at least that lunch is a thing of the past. I'll never admit it to you, but I do feel a little better now." Ha! I knew it. In his heart of hearts, he knew I had done him a favor. Abe looked around. "Pretty gloomy lot, this." He hit the nail on the head there. Those men who were talking were doing so in hushed tones. There was none of the raucous laughter, the bawdy tales and singing that you associate with a large group of men traveling together.

"Sure is."

Clunking and thumping, the ferry churned through the Channel. My old fears of submarines and torpedoes reappeared. Surely the Germans must try to sink these ferries.

The other Americans and I kept to ourselves and didn't try to strike up a conversation with the English officers. This trip to France was a novelty for us, and still had an air of adventure. We did not know what to expect.

But the English soldiers did.

It was after dark when we reached Boulogne. At the quay the English officers walked down the gangplank and into the night, presumably off to somewhere they belonged. That left only Americans on board the ship. We prepared to disembark. Our line of Americans, however, came to a screeching halt. I was third from the front, laden with my bags, when the line stopped. A French official put his hand on the first American's chest and asked for *"papiers, s'il vous plait."* Our man shrugged his shoulders and turned around to look at the rest of us. We, in turn, looked around hoping for someone to appear and solve our predicament. The English had given us orders to go to Folkestone and board a ship to Boulogne, but they hadn't given us any orders to get off. We lacked the necessary *papiers*.

It seemed funny to come so far and not be allowed to disembark. We trudged back up the gangplank, lugging our stuff, and waited in a kind of quarantine until an English official could be found to produce the necessary orders. It was late at night before we were able to tramp off the ferry. One of our fellows threw a jab at the stuffy French official at dockside. *"Vous avez laissé deux million d'allemands dans la France sans permission. Quel difference un poignet d'americains?* (You've let two million Germans in France without permission, what difference does a handful of Americans make?)" That got us a scowl. We were off to a bad start in France.

We stumbled through Boulogne, half asleep, tripping in the blacked out darkness. Some rooms awaited us at the Hotel de Veaux. We slept like logs.

After a few days we got orders sending us to various divisions along the Front, three to five of us to go per division. We were allowed to pick our own group, so I joined up with my old pal Abe Haskell, and a nice guy from North Carolina named Mark Dennis. Our assignment was with an artillery group up in Belgium.

The night before we were to depart for Belgium, I got a nasty surprise. I was sitting down to dinner in a mess tent, when Abe came up with a piece of paper.

"Ben, did you see the assignment list?" He looked agitated.

"What assignment list?" My tray of food was a sorry spectacle—vegetables cooked to death a hundred times over, and beef so tough it could stop an artillery shell.

"The list stating which of us is going where, that list, Ben. I've got it right here." He waved it around.

My knife was making a vain attempt at cutting the beef. Maybe someone had a bayonet I could use.

"Well, I thought it was you and me and that Dennis fellow, going up to Belgium somewhere."

The knife slipped, and went backwards toward me. My life flashed before my eyes, but the knife stopped short of disemboweling me. The beef lay on the tray, not so much as a dent in it.

"It *was*. But, look here." Abe showed me the paper, oblivious to the unfolding drama between me and the beef.

In the mysterious ways of army paperwork, my name had been crossed off and someone named Young was put in my place. My assignment had been changed to somewhere else, farther south. It didn't quite register at first, Abe and I were a team, a winning team. You don't split up a team. Why were they doing this? Who had made this decision?

"Ben, it looks like we'll be parting company. Shame. We've been chumming around since freshman year in medical school." Abe had been a lot of fun back then, too.

"Yes." We'd almost *grown up* together, at least, as far as our medical training was concerned. Medical school, internship, enlistment, the *Orduna*, Chichester. Abe had been no slouch at Chichester, either. He was as eager to learn as I had been. We had often quizzed each other at the end of the day's work.

"As I recall, I did most of the hard work in our labs, you just held the books and told me what to do," Abe said, twisting the facts about medical school. Even now, Abe was good for a joke.

"Funny, Abe. I seem to remember it the other way around." If he wasn't going to put on a long face, neither was I.

We sat there for a while without saying anything. The vegetables on my tray looked like they'd put up less of a fight than the beef, so I took a forkful of them. Awful! I'd eaten some bad food in my day, but this beat all. Just as well, I didn't feel like eating much anyway.

"Are you sure that list is right?" It was a fool's question. Army decisions are final, irreversible, etched in stone. Right and wrong have nothing to do with it.

"Oh yes. I even went to the C.O. His hands were tied. 'The list is the list,' he said." Why should a C.O. care about two first lieutenants?

Abe flicked his finger at the paper, making a tap-tap-tap sound. "I guess I'd just assumed we'd win this war together."

"Me too." Boy, Abe was going his way, and I was going mine. That did not sit well with me. Don Quixote needed his Sancho Panza; I needed Abe. Damn.

In front of our table, a line of men were filling their trays with the inedible English chow.

"You're probably going to get in all kinds of trouble now, you poor Irishman, without me to pull your irons out of the fire." Abe was keeping up the brave front. "And you with the name 'Ben,' no less, you sure there's not a rabbi hidden somewhere in that family tree of yours? We'd love to have you! Plenty of room at the synagogue!" Abe did not follow a Kosher life style, nor did he attend Jewish services regularly, but he liked to read Jewish authors. "Culturally Jewish," he called himself, not "religiously Jewish." As a boy, he'd had a bar mitzvah, but he let his Hebrew studies yield to more secular pursuits.

But in spite of his "falling away" from the faith, Abe had retained an element of the Talmudic scholar in him. He could debate one side of an issue, then turn it around and debate the opposing view with equal skill. It was an act of mental gymnastics that always amazed me. And now Abe was trying to get me to join his synagogue.

"I'd never thought of that, Abe. I'll take a good, long look at my family tree when I get home." I filled his mess cup with tea, then fortified it with a dollop of whisky. I did the same with my cup. Why not? Neither of us were big drinkers, but a farewell toast was a farewell toast. And you can't say good-bye to your best friend with just a cup of tea. "Of course, Abe, you realize that without me as your guiding beacon, you'll fall into wrack and ruin." Two could play this how-will-you-get-by-without-me game.

"No doubt about that."

Looking at the paper, avoiding my eyes, Abe started to swirl his cup around. He was looking for a way to say good-bye.

I was looking for the same thing. People around us were carrying trays, sitting down, eating. Abe kept swirling the cup.

Should I say, "Good luck" or "good hunting"? Too English. "See ya later." Too trivial. Give him a long talk about what a good friend he is? Too gushy, besides, he knew we were close friends already.

Outside the mess tent, a truck went by, honking, the driver shouting some obscenities. Abe's cup kept swirling, around and around. I could hear the gears turning in Abe's head, what was he thinking?

I read somewhere that the hardest thing to say in 25 words or less was good-bye. It sure was proving true as I prepared to say good-bye to my loyal old friend Abe Haskell.

The cup stopped swirling. Abe lifted his eyes, then lifted his cup, as he gave the traditional Jewish toast.

"*Lachayim!*"

To life!

The next day, my friend Abe was gone. I'd hoped to see him off at the train, but an unannounced gas mask drill came along, and I missed my chance to say one last good-bye. Just as well, perhaps.

When I got back to barracks after the drill, Abe's stuff was gone, his cot, empty. That did not leave me *alone*, not by a country mile, for there were hundreds, thousands of other troops in the area, but I felt alone nonetheless.

Abe was certainly not perfect, and he could drive me crazy, like any close friend can. Sometimes when I felt the need to be serious, just for a little while, Abe would keep on with his joking and his talking about the girls. On more than one occasion, I'd told him, "Enough, enough already!" But I'm sure I bothered him a few times, too. That black streak of pessimism every Irishman has would sometimes make itself felt, and Abe didn't like it.

"Oh, you like to hang on that cross and bleed, Ben Gallagher, hang on that cross and bleed," he would tell me. "Why don't you climb down off that cross and join the living?"

And, to tell the truth, he had a point.

In spite of his high jinks and taste for the fairer sex, though, Abe was a tough fellow, inside, he had to be. Abe was a Jew. And there were many people around who didn't like Jews.

"That shopkeeper Jewed me." "Let's Jew him down on the price." "My Dad won't buy me a car, what a Jew!"

These and a hundred other insults I'd heard, and Abe had heard.

"Christ-killers," people would say, when they wanted to insult the Jews. (Roman soldiers had driven in the nails. No one called Italians "Christ-killers.")

Certain universities wouldn't take "them," certain clubs wouldn't allow "them." Even referring to Jews as "them" put their people somehow apart, alien. Something to fear, something to hate.

Abe took it all in stride, shrugged it off as the nonsense it was.

"Shakespeare phrased it best, when his Jewish character Shylock said, 'If you prick me, do I not bleed?'" Abe told me once. Then he got serious, a rare event for Abe Haskell, "Can I change the world? Make every Christian love a Jew? No. Can I pass my anatomy test? Study pharmacology? Be a good doctor? Yes. So that's what I'll do. I'll do what I can do, and go from there. And when I have children, I'll teach them to do the same."

It struck me then, that people hate Jews because Jews work hard, value education, and take care of their children. What sort of reason is that to hate an entire people? We should learn a lesson from them.

But I wasn't going to get any more lessons from Abe for a while. Abe had gone away.

The wind picked up. A shutter on my barracks went bang-bang. Abe's cot was made up, crisp and taut, the pillow smoothed out, as if no one's head had ever laid on it.

A few days later I heard that Young (the man who replaced me) received a severe head injury from an artillery explosion, nearly died, and was sent home, an invalid. It could have been me. No word of Abe getting hurt, though.

Sunday noon, November 25, 1917, we got on a train. Destination—the Front. We were to join the 5th Army, 61st Division, somewhere on the Somme. Several hundred British officers and enlisted men, along with forty American doctors, were also on board. The Americans were split up, assigned four or five per coach. The train was crowded, stuffy, and tense. Every now and then the train would stop and people would get off to go join their outfits. Few people were talking. The men looked like children on the last day of summer vacation.

In my coach were four other Americans, all with orders to report to the chief medical officer (known as the A.D.M.S.—for Army Director of Medical Services) of the 61st Division. The headquarters was located at Arras, on the Somme front. This was a distance of only 70 miles, but the train ride took six and one-half hours, as the train frequently stopped in the middle of nowhere, for no reason, for long periods of time. When we asked our British hosts why there were delays, they regarded us with a "What's the rush?" look. They seemed not to know where they were, nor did they care. And always they were drinking tea. A stop meant a time to "brew up" as they called it. They'd put cream in it, if they had any, but cream was hard to get near the Front. So was sugar. That left only rum or whisky, and the British were *never* short of rum or whisky.

At one of our frequent stops, I was choking down some of that tea, strong as battery acid.

"Say, pardon me, I couldn't help noticing that you Englishmen go for your tea pretty strong. And it seems to be getting stronger as we get closer to the Front," I asked a young infantry captain.

"That's right, Cousin" (ever since the *Cunard Bulletin-Orduna*, the English had referred to us as cousins).

This captain had a jagged scar across his right cheek, and the right side of his mouth drooped. His facial nerve had been cut. So here was yet another Brit who had been wounded, patched up, and sent back to the Front. When *were* the other Americans coming? Even I was asking that question.

"Do you brew it a long time, or, just how do you get it so strong?" I never asked them to add whisky to mine, but they must have sneaked it in while they were brewing it. Or else their tea leaves were soaked in whisky, *something* was making their tea a lethal weapon.

"Well, after we think it's done, we put a piece of rusty barbed wire in it. If the rust comes off, then it's almost strong enough." He spoke to me as if he were the Oracle at Delphi, revealing a great truth.

"Almost?" My eyes went down to my cup. Did I see flakes of rust?

"Yes, that's right, almost strong enough." He was starting to smile, on the left, where his facial nerve was still intact.

"How do you tell when it *is* strong enough?" I shook the cup around. No flakes visible, they must have sunk to the bottom.

"Oh, that's easy, when you go to pull out the barbed wire, and it's completely dissolved. Then, the tea is just right." He poured me another cup. "Cheers!"

My four American compatriots and I speculated if the English poured all their tea toward the Germans at one time, they might be able to wash the Germans back across the Rhine.

The day was rainy. Darkness fell early. As we got within a few miles of Arras we could hear distant thunder, and see irregular flashes of lightning to the east. Odd that there should be a thunderstorm this late in November, thunderstorms occur in spring and summer. In fact, it *was* too late for nature to create a thunderstorm, but not too late for man. The flickering lights and booms were big guns. The thunderstorm was a barrage. We Americans kept looking to the east, at this new thing, an artillery barrage. The British never looked up from their tea or crossword puzzles. A barrage was no novelty to them.

We departed the train at Arras into a cold rain, and took an ambulance to the Field Ambulance Headquarters. It was an old partially destroyed building. The A.D.M.S. there assigned us to service.

In the British Army, at that time, a division consisted of about 14,000 men, divided into three brigades of four infantry battalions each. A brigade was supposed to be four to five thousand men. A battalion was about a thousand men but was often under-strength due to sick and wounded. There had been many killed and wounded in the terrible fighting this year, so most battalions were short of men.

As yet, my assignment was unknown. I was hoping to get assigned to a Casualty Clearing Station. The Casualty Clearing Station was the closest thing to an actual hospital. They had operating facilities, anaesthesia, and could even perform some blood transfusions (arm-to-arm, directly from the blood donor to the recipient). Everything beyond the Casualty Clearing Station (namely, the Main Dressing Station, the Advanced Dressing Station, and the Battalion Aid Post) functioned as a First Aid Post and transit center—no real operations done there. You applied bandages and splints, and evacuated the men. There was one more thing you did in those forward stations, and Maxwell had emphasized that. You gave the men hope. (But all sentiments aside, I still wanted to work at a Casualty Clearing Station. Among front-line doctors, that was clearly the plum assignment.)

But it wasn't up to me to decide, and a first lieutenant was not very high on the medical totem pole, so I suspected my assignment would be in a Battalion Aid Post.

The system, worked out with years of experience in the field, looked like this.

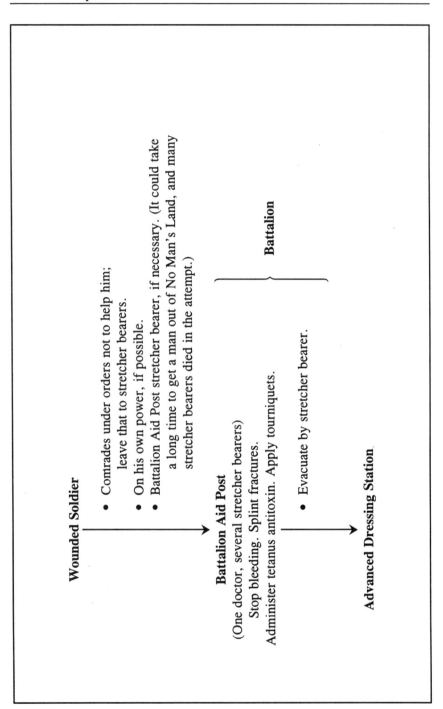

Wounded Soldier

- Comrades under orders not to help him; leave that to stretcher bearers.
- On his own power, if possible.
- Battalion Aid Post stretcher bearer, if necessary. (It could take a long time to get a man out of No Man's Land, and many stretcher bearers died in the attempt.)

Battalion Aid Post

(One doctor, several stretcher bearers)

Stop bleeding. Splint fractures.

Administer tetanus antitoxin. Apply tourniquets.

- Evacuate by stretcher bearer.

Advanced Dressing Station.

Battalion

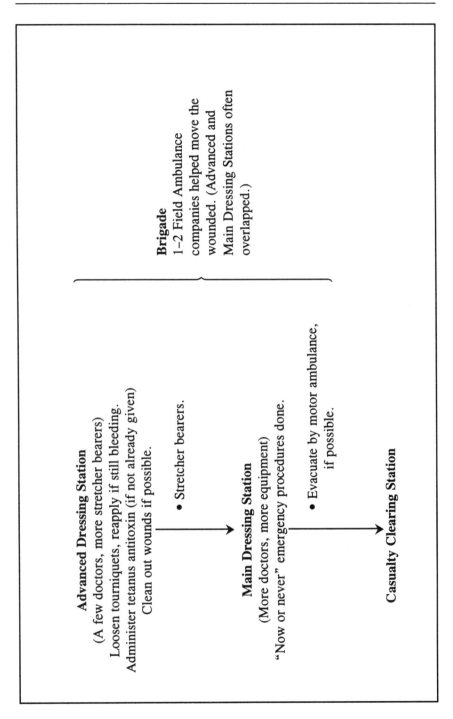

Advanced Dressing Station
(A few doctors, more stretcher bearers)
Loosen tourniquets, reapply if still bleeding.
Administer tetanus antitoxin (if not already given)
Clean out wounds if possible.

• Stretcher bearers.

Main Dressing Station
(More doctors, more equipment)
"Now or never" emergency procedures done.

• Evacuate by motor ambulance, if possible.

Casualty Clearing Station

Brigade
1–2 Field Ambulance companies helped move the wounded. (Advanced and Main Dressing Stations often overlapped.)

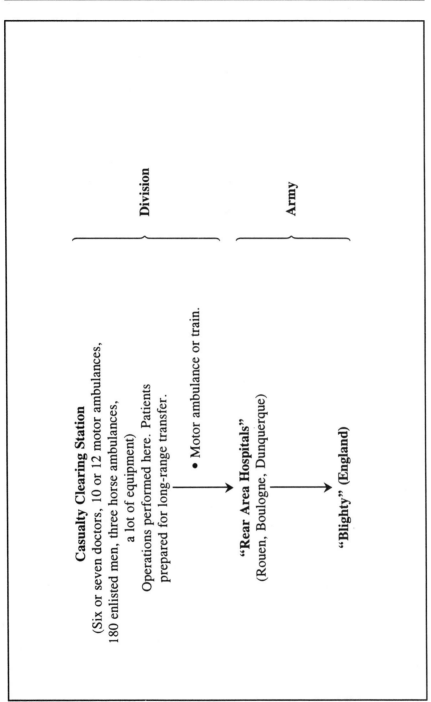

Casualty Clearing Station
(Six or seven doctors, 10 or 12 motor ambulances,
180 enlisted men, three horse ambulances,
a lot of equipment)
Operations performed here. Patients
prepared for long-range transfer.

• Motor ambulance or train.

Division

"Rear Area Hospitals"
(Rouen, Boulogne, Dunquerque)

Army

"Blighty" (England)

An example of a typical soldier's journey:

- Tommy Akins is hit in the thigh with a machine gun bullet.
- Lays in No Man's Land until nightfall, stretcher bearers risk their lives to go out at night and look for wounded men. They pick up Tommy and bring him back to the front line.
- Battalion Aid Post: Doctor sees the wound has stopped bleeding, scrapes the mud out of the wound, sprinkles bismuth powder ("bip") into the wound to prevent infection, puts a bandage on the wound, and gives tetanus antitoxin. Marks Tommy's chest with a T (meaning, tetanus antitoxin given) along with the date.

Stretcher Bearers Carry Tommy to the Advanced Dressing Station

- Advanced Dressing Station: Bandage removed, wound irrigated with water (the Dakin's solution ran out hours ago), morphine tablet given to help relieve pain.

Motor Ambulance Is Able to Take Tommy to the Casualty Clearing Station

- Casualty Clearing Station: Tommy is anaesthetized and the wound surgically cleaned out. Drains are placed and Dakin's solution is flushed through the wound.

Train Takes Tommy to Dunquerque. The Surgical Drains in His Leg Get Clogged While He's on the Train.

- Dunquerque Hospital: Tommy undergoes a second operation, and the wound is definitely cleaned out. All dead tissue is cut away.

Boat to England

- London Hospital: Tommy convalesces for six months.

The system, of course, did not always work in such clockwork fashion, and motor ambulances were often held back by shellfire, or poor road conditions. With heavy casualties, or with movement of the lines, bottlenecks and breakdowns in the strategem could and did occur. (This routine was based on Dr. Jonathan Letterman's system for evacuating the wounded of the army of the Potomac during our Civil War. The emphasis was on skilled First Aid, stabilizing the patients, and rapid evacuation, with facilities for early definitive surgery as close to the front line as possible). The very nature of the military stalemate on the Western Front meant that the Casualty Clearing Stations (again, the closest thing to a true Front Line Hospital) scarcely ever had to be moved unless they were bombed out, which occasionally happened.

The most senior doctors, with the most experience, served in the rear area hospitals, and performed the real operations, the real doctoring. Junior doctors went forward to the Aid Posts. That is, big fish stayed in the back, little fish went to the Front. Having no seniority, being of the lowest medical rank, and coming from America, I was a little fish.

I was assigned to the 183rd Brigade of the 61st Division, and told to go to their Field Ambulance Headquarters in St-Nicholas, a suburb of Arras. The four other Americans with me went to other places, so I was on my own. Once again, I found myself stumbling around in the dark, lost, and getting a lot of curious looks from British soldiers. Most of them seemed to be amused at my American accent. One asked if I had taken a wrong turn at Chicago. Few could provide much in the way of directions.

Arras itself, some kind of big headquarters, had been battered for years and surely looked like the abomination of desolation. Everywhere in the town, houses and buildings were reduced to rubble. Those few structures still standing had a surprised look, as if a giant had torn off a wall to peak inside. Dining rooms, bathrooms, bedrooms stood shamelessly exposed. Plumbing and chimneys poked out like grass growing through the cracks in a sidewalk. And this had once been a city.

At long last I arrived at an old two-story brick house which was somehow intact. All the buildings around this house were in various states of ruin.

I knocked on the door. It opened.

"Yes?" a tall, thin man with sandy-brown hair and dark eyes stood in the doorway.

"First Lieutenant Gallagher. Medical Corps. I've been assigned to . . . " As an after thought, I brought my hand up in a salute.

"Oh yes, yes, do come in," he ushered me in and offered his hand. "Robson, Captain in the Medical Corps. Awfully glad you could make it."

It sounded as if I'd shown up for tea and crumpets.

"We're just sitting down to a spot of dinner. I can't imagine you'd want a little of our cooking, would you? My batman Sykes here is quite a chef!" He held his arm out to introduce Sykes, but all I saw of him was the back of his legs through some doorway. Some pots were banging, the great chef was at work, apparently.

Taking off my jacket, I said, "Oh that would be lovely." (Lovely! When was the last time I had used the word "lovely"? These Britishisms were starting to rub off on me. I would have to be more careful from now on. Soon I'd be saying, "I say," and "Cheerio, old chap!" and all that sort of rot.)

The living room of the house held ammunition boxes for chairs and a broken off door for a table. Tin plates with bully beef, a green paste—possibly peas?—and hard biscuits lay on the table. A few sputtering candles provided dim lighting. Prominent on the table was a bottle of Scotch whisky.

"Colonel Burroughes, this is Lieutenant Gallagher. Lt. Gallagher, this is Colonel Burroughes, commander of the 2nd/2nd South Midland Field Ambulance Company." Burroughes had a long, narrow face, looking not unlike a horse. As I had just met the man, was under his command, and was a foreigner serving in his army, I chose not to tell him he looked like a horse.

"Hello. Tea? Whisky?"

"Tea, please." Why don't they every have coffee? I was getting pretty sick of tea. Were German submarines targeting only coffee freighters? Couldn't they sink a few tea ships?

Robson's batman (a batman was a kind of butler for the officers) fixed up another plate for me, then poured the inevitable tea. There was no barbed wire sticking out of it, so it must have been strong enough. Both Robson and Burroughes looked tired, but Robson made a game effort to make me feel welcome.

"So, a Yank. Pretty exotic commodity in these parts," Robson said.

Sykes, the batman, was *not* the world's greatest chef. He may, in fact, have been counted among the world's *worst* chefs, yet thankfully the food was hot. English cooking, there had to be some way to harness it as an instrument of war. Addressing Robson's comment, I again took on the implied question, "Where are all the Yanks?"

"I hope you'll be seeing more of us soon. In the meantime, I'll do what I can." I started shoveling in the food, trying to chew it without letting it touch my taste buds.

"From New York?" Everyone knew about New York.

"No, actually Minnesota." That gave Robson a puzzled look. No one knew about Minnesota.

"Where's that?"

"Sort of in the middle, up north." Sleep was creeping up on me. I gave up on chewing the food, and started swallowing it whole. It might choke me to death, but it was better than tasting it.

"Isn't Chicago there?" Robson lit up, proud of his knowledge of American geography.

"Yes, more or less. Minnesota's not too far from Chicago." The fine points weren't worth debating. My plate was clean. Sykes came back into the room and looked surprised. Whether he was surprised that the plate was empty or that I was still alive, I didn't know.

Burroughes excused himself and lay down in a separate room.

"I'd love to go to the states some day. See the Grand Canyon. All those wild Indians. That's where they are, aren't they? Aren't there a lot of red Indians riding around in the Grand Canyon, or somewhere near there?" Robson asked.

Like other foreigners I'd met, Robson found the West, the Wild West of frontier days, to be the most interesting aspect of America.

My eyelids were falling fast.

"Yes. There's a lot of them. But they aren't wild anymore, so I hear." Buffalo Bill, Wild Bill Hickock, and Billy the Kid were all gone too, Captain Robson, I thought to myself.

Robson seemed as excited as a child on Christmas Eve, he just couldn't bear to go to sleep when there was this exciting new toy to play with—a real, live American.

"Married, Gallagher, any children?"

"No." Syrupy, clinging sleep was pulling me down, but Robson just had to keep talking.

"Oh, I've got one—child that is," he laughed. "And one wife only, too," more laughter. "That's all we get in England, you know, one wife. No harems allowed." Great laughter now, and he threw his head back. His chin had a lot of nicks and scabs, from shaving, it looked like.

"Here, let me show you a picture of my daughter, my wife, too."

He produced a picture from his wallet. His wife was thin, with great long tresses of hair flowing over her shoulders. She had just a hint of a smile, a tiny glimmer, looking for all the world like the smile on the Mona Lisa. She even had her hands in front, like the Mona Lisa. Did the photographer somehow plan that? Then I saw his daughter.

It is said that all children are beautiful (perhaps by those who do not have them) but this child really *was* beautiful. She looked about two, with ringlets and ribbons in her hair. She had a big smile, nothing Mona Lisa-like or understated about it. If you leaned close to the picture, you could almost hear her laugh. Her nose was crinkled by a smile, and her eyes seemed to say, "Let me ride on your back like a horsey!"

Robson wasn't laughing any more, he had a smile on his face.

"Loves her Daddy, she does, this one," he kissed the picture, then he spoke to it, "and Daddy loves you." He put the picture back in his wallet.

"They're a blessing, Gallagher, children are. Makes it all worthwhile somehow."

I nodded.

"That's why we're here, you see, for them, for the little ones." He rested his back against the wall, put his hands above his head, and laced his fingers together.

"This is it, this war." Robson was in the mood to talk, to philosophize. And I was a complete stranger to this man, he'd first seen only a few minutes before. The term for such a man, I believe, is "he wears his heart upon his sleeve." He continued, "We'll slug it out, straighten out the bastard Hun, and set this world right again. Then my little girl, and who knows, maybe a little boy someday," he winked at me, "won't have to go through all this anymore."

I had heard this sentiment expressed before, in the newspapers. People were calling this "The War to End all Wars." But Robson was making the point more clearly than the newspapers ever could. He would fight this war so his child, or children, would not have to fight another one. A good man, this Robson. If he wanted to "wear his heart upon his sleeve," that was fine by me. But I did so want to go to sleep.

Robson didn't, he wanted to talk.

"I've seen it, Gallagher. The cave-ins, men smothering in dirt. Men drowning in shell holes. Skin peeled off a man like you'd peel the skin off a chicken. Terrible things. As like to drive you mad." He pulled another box over with his foot, then put both feet on top of it, crossing them.

"And some it does drive mad. We sent a captain home in July. A braver man you never saw." Shrugging his shoulders, Robson said, "One day this captain starts crying. Crying and shaking. Shaking all over. We try to buck him up, give him a little whisky, talk to him." Robson shook his head. "Last we saw of him. They sent him home, still crying." Shell shock, oops, NDNYD.

Robson pulled out his wallet again, and tapped it.

"That's my secret, right there," he was indicating the photo of his wife and child. "They keep me in one piece." He smiled at me, "I'd go to hell and back if it'll make this place better for them." He put his wallet back. "Sure you won't have a little tot of whisky before you turn in? Best thing to help you get a good night's sleep?"

"No thanks." Thank God, he was going to let me go to sleep.

"Well then, let's get you all settled in," he lifted his head up and motioned to Sykes.

The great chef showed me to a cot. As I pulled my boots off and crawled under a green woolen blanket, I asked Robson, "What's her name, your daughter?"

"Rachel." Rachel, that's a pretty name.

Lights out.

Arras, wreck that it was, was being shelled regularly. Jerry wanted us to know he was still on the job, apparently.

There was little for me to do those first few days, but of course I was curious to see "the Front." Colonel Burroughes was going up to inspect the lines, and he graciously agreed to take me along. We made our way by ambulance about three miles east of Arras, then got out and walked inside a communication trench leading toward the front line. The subterranean world of trench warfare unfolded in front of me. Nothing happened above ground from here on forward. Eating, sleeping, relieving oneself—all life had to be below ground, below the reach of shrapnel and sniper's bullets. The trenches were deeper than a man's height, a yard wide at the bottom, and a little more at the top. The sides were "revetted," reinforced by a kind of fence work made of tree branches. Where they got the tree branches, I'll never know. All the nearby trees had been blasted apart—they were little more than blackened stumps. The countryside, what I could see of it, was flat, full of shell holes, and devoid of life. Along the bottom of the trench were plank boards—called "duck boards"—to make walking easier.

After a while we came to an officer standing in front of a dugout. Colonel Burroughes and he talked for a few minutes; then I asked the officer if he could show me his dugout. He took me down and gave me the guided tour, showing me a fine, neat dugout, twenty feet under the ground. Afterwards, I thanked the officer, shook his hand, and clapped him on the back like he was an old friend. Col. Burroughes and I headed up the trench and I asked about the officer in the dugout.

"That was General Spooner, commander of the brigade." Col. Burroughes said, smiling at me.

That knocked me for a loop. Not knowing the ranks of insignia in the British Army, or any army for that matter, I'd made a real gaffe, treating a general like a commoner.

"Would you like to see a Battalion Aid Post, Gallagher?" Burroughes asked. With his helmet on, he looked less like a horse than he did that first night. He was my first real commanding officer, and he treated me with every respect. I had no previous commanding officers to compare him with, but he seemed like a genuinely good fellow. He and Robson got along famously, often talking about a common interest of theirs—history.

"Please."

We went a little farther up the zigzagging communication trench. Just behind the front line, there was a small red cross above a doorway. Walking down two steps, I tripped, expecting there to be more steps going farther down. Then I bumped my helmet against the low ceiling, and when I reached up my hand tangled in a cord. Pulling it accidentally, a curtain unrolled on top of me. I had the disquieting sense of not making a good first impression. Colonel Burroughes helped untangle me, and pointed out that this curtain was one of two, set a few feet apart, to protect the Aid Post against poison gas. At the sound of an alarm, the curtains were dropped to keep the wounded men safe from gas. (Just how effective the two flimsy curtains would be was a matter of speculation.) As my eyes adjusted to the gloom, I saw bandages, a heated litter, blankets, an oxygen tank (for resuscitation of gas cases), two splints, space for stretchers on each wall, and a wheeled litter for pushing wounded men to the rear. (How that wheeled litter could make it down that narrow trench, I could not fathom.)

That was it. Dr. Maxwell back in Chichester had been right, a Battalion Aid Post didn't have much in it. Bandage, splint, evacuate. Bandage, splint, evacuate.

That's all you could do. My role up here would be that of an over-qualified orderly, a kind of station master, whose job was to get the men back as quickly as possible.

Battalion Aid Posts during big battles were nightmares, I had heard: men trying to hold their intestines in, only to have the slippery loops of bowel fall through their fingers, bones jutting out through flesh, fountains of blood from cut arteries, eyes and jaws hanging down, and chests opened up so the movement of lungs and heart were visible. In my mind's eye, all those horrors entered into this small, empty Aid Post, plus poison gas seeping under the curtains. Would I be able to do the job? Would I be able to apply the lessons learned at Chichester? Would the ghost of Giancomo come back and sap my confidence? Standing in that Aid Post, imagining its horrors, I realized a trial awaited me. Not here, not now, but sometime, somewhere. God help me when it happened.

At least I wasn't the frightened pup I was in medical school. I had gotten through a tough senior year, and an even tougher internship. And then there was Maxwell and all the experience at Chichester.

Think of the stick man, check off his body parts, remember what's most important. Keep the airway clear, stop the bleeding, clean out the wounds, be methodical. Stabilize and move on, stabilize and move on. Be in charge. Once the patients are stabilized, get that tetanus antitoxin in them, then double check everything. Splint still in place? Has the tourniquet been on too long? Has the artery started bleeding again? Is the wound really cleaned out?

Col. Burroughes interrupted my mental exercise and took me to the front line.

As the communication trench neared the actual frontmost line, it struck me that this was *the* business end of the Western Front. All the supplies, hospitals, ships, reserve areas, kitchens, communication wires—all that, was to serve and maintain this, the front line: the point of contact with the Boche, the Hun, Jerry. Thinking back on all I'd seen before, it struck me there had to be 20, or 50, or maybe 100 people behind us for every one fighting soldier right up in the front line. Inefficient business, war is. And was it smelly; the stench of the Front was pervasive and horrible.

In the last stretch of communication trench (that trench connecting the reserve line of trenches with the front line), there was a dugout on the right with the worst smell of excrement coming out of it. A man emerged holding a large bucket of human feces just as we passed by.

"'Scuse me."

"Of course," Wasn't about to get in *his* way.

"Shit wallahs, Gallagher," Col Burroughes told me. (He never called me anything but Gallagher, never Ben, never doctor, never lieutenant. In the hierarchy of the British Army, I was below Burroughes, so I was addressed appropriately. There was nothing personal in it, for Burroughes was all kindness to me, but the forms of address in a hierarchy are etched in stone.)

"Shit wallahs. The 'wallah' part of it is an Indian term, I think, for "carrier" or something. The 'shit' part I think you know." Burroughes was pointing to the man carrying the bucket of shit. By now, this man had walked some distance away, down the communication trench. Passersby were giving him a wide berth, as wide as you can give in a trench.

"What do they do, exactly, Col. Burroughes, these shit wallahs?" The answer seemed pretty obvious, but I didn't want to look uninterested. This *was* my first day in a trench and I didn't want to look like a know-it-all.

"Keep the trench clean. Clean as they can, anyway. Men can't just be crapping anywhere. They use a bucket in this dugout here," he pointed to the smelliest dugout on earth, above it was a sign, "Rose Hips and Jasmine Lane." The British sure came up with the funniest names for places. Rose hips and jasmine did *not* come to mind when one smelled that dugout! "The shit wallahs—we have two per battalion—carry it away and dump it."

Looking around the crowded, narrow trench, I couldn't imagine where, exactly, "away" was. Just then, a second fellow emerged holding another bucket of excrement. This was proving to be my lucky day.

"Colonel, Leftenant," he gave us a quick salute with his . . . unoccupied . . . hand. "That's a good question you've got there, Leftenant, where to put the, uh, digestive byproducts, you might call 'em." The shit wallah was rolling back on his heels, enjoying his moment in the sun—a real orator, addressing one of the great questions of our time. And all the time holding that bucket. Jeez, Louise.

"Well, it all depends on whether Jerry's got a stunt up his sleeve, or whether we're putting on a show." His free hand gestured to the left, and the right, indicating the great dichotomy of thought on this issue. "If we're expecting a visit from Jerry, we throw it out in front of our lines, so he gets a nasty surprise. And if we're the ones putting on the show, we throw it behind our lines, to encourage our lads to go forward. Har, har, har!" The man was a genius. Someday surely he would be prime minister.

Burroughes had to smile at the shit wallah's explanation.

"Very well, soldier; carry on."

The shit wallah saluted and headed back down the communication trench, still laughing.

We bid "Rose Hips and Jasmine Lane" a fond farewell and got into the front line. My heart caught a little in my throat. This was it. The front line. THE FRONT LINE.

For years I'd followed the progress of the war in the newspapers. I'd read Guy Espy's book *Over the Top*. They'd even shown us newsreels of some trench scenes. But to be in the front line, to actually BE in the front line . . . the reality proved somewhat anti-climactic. The atmosphere was work-a-day, with little drama about it. Every so many feet, a soldier leaned back against the front of the trench, holding upright his rifle and bayonet attached. On the bayonet was attached a small mirror, so he could look out over No Man's Land and not expose himself to danger.

"Don't they use periscopes?" I asked.

"A real periscope is expensive, and Jerry snipers like to pot away at them. These little mirrors do the job just as well, and we can have more of them along the line." That made sense. And they should know, they'd been at it since 1914.

We passed a sniper, as he squinted into the magnifying scope of his rifle. Ever so slowly, he moved the rifle back and forth, back and forth. Draped over him was a camouflage netting, with bits of sand bag, sticks, and some dirt on top. He never fired while I was in the front line.

We came to a kind of dugout in the trench, a soldier was standing there with a box of open potato masher hand grenades.

"Aren't those German?" German grenades were a long stick with a can at the end. British grenades had no stick on them.

"That's right, Leftenant, good old German engineering. That's why we pinched them. The stick handle gives them a better balance, you can throw them farther than you can throw ours." A man with two stripes on his left shoulder was giving this dissertation on the fine points of grenade throwing. He seemed to have graduated from the same school of oratory as the shit wallah. "So, with Kaiser Willy's permission, and sometimes without it," he raised his eyebrows a few times in quick succession, "we pinch these grenades every now and again."

"Carry on, Corporal," Burroughes said. It wasn't the only time I heard that term "carry on." The British seemed to use it all the time.

"Gallagher, go ahead and take a look over the top with this periscope," he handed me a tall rectangular box with two mirrors. "Remember, don't be keeping it up there real long, or Jerry will see the reflection of the mirror and blast away at it. I don't want you getting a piece of mirror in your eye, and I don't want to lose this periscope either."

Using the periscope, I took a quick look over the top, across No Man's Land, to the Hun lines. But for a mass of barbed wire in front of our lines, and a mass of the same a few hundred yards away, No Man's Land was empty. The Germans were not poking their heads up any more than we were. No wonder our sniper hadn't fired, there weren't any targets. A few Boche shells landed about 300 yards away. For the first time, I felt the ground really shake. One of our big guns was "talking back" with thunderous roars.

Shell holes cratered the landscape. Then I noticed that No Man's Land was not entirely empty. Swollen, blackened arms stuck out of the earth, and several bodies were draped across both British and German barbed wire. I was fascinated, and stared harder and harder, trying to pick out details. Burroughes pulled the periscope down. The sights were so hypnotizing I had forgotten his warning about the German snipers.

Overhead a few British aeroplanes were scouting over the German lines. Anti-aircraft shells (Archie—in the British vernacular) were bursting all around. Somehow the birdmen kept emerging from the black puffs unscathed. In the distance, a Hun plane was visible, and I thought I might see a dog fight, but the German kept his distance.

"Seen enough, Gallagher?" Burroughes asked me.

A Boche shell landed just 50 yards away. "Whoomp!"

"Uuh!" a grunting sound came out. The shell's concussion had pushed air out of my chest involuntarily. Dirt clouds sprinkled down on us. My ears rang.

"Yes, Colonel. I've seen enough for today. Very interesting!"

We made our way back down the trenches. The British soldiers we squeezed past were short by American standards and most were thin, with a "lean and hungry look," Shakespeare would say. In cutout shelves in the trench, they kept mills bombs (grenades), bayonets, and ammunition close at hand. Rifles, sawed-off shotguns, sharpened trench shovels, and boards with nails sticking out the end were all held in racks.

"For close-in scrapes," one soldier told me, "in Jerry's trench, at night, there's not enough room to run that Lee-Enfield all (the British rifle) way around. A sawed-off shotgun, that's it, real short. Put it right up against Jerry's chest, so's you can't miss."

The medieval-looking clubs caught my eye, and the soldier commented on that, too.

"Same thing, Leftenant. Most of our work is close-in. Can't be swinging that big old rifle with that long bayonet on it during a night raid on a listening post. Too cramped. Bring that trench shovel down on 'is 'elmet, that stuns 'im. Then swing that sharp end of the shovel into 'is throat. Kills 'im quick, and keeps 'im quiet, too. Don't want 'im waking up all the other Fritzies." The soldier smiled at me, revealing crooked, yellow teeth.

As I turned from the front-line trench into the communication trench, I came to the oddest realization. Those men in the front line, the ones at the business end of the war, they weren't just soldiers. They were killers.

On the way back to Arras, Burroughes and I had some time to sit and talk.

We had just gotten out of the trench system, and were above ground again. Going through those trenches was hard work, as you were forever dodging around and squeezing past people. Burroughes and I found some boxes marked "Explosives. Handle Carefully." They didn't expressly forbid sitting on them, and we were pretty bushed, so we sat ourselves down.

Burroughes started to light up a cigarette, looked down at the boxes, then thought better of it and put out his match.

"It's not like there's loose gunpowder sitting in these boxes, Gallagher, like in Napoleon's day, but still, I should so hate to blow us to kingdom come."

That was fine with me.

"You know, Gallagher, Waterloo's not too terribly far from here." He waved his hand north. "What, maybe a hundred miles, a hundred fifty miles up there in Belgium somewhere. Do you, well . . ." he looked at me quizzically, as if he were embarrassed to ask, "do you read about Waterloo, in your schools? I mean, since you had the Revolution, since you're not part of the Empire anymore . . ."

"Oh, yes, they teach us about it." That was 1815, the Battle of Waterloo; we had just finished fighting the British ourselves, in the War of 1812.

Burroughes nodded, then took his helmet off and ran his fingers through his hair. "Damned scratchy under these helmets. Hell, in the summer, when it's hot!" He scratched his head some more.

"I've heard you and Robson talking about Waterloo," I said.

The colonel smiled, glad I was interested in the battle that had finished off Napoleon. It had even become a fixture in the language, "He met his Waterloo," meaning a man had suffered defeat in some endeavor.

"That Robson, he knows his history. Knows it inside and out." He set his helmet back on, but didn't adjust the chin strap. "Has he shown you that picture of his wife and daughter?"

"Yes. Pretty family," I said.

Burroughes put his hands on his knees and pushed himself up to a stand. "Pretty family indeed. Pretty family indeed. They ought to be. His wife, Robson's, is my niece."

An ambulance brought us back to Arras.

The Britishers in Arras appeared greatly bucked up, for during the week of November 20 they had made a successful attack southeast of Arras on the Cambrai front—advancing four miles deep on a ten mile wide front. Such progress on the Western Front was phenomenal and explained why all the church bells had been ringing in England when we left. For years before this, progress had been measured in a few hundred yards. It was the first time the British had used tanks successfully and there was real hope these wire-smashing mechanical monsters could get this stalemated war on the move again. Was this the long-awaited "Big Push?" This Cambrai attack climaxed a summer and fall of fighting which had produced huge casualties and small gains. (The largest battles had been fought farther north, near the town of Ypres—Wipers, the British pronounced it.)

During this time I got to know Captain Robson (Burroughes' nephew-in-law, if there is such a thing). At our first encounter, I'd been so sleepy I could hardly speak. But now I was rested, had little to do, and neither did Robson, so soon we were thick as thieves. He wanted so much to learn about America, while I was still burning with curiosity about "The Front," so we talked and talked.

The old West was an obsession with him, and I had a difficult time explaining that the days of Indian wars, gunslingers, and cattle drives were largely gone.

"Is it dangerous in Texas, I mean, the Indians with their bows and arrows?" he asked, flushed red himself.

"No. You see, Indians are mostly on reservations now." Robson wouldn't be satisfied with that.

"But wasn't Sitting Bull on a reservation, when he attacked General Custer?"

Robson had the facts, all right, but the timing and the details were forever jumbled. He was going to make those Indians menacing, regardless of the facts. My interest was the Front, this war, the present, so I steered the conversation in that direction.

"How long have you been out here, Captain?" (He was above me in rank, so I didn't presume to call him "Robson," but he could call me "Gallagher," of course.)

"A year, just over a year. Came out last August. The big show on the Somme was quieting down a bit by then. Though not completely quiet, by any stretch.

Robson himself was in his usual state of repose, back against a wall, feet up, hands above his head. We were still in our two-story brick house, and had just finished lunch. (Another masterpiece by Sykes.) Outside, individual messengers were running up and down the streets. Occasionally, a motor car would go past. A far distant boom, boom was barely audible above the conversation.

Robson had gone into medicine, but had read on any and all topics, from the American West (however inaccurate), to poetry (he could recite most of Rudyard Kipling's poems), to foreign languages (French and German he had down pat, now he was trying to teach himself Italian). The Great War may be destroying nations and empires, but it would not distract Robson from his reading or his studies. He was forever with a book open, and often talked to himself, practicing his pronunciation of foreign words.

"So you've been out here a year, that's a long time," I said, trying to keep him focused on *this* war, and not let him slip off to Waterloo or some other historic battle.

"Yes, I suppose so." He could tell I wanted to talk more about the Front. To his thinking, he had told me more than enough that first night. He even seemed a little embarrassed about the lurid tales he'd told about the cave-ins and the men drowning in shell holes. "I guess I was trying to impress you," he'd told me the next day.

I didn't care, he could try to impress me all he wanted. Tell me more stories!

"A year, my goodness." Fishing, I was fishing for another story. Robson was a slippery fish, though.

"Gallagher," there was a tsk! tsk! in his voice, "you're going to the well again, looking for more war stories. I tell you what, we'll work a trade, you tell me about Custer and the Little Big Horn, and I'll tell you a little about Jerry and his tricks."

"Agreed."

Robson got the poor end of that bargain, for I knew damned little about Custer's last stand, just what I'd read in some boy's magazine. But Robson knew plenty about the Front. He opened up a little, and gave me his summary of the war.

"Jerry's dug in there, and we're dug in here," he started out. "Jerry mostly stays put, we mostly attack. If we get a line or two of his, he just digs a few more lines behind those, so we can't break through. There's no going *around* him, so here we sit. There it is."

"So it's a kind of siege?" I asked. "So when will it end? What's the trick?"

Robson shrugged, "There is no trick, we just have to wait it out, starve them out with the naval blockade. Maybe those new tanks will punch a hole in them. We'll eventually get 'em. It may take a while, but we always win the last battle." Robson, like most Britishers, had an undying optimism. Years of stalemate and hundreds of thousands of casualties, and still he had an unshakeable faith they would win the war.

By now Robson was a real friend of mine, and I bit my tongue rather than hurt his feelings. But the British hadn't always won the last battle. He was no fool, though, he had read his history books.

"You're thinking of Yorktown, aren't you, Gallagher?" His left eyebrow went up.

Damn! He'd seen right into my skull.

"Yes, Captain, I was thinking of Yorktown."

(The British lost the last major battle of the Revolutionary War at Yorktown, and lost the war itself.)

Robson threw his arm around my shoulders and gave them a big squeeze, something quite un-British.

"Ah, but you forget one thing, Gallagher. At Yorktown we were *fighting* you Americans. *Now*, we're on the same side!"

Every morning, in front of my adopted brick house, one heard the tramp, tramp of soldiers coming back from the trenches for a few days of rest in Arras. They usually marched to the tune of a drum and bugle band, except the Scotsmen in their kilties, who always had bagpipes skirling away. These men had been at it for three years now, with no real progress. They had suffered huge losses in Flanders (farther north, in Belgium), and here on the Somme. Yet, they marched in time, music playing, often whistling gaily as they tramped along. Tommy (a nickname for a British soldier) had an unbreakable spirit, as I would see for myself in the months to come.

After a few days in Arras, the Ambulance Company I was assigned to—the 2nd/2nd South Midland—was ordered to an area behind the Cambrai front. I stayed with Colonel Burroughes, but my new friend Captain Robson, was sent forward to man a Battalion Aid Post.

"Well, Gallagher, looks like we'll be partying company here. I'm to go up and join the 2nd/4th Gloucesters."

Slung over Robson's shoulder was a knapsack. His chin was still crisscrossed with nicks from shaving. I was forever teasing him about that. What kind of surgeon can't even shave *himself* without drawing blood.

"Captain, it's been a real pleasure. I'm sure we'll meet up before too long."

We were standing in the front door of the brick house in Arras. A messenger/guide was standing impatiently behind Robson, checking his watch.

Robson gave my hand a big shake. "That we will, that we will. It's a small world, Gallagher. I'm sure we'll run into each other again soon."

An Italian book poked up out of his knapsack.

"Cheerio then." He started down the stairs, looked back once and waved, then walked down the road. A half-block away he knelt down to lace his boots, and his Italian book fell out as he leaned over. He picked it up, turned around again and waved the book at me.

" Mmmm BLOODY mmmm mmmm!"

Some aeroplanes went overhead just as he was shouting, and I couldn't make out any word he'd said except "bloody."

Then he turned a corner and was gone.

The area we were going to, Cambrai, had been recently captured from the Germans. If history repeated itself, then the Germans were sure to counterattack.

It was Thanksgiving Day. Our trip started with an 8-mile march from Arras to Warrquetin, with only a little cheese and brown bread to be had at the end of the day. Starting at 6:45 in the morning we marched another 4 miles to Ournencourt, then marched on to Baupaume to catch a train. As we approached the station, Jerry was dropping shells all around. A messenger informed us the Germans had counterattacked, and broken through.

I had heard explosions during the air raid in London, had seen the flicker of distant artillery a number of times, and had even felt a few explosions during my tour of the front line, but this was the first time I *saw* explosions. Black, gray, and brown clouds appeared to spout out of the ground, like mushrooms. A few seconds passed as the cloud dispersed, then, the ground was bare again, and a new crater was born. It struck one as an inefficient way of killing people, for the explosions landed here and there, here and there, almost always finding an empty space. Of course, should it land right on top of you . . .

In Baupaume someone told us to go back through the little town of Metz (not the larger place, which is the capital of Lorraine), to a little clearing in some woods. There was no supper. One couldn't help but wonder who made all these decisions that sent us marching from pillar to post. But it wasn't my job to wonder, so I just kept trudging along with the rest of the men in the Ambulance Company. The woods themselves looked bleak, with no leaves on the trees. There was the sickly sweet tinge of death in the air. Somewhere there was an unburied body, or bodies in these woods.

The Germans were counterattacking strongly, to regain the ground lost in the British Cambrai tank attack. All night long a fierce battle raged a few miles away. The ground shook from the big guns. For the first time I could distinctly hear the tat-tat-tat-tat of machine gun fire. The sheer volume of bullets flying around must have been stupendous. Each machine gun could shoot hundreds of rounds a minute, and they were firing continuously. Nonstop. It didn't seem there was enough steel and gunpowder in the world to support such a magnitude of fire. Whole factories must have been working round the clock just to supply the bullets to this area alone. What a waste of steel.

My body exhausted, not being as used to marching as the "regulars," I crawled into an ambulance, and in spite of the nearby battle, fell asleep in a minute. Dreams of home appeared. All was peace and quiet. It was fall in Waseca, the leaves turning red, yellow and orange. An ice delivery wagon was going down the street, a big brown horse in the harness. He had bells on and they jingled as he walked. That's odd, they put bells on horses around Christmastime, not in the fall. The bells went tinkle, tinkle, tankle, tattle, tat, tat, tat-tat-tat-tat. TAT-TAT-TAT-TAT. The horse and wagon disappeared in a black and gray cloud. Kaboom! I sat bolt upright, shivering with cold, wondering what happened to the ice wagon. Then I looked around the ambulance, heard the shell bursts and tat-tat-tattering of the machine guns. My watch showed I'd only been asleep for a few minutes.

We stayed in the woods until 3:00 A.M. Then we marched back through Metz, and camped out along a roadside near the town of Fins. Across the road from us was a curiously familiar group of men, taller than the average Britisher, and wearing what looked like Boy Scout hats, rather than the British flat-brimmed helmet. The road between my Ambulance Company and this group of fellows was congested with trucks, ambulances, and horse drawn artillery, but I threaded my way across and introduced myself. They were Americans! Boy, was I glad to see some faces from home. And these Americans had rifles! Everyone had been asking me, "Where are the other Americans? When are the Yanks coming?" Well, here they were, in the flesh.

They took me in like the prodigal son, plied me with coffee (no tea, thankfully) and produced some chocolate from their knapsacks. Oh, did that sugary stuff taste good. In spite of Boche shells landing nearby, we kept up a happy American reunion.

These men were part of the 11th Engineers, National Guardsmen from Missouri. (As yet, there were few regular U.S. Army soldiers in France.) These engineers had gone to repair a railroad line in the area recently captured by the British. The Germans gave them a warm welcome.

"Yep, they sent us up here with pick and shovel to fix up a railroad," one of the engineers said, "I been workin' on the railroad, all the liv' long day," he started to sing, the other fellows laughed at that.

"More coffee, Ben?" the Yanks were less worried about rank, sir, and all that stuff. "Where ya from?"

"Minnesota."

"Minnesota! Cold up there, ain't it?" Their voices were twangy, but it was music to my ears.

"Come on up some time, I'll show you!" I told them, knowing that Missouri is nicknamed the "show-me-state." They all caught on, and laughed at my joke.

Our surrounding landscape was flat, not as flat as southern Minnesota, but flat, with mostly farm fields, as far as you could see. All the fighting had wiped out most signs of civilization, such as farmhouses. Men had taken fertile, productive land, and turned it into a barren arena for killing each other.

A hundred yards down the road, a shell hit right in the middle of a team of horses. There was a minute of terrible neighing and whinnying, then a few rifle shots as someone put the horses out of their misery.

"Lucky we brought our own rifles along. Fritzie gave us a little howdie-do yesterday." One of the engineers held up his Springfield and gave it a shake.

"You saw some action?" That coffee was hitting the spot.

"The Boche didn't like us workin' on the railroad, so they came by to tell us as much. Had to dump our picks and shovels, grab our Springfields, and let them know Uncle Sam owned this here railroad now," the engineer said. He wasn't bragging, just stating a fact. The men from Missouri were sent to do a job, and they were going to do it, come hell or high water.

Another engineer jumped in, "They grabbed a few of us, too, were starting to march us back Berlin way, but ol' Jim here popped our guard in the head, and we skedaddled." Captured? Guard shot? Escape? And they'd just gotten here. What would it feel like to be captured? Captured—and freed—all in the space of a few minutes.

"How far was that, anyways, Jim? Two hundred yards? And still, you hit that Fritzie right in the middle of his square old head." An engineer poked himself right in the middle of his forehead. At two hundred yards? That was a hell of a shot. These Missouri men wouldn't be stretching the truth on this story, would they? Should I ask *them* to show me?

"Lucky shot, I guess." Jim, the marksman, was scuffing his feet in the ground. "That weren't no two hundred yards, neither. Y'all just tryin' to impress our friend from Minnesota." He looked at me, "It was only 195 yards, not an inch farther." Everybody broke out laughing.

Jerry was dropping shells a little too close for comfort, so my new-found friends had to decamp and move into the lee of a small hill. We had a warm good-bye, they handed me another chocolate bar, and off they went. They were the first Americans I'd seen, except for the few American doctors, and they looked pretty darned good to me. It was great to say "So long!" and "See ya, boys! Good luck!"

And I had never tasted better coffee.

Our Ambulance Company moved up the road and found some huts left behind by a transport company. Jerry had slowed down his shelling some, and those huts looked a lot better than another night under the stars, so we moved in. Hours later the transport company returned and demanded their huts back. The discussion heated up, a lot of jurisprudence was bandied about (possession was nine-tenths of the law, for example, our side argued), idle threats were shouted back and forth, and soon the Germans seemed less a hazard than this transport company. Finally, we achieved "Peace without Victory" as President Wilson had urged. We reached a compromise, and all of us packed into the little huts together. My two-story brick mansion in Arras seemed a long way off, and I thought *that* was primitive.

There we stayed, from December 1 to December 2. The shelling was on and off. On the evening of December 2, we received a note saying Captain Robson had been killed.

Robson—dead. Dead. Captain Robson. My friend Captain Robson was dead. That was what the note said. "Confirmed. Cpt. Robson. Killed in action." But just a few days ago he'd shaken my hand, stooped to lace his boots, waved that Italian book at me. And now he was dead?

There had to be some mistake. Robson was a doctor. Yes, doctors got killed, just like any other soldier, BUT HE WASN'T JUST ANY OTHER SOLDIER. He wanted to see the Grand Canyon, wanted to see the wild Indians, wanted to have a son, wanted to play with his daughter, wanted to hear about Custer's last stand, wanted to learn Italian.

He wanted to live.

But Robson was dead.

Colonel Burroughes winced, looked up from the paper, sighed, then tucked the note into his breast pocket. He would be writing a letter to Robson's wife, his own niece, soon. Then he looked at me.

"Gallagher, you're the only one I've got. You will replace Robson."

Chapter 5

OVER THE TOP

2nd/4th Gloucester Battalion
December 3–4, 1917

"God, how he loved that daughter of his," Burroughes said. Three years old she was, still in the forgetful years. When Rachel Robson grew up, she would have no living memory of her father.

Burroughes shook it off. He had to. It was his duty to distance himself from lost men. He had been doing it for years. But *I* hadn't, I was shook to the bone.

"Gallagher, you will go join the 2nd/4th Gloucester Battalion, 183rd Brigade." There was the slightest hint of detachment in his voice, as if he were preparing to distance himself from me.

"Yes, sir. Colonel Burroughes. Where will I find the 2nd/4th Gloucesters?" We were still living in the small huts the transport company had set up. Wooden and spartan, they still beat living in a tent by a long shot. I forced myself to concentrate on Burroughes' words, I would be going to the Front now, there was no time to dwell on Robson's death.

"They'd be able to tell you where the 2nd/4th Gloucesters are at 183rd Brigade Headquarters."

"All right." Picking up my kit bag, I headed out of the hut. Robson was gone. Forget about it, get yourself up to the 2nd/4th Gloucesters. I needed to be busy, to be doing something, going somewhere, not sitting around thinking about my friend, my dead friend. This was war. People died. Friends died.

"A moment, please, Gallagher."

"Yes?" Why was he holding me up? I started to get angry at Burroughes, to blame him for Robson's death. Burroughes *had* ordered Robson forward. He had, in effect, sent Robson to his death. But, no, that was stupid of me. It wasn't Burroughes' fault.

"Do you know where the 183rd Brigade is?" Burroughes asked.

He had a point.

"Well, no, now that you mention it." I hadn't given it a thought. My mind was going a hundred miles an hour; Robson was dead, I was going forward, alone, men's lives might depend on me, soon. The stick man I had first envisioned at Chichester appeared, the stick man who reminded me to check off each body part, save the most important aspect of that body part, and move on. I'd better calm down, I wouldn't do anybody any good if I was all frazzled like this.

Colonel Burroughes smiled at me. "If it makes you feel any better, neither do I. Here, have a seat." He pointed to an empty box, the only item of luxury in the hut. He started writing some orders on a piece of paper. "I'll get a motor ambulance to take you to Division Headquarters at Metz. They should be able to tell you where the 183rd Brigade is, and they, in turn, should be able to tell you where the 2nd/4th Gloucester Battalion is located." Good. A plan. A set of instructions to follow, that should help settle me down. My stomach was full of butterflies, the way I used to feel when I would walk out to the mound at the start of a baseball game. This was it. THIS WAS IT.

He handed me the orders.

"I know I'm insulting your intelligence when I say this, Gallagher, but I must point out a few things." Still, the butterflies were going and going. And I knew they'd keep going until I actually got to work. Once I started in, I'd be all right. Or so I hoped.

"Yes." Flutter, flutter.

"Even the most casual observer would note that it is night."

A glance outside the door confirmed that very fact.

"And night tends to darkness," Burroughes added, raising his eyebrows. There was no arguing with this man. His logic was impeccable.

"Right again, sir." Flutter. Less bothersome now. Concentrate on the directions. Don't worry about what you'll *do* once you get there, just concentrate on *getting* there.

Outside, light flickered and artillery boomed.

"And Jerry's been putting up quite a stunt lately, so the lines may have, shall we say, shifted a little." Burroughes used the British slang word "stunt," which meant an attack. They tended to say "stunt" when the Germans attacked, and "show" when the English attacked, though it wasn't an absolute rule.

More flickers outside, but the wind must have changed, for there were no sounds of explosions. The colonel was silent a moment. He seemed to be thinking about Robson. Perhaps he was thinking of me.

"So, I guess I'm saying, get up to the 2nd/4th Gloucesters as soon as you can, but don't push your luck." Burroughes was being the kindly father, who had just lost one son. "It's easy to get lost in the best of circumstances, and these aren't the best of circumstances. This is a new area; Jerry's on the prowl. You yourself have only been in the trenches once. Well, you know what I'm saying. Do be careful." He did not want to lose a second son. "And try to sound English when you open your mouth, for God's sake. We don't want you getting shot as a spy." This last remark came out of the clear, blue sky. One more thing to worry about, getting shot by the English as a spy! Whether Burroughes threw that in as a joke, I didn't know, but it helped my nervousness. My last butterfly flew out of my stomach and headed out into the dark, flickering December night. I followed.

An ambulance was to drive me to Metz. My driver took off at breakneck speed down the shell-torn road. We had to travel without lights, so as not to draw enemy fire, and the moon had not come up yet. Traffic was going both ways, it was pitch black. Might it not be safer to get out and walk?

"Must we go this fast?" I asked, trying to sound calm.

"Oh, it's not that fast we're going, Leftenant, whooooah!" my driver swerved hard right to avoid a shell hole, sliding me against the door, then he swerved just as hard left, to avoid an oncoming truck, sliding me back the other way, smacking right into the side of him. "Just seems we're going fast, what with all these bad drivers on the road tonight." Lucky for me I had a "good" driver.

We bounced over something, it seemed to "give" as we went over it, and there was the faintest neighing sound, though hard to hear over the noise of the motor.

"That wasn't . . . " No, it couldn't have been.

"Gotta keep movin', Leftenant, can't stop for every little bump in the road." Little bump? How many "little bumps" let out a neighing sound when you drove over them?

Swerving, squishing, and lurching down the road, we arrived at Metz about 9:00 P.M. Division Headquarters told us the brigade was at a place called Villiers-Plouich, four miles away as the crow flies (Viller Ploosh, the British pronounced it, making no attempt to use the correct French). Near the Front, of course, one could rarely travel as the crow flies. Division Headquarters staff told me the ambulance could go no farther due to heavy shelling (that was fine by me, that ambulance was more dangerous than any German artillery fire). But heavy shelling did not preclude *me* from going forward. (Ambulances are expensive and hard to replace. First lieutenants are a dime a dozen.) I sent the driver back, got some directions, and set out alone, with "me pack upon me back."

I had a map, and tried to read it in the flickering light of artillery fire. Perhaps it was just as well that I couldn't see it, for maps had never agreed with me through the years. At some point, I remembered that a compass might help, but no luck, I went through all my pockets, it was lost. A mile from Metz there was an intersection called Queen's Cross Roads. Division Headquarters had told me to avoid this place, as Jerry shelled it continuously, and take instead a track through a field around the intersection. Starting out into the field, I soon found tracks running in very possible direction and feared becoming hopelessly lost. Returning to the main road, I cautiously made my way through the intersection. All was serene, not a truck or a soldier was there. No shells fell as I walked right on through. Jerry must be resting.

Walking through the intersection, I felt very much alone. This would be the test, the moment I had prepared for so long. A doctor, alone, at the Front. Yes, I had gone through medical school; yes, I had done a busy internship; and yes, I had gained great experience at Graylingwell with Dr. Maxwell. But there had always been an extra pair of hands around, an extra head to think through the problems. In medical school, there was an intern to help me. Even on that awful day in Minneapolis when Giancomo died, my resident Hansen came to help me in a few minutes. Later, as an intern, if I couldn't reduce a hernia, or set a wrist fracture, a more senior resident or staff physician could always show the way. At Graylingwell War Hospital in Chichester, Dr. Maxwell gave me a lot of rope, but he'd never quite let me hang myself.

But now, it was different. I was all alone in that intersection, all alone. And up at the Battalion Aid Post, I would be the lone doctor. If I got in trouble there, I couldn't ask for Hansen, or Maxwell, or anybody. Men's lives would depend on me, just as Giancomo's life had depended on me years before. If my confidence faltered in that Aid Post; if I started hesitating, dawdling, and fumbling, some men might die who might otherwise live. Like Giancomo. That thought weighed heavily on me. But at least now I had a system. The stick man. Consider each patient the stick man, work your way down. Keep the airway clear, stop the bleeding, stabilize the fracture, move on. Check them out from head to toe, then check them again. At Chichester, I had tested myself again and again on the treatment of wounded soldiers. And I hadn't just done the mental exercises.

I had changed the bandages, splinted the fractures, irrigated the wounds, operated on the legs, the arms, the chests, the heads. Anything and everything came to us at that hospital, and I thanked my lucky stars I had worked so hard there. Front line work would, of course, be different. Patients at Chichester were over the acute injury, they were days or weeks out from combat. At the Battalion Aid Post, the men would be only minutes, or possibly hours out from their injury. There would be a lot more acute hemorrhaging than we ever saw at Chichester. All right then, so be it. I'll treat the hemorrhaging and be right quick about it. Then I'll be methodical about checking off the rest of the injured parts. Fix what you can fix, the send them back. Fix what you can fix. Do the job. That's all you can do. Don't forget tetanus antitoxin either. So, alone in that intersection, with the great front line trial ahead of me, I felt nervous, but not helpless. Maxwell had said "You're ready." Whether he was right or not, I would soon see.

Passing a battery of artillery, I again asked for directions. Unlike the infantry, the artillerymen usually had some sense of direction. One certainly hoped so—hate to have them pointing those big guns in the wrong direction. The artillerymen told me there was some kind of ambulance station up ahead in a sunken road. I went ahead and found a carved out dent in the side of the road, and this was, indeed, an Ambulance Company.

"Colonel, someone here to see you," a big, husky sergeant introduced me to the head of the Ambulance Company. It was hard to make out people's features at night in the trenches—lighting was all by candles and hooded lamps. You could see the gleam of teeth when they smiled, though, and these fine fellows were smiling.

"Oh, hello, Leftenant, sit down. Sergeant! Fetch us up some tea, and some eats, too, something from the Savoy Grill, if you can. If not, a little bully beef and bung will do nicely."

"Bung?" I asked, sitting down.

"Cheese, actually. The men call it 'bung" because it tends to stuff them up, constipate them, as it were." Another big gleam of teeth against a shadowy face.

"Oh." In a hundred years I couldn't learn all the slang the British used.

"Say, you don't sound like your from Manchester or Birmingham. Are you Canadian?" Canadians sounded a lot like Minnesotans. And the Canadians had been fighting alongside the British since 1914.

The sergeant handed me a plate of beef and cheese, and a cup of liquid high explosive that must have gotten mixed in with the company tea. I took one swallow and felt like I should get a Victoria Cross for the effort.

"Strong enough for you, Leftenant?" the sergeant asked solicitously.

"Fine," I croaked.

"So, are you Canadian?" the Colonel asked me again, drinking his tea straight down as if it were a cup of mountain spring water.

"No. American."

"Well, what do you know," the Colonel said. "Our cousins are finally starting to show up. The men had started a little variation on your song, 'Over There'."

"Oh, how does it go?" The stringy beef and rock hard cheese may or may not have tasted good. The tea had killed any ability to discern taste.

"Well, I don't know exactly, but the last line goes:

'And we won't go there, 'til it's over, Over There.'

"No offense intended." Gleam. Those teeth were gleaming in the night. The sergeant, too, unveiled a ribbon of white.

"None taken." Hmm. The rapier thrust of British wit was now aimed at us Americans.

"So what brings you out here at this time of night?" the Colonel asked.

"I'm supposed to get to 183rd Brigade. They'll tell me how to get to the 2nd/4th Gloucester, to take over as their battalion medical officer." Battalion medical officer. A thousand men in a battalion. A thousand men under my care. The butterflies tried to fly back into my stomach, but I fought them off. Calm down. Do your job as you know it. Apply the lessons of Chichester. Stop the hemorrhaging. Splint the fracture. Keep moving.

"And you want to get there tonight? In the dark? While he's dropping shells here and there. He's even got a bit of a stunt up, trying to take back all the ground we took with our tanks a week ago." In addition to using the terms Jerry, Hun, or Boche, the British sometimes referred to the Germans as simply "he."

"Well, yes. Colonel, but my orders . . . "

"You'd better bunk down here tonight, get up to the 2nd/4th in the morning." The gleam of his teeth was gone, he had a concerned look, as nearly as could be discerned in the shadowy light.

"No, no thank you, Colonel. I truly do appreciate the offer, but I should get moving on. Thanks so much for the food. Now I'd better get moving on." This was my first, my very first assignment. No dawdling. My orders said get there, and I was going to get there.

"Well, all right, if you insist. Let me at least give you a couple guides. Sergeant!"

The sergeant appeared out of the dark.

"Sir."

"Get Clooney and Braithwaite up here. I want them to escort the Leftenant here to wherever he needs to go."

"Yes, Colonel."

Only later did I learn the identity of this kind colonel; Simon-Leek, one of the best-known men in the British Army. He was the first man to win the Victoria Cross twice (Britain's highest military decoration). He had won his first one in the Boer War, back in 1902.

What my guides thought of me, I did not know, but they didn't grumble as they led me up the sunken road, and into a cross-wise running trench. They didn't know whether to go left or right, went right on a hunch, and started asking some infantrymen for directions. (Among the infantry, accurate directions were as rare as hen's teeth.) Through sheer bad luck, we came across a dugout which turned out to be the headquarters for the 20th Division. In the course of walking around for hours, I'd succeeded in going from my *own* Division's headquarters to *another* Division's headquarters. No progress whatsoever.

"Well, Leftenant, there you are, all delivered in one piece, and to a fine place, too, you are delivered," my guide Braithwaite said. He looked just like my other guide, Clooney, and their lively banter sounded like a vaudeville act—so effortlessly they played off each other.

"But this is the 20th Division Headquarters, I was . . . " They wouldn't leave me marooned here, would they?

"The 20th, a fine division. Braver men you will not find," Clooney said, nodding vigorously to emphasize their bravery. "And an unerring sense of direction, too. Surely the brave lads of the 20th Division will get you where you need to go." His hand reached out with a magnanimous, sweeping gesture. All hail to the courageous 20th Division and their magnificent sense of direction.

"Now, by your leave, Leftenant, my mate here and I will retire to our humble abode and catch forty winks before 'night's candles are burned out, and jocund day stands tiptoe on the misty mountaintops,'" Braithwaite said, quoting Shakespeare.

"'Let's away, before the break of day,' ta ta, Leftenant," Clooney said, waving good-bye. He, too, was quoting Shakespeare for his purpose. Before I could protest, the night had swallowed them up.

That left me to the tender mercies of the 20th Division staff, who wondered about my accent (German spy, maybe?), my story (why was a doctor from the 61st here in the 20th?), and my timing (who moved around alone at night in an unfamiliar sector?). I'd experienced stiff British treatment before, but this topped all. No one asked me to stay 'til morning; no one offered a guide, or food, or even tea. No tea? Unheard of! Getting what directions I could, I set out on my own down the labyrinth of trenches. By now, I had no energy left for nervousness or idle reflection. Maybe I was ready, maybe not, but one thing was for sure. I was tired.

The British were forever giving their trenches interesting names. Pope Avenue. Picadilly Circus, and the like. My directions were to follow a certain trench called Blenheim Avenue, until I came to a road, then follow the road into a ruined village. In a dugout along a railroad cutting I would find the headquarters of the 183rd Brigade. Probably.

I followed Blenheim Avenue for a few miles, staying in the trench at first, making slow progress. Here and there men were sleeping right in the middle of the trench, so I had to climb out, crawl along the top, then fall back in on the other side. As it turned out, I was far enough back to safely walk on top of the trench, but this was all so new to me I didn't know what was safe and what posed a danger.

Foolishly, I continued to ask directions of the English soldiers. In general, they didn't know, or care where they were. They left all that to their officers. In the trenches, the men would sprawl and curl in all kinds of impossible angles, and sleep, while one of their number sat up, tending a small fire, brewing tea. About the only answer I ever got was, "Don't know, sir."

Tired of the slogging, I threw caution to the wind, and climbed out of the trench, to where the going was much easier. By now the moon was up, and visibility was good. Parties of men with pack mules were going in various directions bringing rations and ammunition. One dead mule frightened the hell out of me. Just as I passed by, a bunch of rats ran out from underneath it, one of them running right over my boot. Those rats were big and fat. Well fed, they were.

Upon reaching the road crossing the trench, I could see in the distance to the right the ruins of a good-sized village. It was Villiers-Plouich, my goal. "He" was dropping shells all over it. It looked, even to my inexperienced eyes, like the Hun had a stunt up, and Villiers-Plouich was the target of that stunt.

I went into the village, crouching low. On the far side, there was a railroad cutting, where Brigade Headquarters should be. As I made my way around the embankment of the cutting, something most curious appeared. In the midst of the heavy bombardment were 50 or so British soldiers, sleeping, in the same odd angles and curls as they had in the trenches. What were those men thinking, out there in the middle of the road, sleeping through all this? By the moon's light, I saw they were not sleeping at odd angles, but rather lay at impossible angles—legs bent around so a foot was by the head, chests cracked open, arms missing. When a shell landed close, it lifted the men up, killing them again, and tossed them, rag doll, into an awkward new posture. I ran past the bodies, frequently throwing myself on the ground as a shell hit nearby and showered me with dirt. Dead mules and horses lay everywhere.

There were dugouts slit into the sides of this murderous railway cutting. Sentries stood in the entrances, leaning back into the doorways to avoid shrapnel. As usual, none of them knew where anything was. The fifth dugout I came to, and by now any would do, was indeed Brigade Headquarters. I dashed down the steps and out of the barrage.

At the bottom I ran into my old friend General Spooner, the fellow who'd shown me his dugout a few days earlier. He was as friendly as before, gave me something to eat plus some warm tea, and told me to lie down and rest. This time I was too tired to play the hero; I curled up in a blanket, lay down on the floor, and fell sound asleep.

They woke me a few hours later, just before dawn, and told me to join a group of men going up to La Vacquerie. It was a town about a mile ahead, where the 2nd/4th Gloucesters were entrenched. At long last, I was to get to my Battalion assignment. Leading this group was a Captain Gardiner, who'd come down from La Vacquerie with his men in order to pick up rations.

"A Yank, no less," Gardiner held out his hand. Flaming red hair peaked out from his helmet, and freckles covered his face. His smile revealed a huge gap between his front teeth. He could eat watermelon through a picket fence with that gap.

"That's right, Captain Gardiner, nice to meet you." Still pretty sleepy, I slurred some of my words. My side ached from sleeping on the hard ground and my neck felt stiff. My right arm had fallen asleep. When I shook it, my little finger and half of my ring finger burned a little. I must have compressed my ulnar nerve on that side.

"Grab your kit, then, and stick close to me. Jerry's trying to take La Vacquerie, but we've scuppered him pretty good so far."

The early hour, lack of sleep, and thundering explosions all put me into kind of a haze. And I wasn't quite sure what "scuppered" meant, but didn't want to look the fool in front of the Englishmen, so I just picked up my bag. My arm was waking up, but still felt a little tingly.

"We'll be going up a sunken road, so we should be safe until we get to town. Unless of course, one lands right on top of us. But I don't think that'll happen, you look like the lucky type," Gardiner bellowed with laughter. His men cracked up, too. With that red hair, freckles, and gap-toothed smile, Gardiner looked like an eight-year-old kid.

"Right near town the road shallows out quite a bit, so you'll be needing to do your shrinking violet imitation." Another laugh. Gardiner found humor in everything.

"Right, lads! Let's not be getting the wind up, just because Jerry's in a snit. Out we go."

Up the stairs we went, out of the safety of the dugout. I was the last man out. By the time I stepped out that doorway, I was wide awake, arm and all.

We started up the sunken road, which seemed more like a pre-built, wide trench, so our heads were kept below ground level. The Germans continued to shell this road, and I was getting a little more adept at knowing when a shell was close, and when one was far away. Over our heads I heard a peculiar whistling noise, similar to the twang-ang-ang of a telegraph wire when you hit it with a stone. But, there were no telegraph wires near. After a few hundred yards of walking, we crouched down against the side of the embankment, giving the enlisted men a breather. The ration boxes they were carrying were heavy.

Twang-twa-aa-ang overhead.

"Captain Gardiner, what is that sound?" I asked.

"Oh that," he pointed upward, careful not to lift his finger above the top of the sunken road, "bullets, machine gun bullets."

Twang-twa-aa-aang.

The road was well bedecked with dead men. Nearing La Vacquerie, I stepped to one side to avoid walking over the body of a man. Something about his uniform looked familiar. He had a medical insignia. Next to his head was a knapsack. Fluttering at the top of it was a book. The words looked foreign. Not French, not German—Italian. The body lay there, arms splayed out, chin jutting up. The chin was crisscrossed with razor cuts. It was Robson. He had never made it to the 2nd/4th Gloucesters. His trip, his life, had ended here, on this road to La Vacquerie.

He lay on his back, no sign of violent death apparent, but the ground beneath him was stained, not red, just dark. The dried blood had lost its bright hue and made the earth look dark, stained, dirty. Robson's face was ashen, his eyes—half-open—looked milky. His helmet had come off and the wind blew his hair around, sandy-brown hair.

Dead.

The night before he left, he had recited Kipling's poem. "If." The last verse went:

"If you can fill the unforgiving minute,
With sixty seconds' worth of distance run.
Yours is the earth and everything in it,
And, which is more, you'll be a man, my son."

Robson had done that. He had filled every unforgiving minute with sixty seconds' worth of distance run.

Sleep well, Captain, you've earned it.

"Leftenant! Leftenant!" Gardiner was yanking at my arm. These thoughts about Robson would have to wait, there was no time. There was no time.

At La Vacquerie, the sunken road gradually became less sunken, and we had to crouch lower and lower. In the town itself, the road offered us no protection, so we had to hurry along from broken brick wall to broken brick wall. No houses were intact. Shells were landing all over. Machine gun bullets were no longer whizzing overhead, now they were slap-slapping into the walls. Captain Gardiner pulled me down a stairway which seemed to appear out of nowhere. It went down to a very deep dugout, the 2nd/4th Gloucester Battalion Headquarters. A sigh of relief, I had made it, in one piece. Colonel Barnsley, the C.O., and four other officers were preparing to eat breakfast, which was sizzling on an oil stove in the corner. All of the officers looked haggard and unshaven. It had been a tough night for them.

As always, tea was brewing, and one of the officers handed me a tin cup. No sooner had I laid down my pack, taken a sip, when a series of heavy thuds overhead announced an intensification of the German barrage. The officers looked up at the ceiling of the dugout, as if to "see" the bombardment. Dust filtered down with each thud.

"Five-nines," one of them said.

That meant nothing to me, but it apparently meant something to them, for the officers looked worried. Before I could take a second sip of tea, another officer came running down the steps of the dugout.

"Get out! Jerry's come over the top, and our men are leaving the trenches."

But I just got here. Where's the Aid Post? What should I do? My mind was racing.

Barnsley spoke, "Step lively, boys. We'll finish breakfast later." Major Day, his adjutant, set fire to some papers.

The officers dropped their tin cups, grabbed their pistols, and bolted up the stairs. Colonel Barnsley suggested I follow him as he knew a line of retreat. It was all I needed to hear, and I fell in step behind the Colonel, up the long, narrow entrance I had walked down a few minutes before. The sun had come up and was shining brightly now. From the top of the stairs, I could see dozens of English soldiers running toward, and past me, dropping behind fragments of walls to fire back at dozens of German soldiers now entering the far side of the village.

I could see their coal scuttle helmets, gray uniforms, and Mauser rifles. One of the Germans leveled his gun and pointed it right at me. Whether from his gun, or another, a piece of wood snapped off right by my ear. Feeling that discretion was the better part of valor, I chose that very moment to join the retreating Englishman.

Barnsley and Day and the other officers had disappeared in the mass of retreating men, but the line of retreat was obvious, a wide open field with no cover whatsoever. To the right, a couple hundred yards away, German machine guns were sputtering their lead at the fleeing men. Soldiers were falling, sometimes a single man, sometimes in bunches. Sometimes they dropped like a stone, other times they would jump high in the air when hit, then drag on as best they could. The barrage, which had been falling on top of the village, had now lifted and was falling about 200 yards west of the village, in the exact direction of our retreat. This line of explosions was hitting in a straight line across the field, and it went to either side, as far as you could see. There was no getting around it, and it seemed impossible to get through it, so thick were the shells falling. I ran right at it.

Just before I reached the solid line of explosions, to my great surprise and wonder, the explosions stopped. The barrage lifted, then advanced to a line about a hundred yards ahead, forming a new solid line of explosions. It had lifted and moved as easily as the stream from a hose, as a man directs the stream with his thumb. I kept running. Men kept falling, falling, falling. Ahead of me a man ran into the barrage and disintegrated, both arms flying high into the air, spinning around pinwheel fashion, almost landing on me. Bits of flesh spattered at me.

Any tendency to tarry was dispelled by the machine gun bullets picking off many a poor fellow in his tracks. There indeed "he who hesitates is lost," so I entered the barrage at the same spot where the man had been blown to bits. I plunged wildly on, holding my forearms in front of my face, shouting at the top of my lungs. All was darkness, a brown, earthy darkness, and hot waves of air pushed me first one way, then another, as if in a great wind storm. Something tripped me and I fell hands down into a warm and sticky mass. I tried to push off, to get up and get going again, but the slippery mass gave way, and I fell face first into it. It smelled like a butcher shop, only warm. To describe my sensations in crossing that field and as I lay face down in that sticky stuff, with explosions buffeting me, would be very difficult. To say I was not scared would not be the truth, but the suddenness of it all, the novelty of the situation to me, who only a few days before had heard a big gun for the first time, and the necessity for quick action served to allay some of the sensations of fear.

A searing hot blast of air passed over me from behind, then I was up again, peeling slippery stuff off my face so I could see. Ten more feet, and I was out of the brown curtain of explosions. Ahead, there was a trench and I dove into it, head first. How many of the retreating English had made it? It didn't seem like anyone could have.

But somehow, they had. Men were jumping into the trench all around me. Instinctively, I started putting emergency dressings on the injured. The time had come to "do the job." My stick man theory went out the window, I just looked for the blood and slapped on the dressing. It was like a piano player who knows the piece so well that he doesn't have to "think" about where the fingers are going. He just plays the song. I just plugged the holes. Quickly we all moved along to the right and down a communicating trench running farther back. We crossed another trench, named "Hindenburg Line," and I was afraid, somehow or another, we had gone the wrong way and had jumped into the Hun's own trench. The joke was on me. It didn't occur to me the Germans wouldn't write their signs in English. The Germans would call it the "*Siegfried Linie.*"

Fresh British troops manned the next line of trenches. They were "standing to" with guns in hand, waiting for us to get back before opening up on the Germans. All the while Jerry lay a murderous shell fire right along this trench, and his machine guns were sweeping the parapet, flicking off dust. I found a dugout, and immediately set up an impromptu Aid Post. At first, my only equipment was the emergency dressing each man carried with him, until I located a cache of extra dressings, including some with German writing. I was indeed, as Dr. Maxwell had pointed out, functioning as an orderly, slapping bandages on wounds, trying to stem the bleeding. My stay in that dugout lasted only a few minutes.

The last of our men ran past the dugout and hollered down to get out of there, Jerry was in the trench and coming up fast. We had to keep moving back like a flock of sheep. I helped the wounded out of the dugout, told them to get a move on, and followed the retreating men. Behind me, a German machine gun was working its way up the trench. I didn't look back.

Making my way down the trench, shells landing everywhere, I saw for the first time what I'd only read about—men killed, and buried in a trench with just a head, arm, or leg sticking out of the dirt. Once my head actually hit a human foot—the top of its boot had been blown off, and I could see the poor fellow's dirty toes and toenails. Ducking, I kept running. In some places, the trench had caved in, so we were forced to crawl over the piles of dirt to avoid the machine gun fire playing at our heels and head. I distinctly remember pressing my pelvis into the dirt to keep from getting shot in the buttocks. (The advice the Welsh lieutenant had given me.) Within a hundred yards we reached a diagonal trench, and here the English were making a stand. A little farther on, there was a big dugout with a Red Cross above it.

That Red Cross guarded the door to the seventh circle of hell. Before I even crossed the threshold, men were crying out to me for help. This would be my baptism of fire as a doctor.

One step in the door and I heard a chorus of misery.

"Aaaa! Jesus! Jesus, Jesus!"

"My leg, oh God! Help me!"

"Mother, Mother!"

"Doctor! Doctor! Orderly! Anybody!" A soldier was using one hand to shake an unconscious man, and his other hand to wave for help.

"I'm gonna be sick." Another soldier doubled over and emptied his stomach all over the stairs, and several men. Dark blood was mixed with chewed up food.

"I can't breathe, I can't breathe!" A man stood on the stairs, arms holding on to the wall. His eyes and face were swollen up, and his chest was retracting—pulling in—with each breath. There must have been some poison gas used in the German assault, but I hadn't seen any.

"I can't see. I'm blind, oh God Almighty, the bastards shot me eyes out!" A poor fellow rocked back and forth, his hands in front of his eyes, a clear liquid slithering down his cheeks—the clear liquid was vitreous humor, the liquid inside your eyeball.

Men were sitting, holding their arms or legs, or holding their bellies. One man was squeezing the stump of his wrist, trying to make a tourniquet with his fingers.

"Here, let me," I said. "Lieutenant Gallagher, Medical Corps. Anything else? Other than this scratch, I mean?" He'd live. It was an arm wound, best to let him evacuate himself, the sooner the better. Of course, it was more than a scratch, but I had to keep his spirits up enough to get him to walk back himself.

I tore his good sleeve off and tied it around the stump. He was as pale as a ghost.

"No. Nothing else. Just this." Just this. His hand lost. But that's how I wanted him to think of it. That might get him back, and it would save me some stretcher bearers.

"Not much more we'll do for you here, think you can make it a little farther back?" I asked, looking him right in the eye.

"I don't know, sir." He looked down at the stump. The jagged ends of bones were exposed. Some tendons dangled like cut electrical wires.

"Sure you can, up you go." I helped him up, got to the top of the dugout, and grabbed a passing soldier.

"Help this man back to the Advanced Dressing Station, will you? Good." Not waiting for an answer, I pushed the two down the trench, towards the Advanced Dressing Station. Don't give the wounded man time to think about it. Get him walking. Get him moving. Get him back.

I hadn't even made it all the way down the stairs yet, and I had treated and evacuated my first patient. Heading down the stairs, I got assailed again by every kind of pitiful cry you could imagine. Everyone wanted help, men cried out for their mother, their wife, their sweetheart. The sounds of vomiting, coughing, and choking came from all sides. A few men were curled up, not moving, not breathing—live dead men. There *must* be another doctor down in that dugout somewhere. I slipped on some vomitus, caught myself on the wall, and kept going down, down, descending into the dugout. This was the descent into hell that Maxwell had told me about. No nervousness assailed me, no doubts nagged me. Giancomo's ghost blew away like a will-o'-the-wisp. Robson's death was tragic, and painful, and behind me. Maxwell's teaching was there, in my head, and in my hands. And Sister Marie Francis' prayer was in my heart.

"God will guide your hands, Ben," she had told me once.

Ignoring, for a moment, the men who reached out for me on the stairs, I made it to the bottom. There was room in this huge dugout for a couple hundred men, but it was already jammed, wall to wall, with wounded men. And stretcher bearers were bumping their way down the stairs with more.

A man with sleeves rolled up was standing next to a heated trestle in the center of the room. He was cutting the last shreds of flesh that held a man's leg on. Two assistants were holding the patient down. The wounded man had a bayonet scabbard in his teeth and was biting down for all he was worth, his face bathed in sweat.

"Won't take a minute, lad." The doctor's forearms and hands were covered in blood. His shirt had huge sweat rings under his armpits. He was working fast, but not frantically, and his voice was even and reassuring. This man did not shout, he did not have to shout.

"Gallagher. Medical Corps. Can I help?" I started rolling up my sleeves.

"Craig. Help hold him down." Firm, smooth. The voice of command.

The man's leg was off in a minute, but the pain did not magically stop. The wounded man kept biting on the scabbard. A snap announced that he'd broken off a tooth.

"Tie off the bleeders, and toss in two stitches, just enough to keep the skin flap over the stump. Nothing fancy. I'll take a look 'round and see if I can't thin it out here a bit." Dr. Craig flashed me a smile, then walked off, wiping his hands on a towel.

In the weeks and months leading up to this, my trial of fire, I had worried and fretted so much about being alone, ALONE. And now fate had thrown me in this dugout with *another* doctor. By all appearances, he looked like he knew what he was doing, too. There were so many men in the dugout, and so many more were coming that I would almost *be* working alone, but it comforted me to know that Craig was nearby.

"Right," I said. One artery was spouting all over one of the assistants, I tied it off. One stitch, two stitches, gauze pack, wrap, tie. Next!

In my earlier visit to an empty Aid Post, I had used my mind's eye to fill the room with horror. In this Aid Post, no imagination was necessary. Anything that could be torn off, crushed, pierced, or broken, was. Our job was to treat the men briefly, then send them back to the Advanced Dressing Station in Villiers-Plouich, a mile away. Easier said than done. Just getting in and out of the dugout was cumbersome for the stretcher bearers, tripping down a small stairway, bumping into people, jolting the wounded, then reversing the whole process on the way out. Once out of the dugout, these same stretcher bearers had to push down a crowded, narrow trench, under fire, for a full mile, remove the wounded, then pick up some water, for we were desperately short, and thread their way back again. It might take an hour to get one man back, and in that time dozens would come in. Captain Craig and I were overwhelmed.

I worked my way through the dugout, trying to do a *little* for all the men first, rather than trying to do a *lot* for any one man. Triage in its most basic form. The first few dozen patients I remembered, then they all blurred.

—The first man was choking, his mouth full of broken teeth. Shrapnel, or a German rifle butt (it didn't really matter) had stove in his face.

Protect his airway. I reached my finger into his mouth, swept out the broken teeth, and jammed a role of gauze into the side of the mouth to prop it open.

Next!

—The second man's upper arm was shaped like an "S," obviously broken in several places.

"Splint!" an orderly handed me one. "You got any whisky?" He nodded and pulled a flask out of his jacket. "Drink this." The wounded man took a bolt. "Hold on." Putting my foot on his chest, I pulled his arm out straight, the cracking of bones drowned out by his screaming. When his arm was—approximately—straight, I told the orderly to affix a splint on either side of it and wrap it up tight.

Next!

—The third man did not have a scratch on him. I rolled him over, no wounds on his back either. (That was one of Maxwell's pearls—"Don't forget to look on the backside! Wounds don't just occur on the front.") I rolled him back. Odd. Why should he be in this dugout, if he hasn't any wounds?

"'E's dead, sir," my orderly said. A great, muscular man, he was with large tattoos of anchors on his forearms, he looked like he should be strolling the deck of a ship, rather than an army dugout. He had latched on to me after I separated from Craig.

I looked at the orderly, than at the unmarked man. No pulse. No breathing. He *was* dead. I'd been so intent on finding the *wound*, I had forgotten about the *patient*.

"Right, then. Let's get him out of here. By the way, I'm Lieutenant Gallagher, and you are . . ."

"Kingston. Corporal Kingston. They call me 'Tiny,' Leftenant," he said.

Tiny proceeded to pick up the dead man singlehandedly, sling him over his shoulder (the dead man must have weighed 200 pounds himself) and go up the stairs. In just a few minutes he was back, looking none the worse for wear. Tiny would prove quite useful.

—The fourth and fifth soldiers both had belly wounds. I slapped a large binding dressing on each and made a note to come back later and wash out the wounds, if we could ever get any water. These men would be high priority for evacuation when a stretcher bearer became available.

Next!

On and on it went. Bandages on, splints applied. My list of who-should-get-evacuated-first kept growing. At one point, there was only one stretcher bearer team available. Who should go first? The belly wound (an early operation could save him) or the head injury (an early operation could save him, too)? I opted for the head injury, for the belly wound patient began to have agonal respirations (deep gasps punctuated by long pauses, indicating that death was near). Save who you can save.

The dugout had a surprisingly high ceiling, about eight feet, and was well supported with thick timbers. Shells were landing overhead, but our sturdy shelter neither shook nor poured dust down onto our heads. The walls were rough planks, but the floor was dirt. It was like a crude, underground log cabin.

Craig, short and wiry, in his 40s but looking much younger, worked one side of the shelter and I worked the other side. We would come together every now and then to do an "operation" on the heated trestle (bed) in the middle of the room. There was no anesthetic, only Tiny and another orderly, holding down the patient as we pulled out a piece of shrapnel or splintered a broken leg.

Craig and I took a breather a few hours later, just for a few minutes. Fifty men or more had come under my care. Two had died while I was working on them.

"Gallagher, you said your name was?" Craig asked, munching on some dry crackers. He didn't eat too many, for there was no water to wash them down.

"Yes." The air around us was thick with the stench of feces. Dying men tended to relax their sphincters at the time of death and soil themselves. Some men with belly wounds had feces running straight out of their exposed intestines.

"That's not an Irish brogue I hear, though," Craig said. Tiny squeezed past us, another dead body slung over his shoulder. Blood was dripping out of the dead man's mouth, running down his face and forming a gruesome streak down Tiny's back.

"Irish by descent, American now." The high-pitched screams from the wounded had slowed down, but many were still moaning and muttering to themselves. Tiny was oblivious to the bloody trail, now running down onto the back of his pants. He headed up the stairs. Where was he putting those bodies?

"How long you been up here?" Craig asked, his mouth sounding dry as dust from the crackers.

"To tell you the truth, it's my first day at the Front." I had aged a hundred years this day.

"No. Your very first day? Looks like you've been at it for years," Craig said.

"As long as the *men* think that." My doctor "presence" had held, thank God for that. "How about you, Captain Craig?" Craig knew his business, no doubt about that. He must have been treating casualties for years.

"Started out in Gallipoli. Bad business, that." Craig lifted his head up and looked around the room, "Not that this business is overly good. Guess we might as well stick it out here. Where are you supposed to be, Gallagher?" I had almost forgotten that. My official assignment was swept away by the German attack on La Vacquerie. But *this* was my real assignment—treating wounded men.

"2nd/4th Gloucesters." Some of the Gloucesters were in this dugout. Some of them had been carried out, dead. The wounded men in here were from all different units, jumbled together in the retreat.

"I'm with the Warwicks, wherever they might be." A private with the Warwicks had bled to death right in front of me 30 minutes earlier. His neck had been pumping blood furiously, no amount of pressure could stop it.

"Captain Craig! Leftenant Gallagher! Four casualties up here at the top of the stairs. Got room?" Tiny's voice shouted down the stairs.

Craig looked too tired to go up the stairs. He waved a hand in that direction.

"Gallagher, take a look."

In the dugout, the wounded were packed in like sardines. We'd just emptied out about 15 bodies, still there wasn't much room.

Craig gave me a significant look. "You know what you need to do."

Up the stairs I went. Someone had thrown some dirt on each step, to absorb blood and vomit, and keep people from slipping. At the top, there were two men standing, holding their arms.

"You don't look too bad, fellows, let's have a look. Looks like you might have gotten a trip to Blighty," (a term for a wound that was not so serious as to maim or kill you, but serious enough to get you out of the line, and home).

Both men brightened at the mention of Blighty. They walked back on their own power, talking eagerly to one another, making plans for their new life, out of the trenches.

"How about the other two?" a stretcher bearer asked. He himself looked ready to drop, the veins on his arm bulging from the strain of carrying heavy stretchers down the crowded trenches.

"Bring up the first one," I said.

He was unconscious, pasty-complexioned, his skin cool and clammy to the touch. Shrapnel had torn into his thigh and pelvis, blood had soaked the blanket over him. His pulse—weak, thready. The man was in shock and beyond my power to help.

"Take him over there," I pointed to a little dent in the side of the trench.

"'E's not goin' into the dugout?" the stretcher bearer asked, knowing what it meant when a man was denied admission. Another wasted trip. All that carrying for nothing.

"Let's see the next one." I was sorry he had carried the man this far, only to get the bad news.

The next one had almost the same injury, his pulse also bespoke a lost cause, only this soldier was still conscious.

"Lay him in the trench, too, he's not going into the dugout." Another trip in vain for the stretcher bearers. How they must tire of this.

"Doctor, Doctor," the wounded man whispered, "Doctor." He spoke without opening his eyes, he kept moving his head from side to side.

"What is it son?" This man would die, and die soon. There was no time to treat him, no reason to use up bandages, clamps, or tourniquets on him. But he deserved a kind word. Every man deserved that.

"Doctor."

"Yes." Ready to say the usual things—you'll be all right—home soon—you've got your ticket to Blighty. But he was delirious, too far gone to register my platitudes.

"Doctor." He stopped talking, and started taking deep breaths. Deep breaths with a long pause in between.

"That's all 'e's been sayin'. Just 'Doctor'. We'll let him rest out 'ere. 'Ere you go, laddy, we'll let you stay out 'ere, get some fresh air." The stretcher bearer, lean as a whippet and all muscle, laid the dying man down as if on a feather bed.

"Carry on," I said, and turned toward the dugout. Just before I ducked into the doorway, I saw where they had been putting the dead men—up on the parapet, the top of the trench. That was how Tiny got rid of the bodies and got back so fast. Both of the wounded men I had just written off would graduate from the trench to the parapet, where they would form human sandbags. Their inert forms would absorb bullets and shrapnel, and protect the living. My eyes went from the parapet, their future, to the two dying men still on their stretchers.

It seemed like a brutal thing to leave a man in a trench to die. But we had no choice.

The English apparently were not prepared for such a massive counterattack. There was little water and nothing to eat. Men cried madly for something, anything to drink, and often waited for hours before a returning stretcher bearer brought a canteen. Even with that, they got only a swallow or two. Many men lay on the floor, suffering an agonizing death with the most awful combinations of wounds—a missing eye, plus a crushed pelvis, all four limbs broken, faces torn off with only a frothy red bubble for a mouth—and we had little but our presence to give them comfort. One's heart ached at the hopelessness of it all.

Madness. This dispute between nations—whatever the original cause—was not worth all this blood, anguish, and misery. There must be another way of settling conflicts, a way that did not involve packing an underground Aid Post with dying young men. If the heads of all the warring governments had to spend one hour in this hell hole, the war would be over in short order. Foolish me, I had not been here long enough to realize that human life was the cheapest thing in the war.

On a personal level, I felt somewhat vindicated for Giancomo's death so long ago. Whatever I may have lacked in doctor "presence" back then, I had now. I could "hold my own with the best of them." I had been through the fire, and fire is what forges steel. In this jam packed Aid Post, I had fixed what I could fix, and saved who I could save. And that is what a doctor does. I guess that made me a doctor.

My great fears of falling apart under the stress, or fumbling and being indecisive, had not materialized. A milestone in my development as a front-line doctor had arrived. But my personal triumph paled before all the misery and suffering around me. I had taken one step forward, but the men piled on the parapet didn't know that.

By afternoon of the next day things had quieted down a little. Jerry was still shelling, but was not attacking with his infantry. Captain Craig wished me well, as I joined up with three stretcher bearers, and headed back to Brigade Headquarters. Once again I would try to find that elusive quarry of mine, the 2nd/4th Gloucesters.

Coming out of the Aid Post, I saw the parapet lined for hundreds of yards with human bodies. Two of them I recognized.

When I got back to Villiers-Plouich Brigade Headquarters, I learned the 2nd/4th Gloucesters were assembling nearby. The Battalion Headquarters was in a dugout off a trench called "10 Downing Street." Inside, I found some familiar faces—Col. Barnsley, Major Day, and some of the officers who had been about to eat breakfast the day before.

"Something to eat, Gallagher? It seems we were rather rudely interrupted yesterday," Colonel Barnsley quipped, cool as a cucumber. He had just lost half his battalion, 300 men or so, and he was completely composed. No wonder the English conquered the world. They seemed to take disaster in perfect stride.

"Yes, please, Colonel Barnsley." My knapsack was back in La Vacquerie, my shirt was torn from my run through the barrage, I was dirty, and I was soaked in blood from the Aid Post.

"Let's get a brew up," I said, using the British term. Major Day started looking around for a cup to hand me.

From inside my jacket, I pulled out the tin cup they'd given me yesterday.

"Don't have to get a cup for me, thanks. I brought my own."

Chapter 6

DEBATE

December 1917

Major Day, Barnsley's adjutant, poured some tea into my cup. Something warm dripped on my pant leg.

"I had heard our cousins had trouble holding their tea," Day said, a smirk on his face.

"Looks like you've got a bit of a drinking problem there, Gallagher," Barnsley said, smiling.

The tea had dripped out the bottom of the tin cup. Holding it up, one could see three tiny holes poked through the bottom. How had those holes gotten there?

"Here you go, Gallagher," Day said, handing me a new cup. "Our men are holding a new bit of line here. Lot of the lads have made it back these last few days. Looks like about 300 or so are lost, though. Bad bit of luck, that. Lost two company commanders." He looked saddened, but not devastated by the news. Major Day exemplified the British ability to absorb a punishing blow and come bouncing right back.

"Any of the medical people lost?" I asked, trying to build up the nerve to choke down another cup of front-line British tea.

"Yes, the medical corporal and his assistant up in the Battalion Aid Post," Barnsley said.

If I hadn't stopped to sleep in that Brigade dugout, *I* would have been in that Aid Post. And now *I* would be captured, or worse.

"Any word on whether they were captured?" I asked.

Day shook his head, "No word."

I reached up and touched my Saint Christopher medal Sister Marie Francis had given me. It had worked. It had protected me during my fearful journey to and from La Vacquerie. But why should that be? The bodies lining the parapets probably had religious medals or lucky charms on them, too. Why had mine worked? Why had theirs failed? There was no answer to these questions.

My official assignment to the 2nd/4th Gloucesters had come only two days before, and I hardly knew anyone in the battalion, but I already felt quite at home, for I had received my baptism of fire with them. U-Boat Alley had been a baptism, of sorts, but the threat there was implied, rather than real. A torpedo attack, and a dive into icy-cold, oil-covered water would have been a terrible experience. But nothing like that happened. No torpedoes, no explosions, no scramble for the lifeboats on a listing deck. Nothing. Just a ride across the ocean on a zigzagging ship.

The air raid in London, too, had exposed me to the enemy, and the bombs there were real enough, but the searchlights, the cool response of the Londoners, all served to make the air raid more of a fireworks show than an earnest attempt on my life.

Yesterday was the real thing. Those men falling in the field were not play acting. Nor was the man who disappeared into a red mist and a pair of spinning arms. That German who leveled his Mauser at me was not just shooting at anybody. He was gunning for me. And to think the British had been enduring this punishment for years.

My shirt was bloody, torn, dirty, and had two buttons missing. My backpack must be in German hands by now.

"Colonel Barnsley, I'm looking a bit 'scuppered,' I believe is the term. Not fit even for shit wallah duty." If the British could take a pounding, and still joke about it, so could I.

That brought a round of grins. This Yank can even speak the lingo, they seemed to be thinking.

"I'd tell you to put on your formal wear for dinner, Gallagher, but I see you've lost your kit bag," Barnsley said.

"Left it in La Vacquerie, I fear. Too much of a hurry to get out of there," I said.

"You weren't alone," he indicated around the floor of the headquarters. No kit bags anywhere. "You see that poverty is our common lot."

Tired, bedraggled, filthy we were. Each of us had stared into the face of death. Every man standing around me had dodged a thousand shells, ten thousand bullets as they crossed that field near La Vacquerie. All had lost friends; I had lost Robson.

Yet, we were alive! There was an exultation to it, a guilty happiness. The shadow of death had passed over us, but had not taken us. Maybe next time, maybe tomorrow, maybe in an hour, maybe in ten minutes . . . but now, right now, we were alive. We had made it. We had made it through, each of us, individually, and here we were, together.

The words of Henry the Fifth came to mind, when he talked to his men before a great battle:

> "We few, we happy few, we band of brothers;
> For he to-day that sheds his blood with me
> Shall be my brother;"

The bond I felt with that "happy few," that "bond of brothers" was something you can't even put into words. Shared danger, shared sacrifice—these terms approach it. Perhaps the English language lacks the appropriate word, and we must settle for the words of Henry V.

> ". . . he to-day that sheds his blood with me
> Shall be my brother."

We sat down on ammunition boxes, the universal furniture of the Western Front. Some maps were laid out, blue lines indicating our positions, red ones—the German positions. Holsters with pistols lay on another box.

"Jerry took back most of what we took on the 20th. The lines are back to where they were, I fear. Jerry doesn't appear to be greedy, at least—guess he was homesick for his old dugouts. Doesn't seem to want to take any of ours," Barnsley said, pointing out the various positions on the map.

So this was how the war had dragged on for three long years. One side advances, then retreats. The other side advances, then retreats. Attack produces counterattack. No change, except for the hundreds of lives lost or ruined. Stalemate. Then, the letters go out. "It is our duty to inform you . . . sacrificed for his country . . . a heroic death . . ." During the retreat, I saw nothing heroic, beautiful, or noble. Most of the killing was done at great long distances, by artillery crews firing at a point on a map. Much of the dying was done by fellows who were running away as fast as they could. Year after year this had gone on, and not just here. Up north, in Belgium, farther south, in France. And in Italy, Russia, and far off Syria, Africa, and Turkey. Lives swallowed up, wholesale, day after day, across the entire face of the earth.

Everyday, somewhere in some battle zone, men were raining steel upon other men, tearing them to pieces. I had seen one small sector of one small battle. When I multiplied what I saw by the total number of battles, and the total number of years, it staggered the imagination. An entire generation of the planet's men were evaporating.

After three days we left the danger of the front-line trenches, and went into the "safety and comfort" of the reserve in Havrincourt Woods, a few miles back. "Safety" meant no trench protection against the daily shelling and bombing, and "comfort" meant laying tents on mushy, snowy ground. But we got some bedrolls and blankets. That, plus Boche shelling, kept us plenty warm.

One day a couple of German planes came over right at treetop level, so our fellows tilted up their Lewis guns and fired. This did not seem to scare the German fliers one bit, for they immediately turned around and fired their machine guns at us. We all jumped into our tents as the bullets came through the treetops. Later, we laughed at our folly, for the folds of a canvas tent offered little protection against a machine gun bullet. No one was the worse for wear, but I took to regarding the sky with some apprehension afterwards. It is a particularly helpless feeling to have a plane boring in on you, and suddenly hear rat-tat-tatting above the engine roar.

After four "relaxing" days in the Havrincourt Woods, we moved up into a support trench, one mile behind the front-line trench. Better to be closer to the enemy, but in a trench, any day.

December was cold, and we suffered. There were no dugouts, and the men weren't allowed to bring their blankets with them, something about "interfering with their vigilance," which struck me as nonsense. Pieces of canvas were stretched across the trench in various places, and a half-dozen men would huddle around a fire to keep warm. I was in the relative luxury of Battalion Headquarters, a sheet iron shelter, eight by twelve feet long. The weather had little trouble finding its way into our little abode; it proved to be a bracing few days indeed. In spite of the cold, the men did not get sick, and casualties were few, so there was little medical work to do. We passed the time in conversation.

"You know, Lt. Gallagher," Colonel Barnsley opened up, "I was wondering a little about the States." Barnsley, like Burroughes, had a long, narrow face. But Barnsley looked more like a basset hound than a horse. I wondered what we Americans must look like to the British. Poodles? Donkeys?

I was leaning over a cup of tea, breathing in the steam. It was the only warm air in the shelter.

"How many servants do you have?" he asked.

"Servants?" The term was just not used, in my experience. Servants hearkened back to another age, an age long ago, before all the modern advances—automobiles, aeroplanes, telephones, wireless. Servants stayed in castles, worked for kings, lived in fairly tales. *Cinderella* was a servant, for God's sake.

"Servants. You know, personal servants, aside from the cook and kitchen help."

"Well, we have a cleaning lady come once a week, in the morning. I've never really thought of her as a *servant*." What did he mean—aside from kitchen help?

Barnsley looked at me, unbelieving, shocked—if, that is, a basset hound is capable of looking shocked.

"She doesn't live with you? Does the cook live with you, at least?" I somehow expected his ears to pop up in surprise.

"We don't have a cook. Mom does the cooking." And it's a damn sight better than the stuff I'm getting here! Better not say that, he might bite me.

He didn't know where to go from there. America must have struck him as a rather odd place.

Outside the shelter, there was a banging and a string of curses.

"Ammo wallah, coming through, one side mates, one side!"

The ammo wallah was to ammo what the shit wallah was to shit. The British Army also had grub wallahs—they carried food up to the men. A rumor about the wallahs had recently made the rounds. German spies, who spoke perfect English, had slipped under our wire a few miles north of our position, slit the throats of our shit wallahs and grub wallahs, and had switched their respective burdens. With this, the Germans hoped to achieve the decisive "breakthrough," but the plan failed. None of our men noticed any difference at mealtime.

Barnsley picked up the discussion.

"We had an American professor come to visit us at Eton once, you know, so I'm not a complete stranger to the, uh, colonies," Barnsley said.

"Former colonies," I corrected. Need I remind him that *we* won the Revolutionary War?

"Yes, quite, former colonies." He pointed to my cup. "I'm glad to see you've reacquired a taste for tea." A clear dig at the Boston Tea Party.

I was about to say, "I prefer coffee," but thought better of it. We were allies, after all.

"So you see," Barnsley went on, "this professor debated with us the nature of good breeding, the origin of gentlemen."

There were four other officers in the dugout. They looked up from their tea at me, for they could smell a debate brewing, and Barnsley had been a champion debater at Eton. Everyone was breathing in the steam from their tea, too, and keeping their hands warm on their cups.

"A gentleman is born, you see. It's in the blood, in the very blood." In a formal debate, this would be the presentation of the topic, the issue of discussion.

I had not attended Eton, *the* elite school in England. I had attended the University of Minnesota, thank you, and had done a little debating in my day, too.

"Really?" I asked. *En garde!*

"You can see it, feel it. Look around you, these five officers, gentlemen all. Each one born to it. Why, it's in their *blood*." He made a magnanimous gesture. They were good men, true, but they didn't look any "better" than the enlisted men, shivering out there in the open trench.

"Look at the enlisted men," Barnsley's adjutant, Major Day, spoke up, "born of humble parents. Good men all, don't get me wrong, Gallagher, but it is their's to serve, and ours to lead. That is what a gentleman does, he leads. Guide the men with a firm but gentle hand. And the men know it. And respect us for it."

"That's what keeps order in the ranks, you see." Barnsley took up where his adjutant left off. "Now this American professor had no grasp of this. 'Gentlemen are made, not born,' he said. What kind of nonsense is that?" He looked around the shelter. His fellow Englishmen nodded and harrumphed their approval.

"Gentlemen, I know I'm outnumbered here, but I beg to differ," I said.

Major Day bowed his head and held out his left hand, palm up, "Quite all right Gallagher, gentlemen can disagree in gentlemanly fashion. Pray, go on." Maddeningly polite, these English.

A cold wind blew under the door of the shelter. One of the officers got up and shoved a blanket into the crack below the door. Officers got blankets, enlisted men didn't.

"Would you call *me* a gentleman?" I asked, leading them down the primrose path.

"Of course. Yes. Quite!" they all said at once. One or two even harrumphed for *me*.

"Well then, 'bid me discourse. I will enchant your ear,' as your very own Shakespeare said."

That got them. Quoting Shakespeare always did. It gave me fiendish pleasure to get them eating out of my hand.

"Twelve children in a family in County Donegal, Ireland. The potato famine had taken the other four. Somehow they scrape together twelve dollars and fifty cents, the price of a ticket to America. But only enough for one ticket. The oldest son gets the nod."

Crump! Crump! Crump! Dust settled down on us. The Germans had sent three shells down for no particular reason.

"This man, the oldest son, sails to America on a coffin ship, as they called the emigrant ships then. Thirty fellow Irishmen die during the passage. This man lands in America, and makes his way west, arriving in Minnesota with a wagon, a wife, an 18-month-old son, a cow, a pig, and twenty-five cents cash."

"Twenty-five cents?" Barnsley asked, falling into the trap.

"Twenty-five cents. 'For investment purposes,' he told us later on."

"You talked to this man?" It was Major Day, wrapped up in his coat, the wind had found its way back into our shelter.

"Of course. He was my grandfather." Take that! So much for your servants, your blue blood, your class system. In America, we grab our own bootstraps, and do all the pulling ourselves.

No one said anything.

"In America, we do not ask, 'What is your bloodline?' we ask, 'What can you do?'" Touché. The score now stood, University of Minnesota debate team - one: Eton - zero.

One of the officers played sore loser and threw a little dig at me, and America in general.

"So, I suppose you Americans are quite excited at the prospect of coming over here? You win the war for us poor Brits." Sharp. As sharp as barbed wire that was.

The cold, tin shelter had just gotten considerably colder. The English eyes bored in on me, waiting for my response. The officer's question had been impolite and blunt by English standards, but it hit the nail on the head. Just what was the American attitude? The English wanted to know.

I swallowed hard, for I knew I was talking for all Americans, "I am not so vain, and we Americans are not so naive, as to think we are going to come over here and teach you how to fight. You and the French . . . "

"The frogs," Major Day corrected. They always called the French "frogs," something I did not like.

"The FRENCH," pausing for effect, I looked right at Major Day, "You and the French have proven you know how to fight. We are coming over as fast as we can to *help* you win it. If it weren't for the bravery of you, the French, and the Belgians, the Hun might be at *our* throat right now. But you held him off, and now we're in it."

This wasn't a debate now, I wasn't looking to "win" this argument. I was functioning as ambassador, spokesman for America, and I took the responsibility seriously.

"You could say we should have joined in when you did, back when Germany invaded Belgium. You could say we should have joined in when the *Lusitania* sank. And many Americans *did* want to. But others didn't. Our opinion was divided, maybe because we are a nation of immigrants, many from Germany, Austria, and the neutral Scandinavian countries. A Swedish farmer in Minnesota, for example, might say, 'Why should I send my sons to fight the Germans in France? I need my sons here on the farm. I got no fight with Germany.'"

They were listening, the Englishmen, listening but good.

"But that all changed when the Germans kept sinking our ships, and especially when they started intriguing with Mexico to take away some of our southern states. Now, we *do* have a fight with Germany."

Some nods. Still, it was quiet.

"It has been a tough go for you fellows over here, and a lot of us are a little red-faced we didn't come over earlier. But that's all water under the bridge. And you can bet that Swedish farmer in Minnesota is putting at least one son on the train right now. And sometime soon, I hope real soon, you're going to blow that whistle, and the first man over the top will be a big, husky, blond-haired farmboy who talks just like I do."

You could have heard a pin drop in our shelter.

Regardless of our disagreements, I had seen these officers under fire, and my respect for them as brave men, and good soldiers, was immense.

Four days passed, and we went up to the front line at Villiers-Plouich. Dead men, horses, and mules littered the landscape. The cold weather preserved them to a certain extent, but they still sent up an awful smell. Bellies of men and beasts swelled to tremendous size, and sometimes burst open from the pressure. Rats feasted. They seemed to look at us and say, "You're next."

There were enough discarded weapons to equip a good-sized army. Rifles, Lewis guns, pistols, trench mortars, grenades, all lay about. Didn't they think of picking these things up, at least preventing them from getting rusted? Numerous tanks were stuck in ditches and trenches, their treads snapped off, hatches opened, noses and tails pointed at all angles. One was completely blackened, and smelled, for lack of a better term, like a roasted chicken. The Germans had learned a valuable lesson, a flamethrower could stop a tank. Not that there's any good way to die, but somehow being inside a metal tank covered in flaming gasoline, with some of that fire coming in through the slits and apertures, struck me as a gruesome way to go. To my thinking, the tank as a useful weapon of war seemed a long way off. Some of the British had great hopes for the tanks; others were dubious.

As we went into the line that night I saw the prettiest fireworks I had ever seen—a shrapnel barrage over the German lines a mile or two away. Each shell burst above the ground with a colored flare, and the line of fire was as straight as a ruler. Though beautiful to me, it was no doubt awful to the men beneath it; men were dying out there under those lovely fireworks.

The front line was quiet. Every now and then one could hear the crack, crack of the snipers, both ours, and theirs. There was a cold-bloodedness about the snipers, sitting at times for hours, looking through their scoped rifles, waiting for their quarry. They tended to keep to themselves. I couldn't help but wonder, "What would a sniper do after the war?"

After a few days I was replaced and sent back to the Main Dressing Station. Later, I was sent farther back to the headquarters of the 2nd/2nd South Midland Field Ambulance Company (Col. Burroughes' command) in the village of Equancourt. My confidence had grown immensely, and I was not the same "nervous pup" I had been just a few weeks before. My "blooding" near La Vacquerie had done me a world of good. I was not cocky, by any stretch, but now felt able to handle most things. Experience had been a great teacher. I was happy to see Colonel Burroughes again, and felt I could actually do him some good now. We held sick call for the transport companies, and I observed something interesting: the farther men were from the Front, the more likely they were to get sick. Maybe, just being at the Front, kept some men in such a state of "nervous excitement" it didn't *allow* them to get sick. Then, once they were out of immediate danger, their nervous systems "relaxed," and they got sick. No scientific study had ever explained this, but other medical officers had observed it, too. As for myself, I didn't get sick at all, and rather enjoyed being "out of the line." I had endured enough thrills and danger for a whole lifetime, and would be happy to stay in a safe area for the duration of the war.

Unfortunately, few places were safe, even in the rear. We were bombed a few times at night, eeeeEEEEE BOOM! eeeeeEEEEE BOOM! Sleeping through the air raid was the most logical approach, for if the bomb missed, it wasn't worth waking up for, and if it hit, well, that wasn't worth waking up for either. But it was hard to be logical during an air raid. When the bombs came down, I was up. An air raid was a frightening thing.

For the first time since landing in France, I attended Mass. (No doubt Sister Marie Francis would have been horrified I hadn't gone earlier, but I didn't feel it necessary to burden her with this unnecessary information.) Mass was held in a little cellar under a ruined church. A small, but fervent number of English Catholic soldiers attended (England was a largely Protestant country). A Hun plane buzzed around overhead and dropped bombs. Debris shook down onto us in the cellar, but the cellar was as strong as our faith, and the Hun pilot failed to reduce us "faithful few" to a "faithful fewer."

Christmas was almost upon us when, to our delight, the 61st Division was relieved and sent back for a rest, not to a relief position in a dangerous woods, but for a real rest, in a safe haven. We marched back a few miles, and boarded a train. The benches on the train were hard, but it beat marching all hollow.

About 11 P.M., on a snow-covered, moonlit night, we arrived at the town of Corbie. Our bellies growled for food, yet we still had to march a few miles more to our billet in Sailly-le-Sec. Napoleon was right, an army does "march on its stomach." Most often the British Army marched on an empty stomach. Though cold and hungry, I enjoyed the marching through the silent, beautiful countryside. Corbie was on the Somme River, which twisted and bent like a snake through peaceful farmland. The moon gave the snow a bluish appearance, something I remembered from back home in Minnesota. Like a Christmas card it was, this scene.

We tramped into Sailly-le-Sec at 3 A.M., eager for a hot meal. To our dismay, we learned our transport trucks had gotten stuck in a snowdrift a few miles away, and we'd have to go to sleep on an empty stomach. Another American doctor and I were posted to a cold attic room in a French peasant's house. Hunger and cold did their best to keep us awake, but fatigue did its best to put us to sleep. Fatigue won out—we fell fast asleep. By morning our trucks were there, after battling their way through snowdrifts. We all had some dandy eats. They say exhaustion makes the softest pillow, and hunger makes the best seasoning. If that were the case, then we had soft pillows and the best seasoning in Sailly-le-Sec.

Some of the talent in the Division put on a show, and very good it was, too! What with new drafts and all, plus transfers, the 61st Division was back up to 10,000 men, so they were able to distill out a fair number of musicians, singers, and jokesters, and put on as good a show as I saw in London. Most amazing of all, was the transformation I witnessed men go through. One minute they were soldiers, the next, performers.

A man who dove into the trench right after me in La Vacquerie was now up on stage playing a piccolo! The cold-blooded sniper was now in a line of "girls" doing a can-can dance. A shit wallah became an amateur magician, making coins disappear and reappear. The Lewis gunner played the keys of a piano instead of pulling a trigger. The show gave the men a humanity, an individuality, which they lacked in the trenches.

The songs were great.

"Tyke me back to dear old Blighty"—they loved that one. Everyone wanted that Blighty ticket home. I myself thought about it more than once.

"Kaiser Willy," meaning the German leader, Kaiser Wilhelm II, was ridiculed over and over again. But the individual German infantryman was never mocked, for the men didn't really hate "Brother Hun." He was as much a victim as they were. Someone high up in political circles had brought this war on; not the poor, freezing, sleepless German fellow lying out there in his listening post in No Man's Land. Brother Hun was doing his job, as he understood it. And the British didn't hold it against him.

Near the end of the performance, the British just couldn't help throwing a little jab at their cousins. A painted mock-up of the Atlantic Ocean, with a Statue of Liberty at the far end (with a *Made in France* sign on her, no less), was set up. An Uncle Sam appeared, along with a chorus of cowboys. Where on earth did they get the cowboy hats? Then these displaced artists started a distorted version of "Over There," ending with the line,

"And we won't go there, 'til it's over, over there."

Uncle Sam and the cowboys waved good-bye, and *stayed* on their side of the Atlantic.

Later in the show, an excellent, four-part chorus sang "It's a Long Way to Tipperary." The tune got the men all excited, me, too. We were stomping our feet on the wooden floor, threatening to collapse the whole building!

The finale, with "There's a Long, Long Trail a-Winding," didn't leave a dry eye in the house. What a show!

Sailly-le-Sec was beyond the point the Germans had ever been (except for a few days in August 1914) and the French were still living there, in typical French fashion. They didn't seem to have actual farmhouses, as we did in America; rather they had little villages, with several houses clustered together. Each morning the farmers would meander out in different directions to their respective fields, returning late at night. A house had its horse, cow, and chickens nearby, and a manure pile—in front of the house—which made for a pungent domestic setting. Beauty and cleanliness did not come to mind when I thought of these villages, though the churches and schools were neat, and well built. Perhaps to some extent, this earthy, and unsanitary setting made it easier for the French *poilu* to adapt to trench life. (Poilu meant "hairy one," and was an endearing term for the unshaven French soldier.) Everyone referred to them as poilus, except the poilus themselves, just like everyone called the British soldiers "Tommy," except the British soldiers themselves.

Nearly every village sported one chateau, a two- or three-story brick affair, with surrounding hedge. No unsanitary sheds or stables here, just a well-kept yard. Being wealthy in France might not have bought happiness, but it did bring a breath of fresh air.

Most of the townspeople were friendly and sociable—they seemed happy in their village life, not knowing much about any other. I tried out my fledgling French on them, but it didn't go over too well. My pronunciation seemed to hurt their ears. No matter how poor, aged, or infirm, each and every Frenchman felt himself the guardian of the language, and they promptly corrected my pronunciation, diligently repeating the words until I got it right, or at least got it close. One sensed that the French language was viewed as a national treasure, to be guarded at all costs.

We spent a pleasant Christmas at Sailly-le-Sec. How could any of us know that in three short months, the Germans would again threaten this little village, and the whole Allied cause.

Chapter 7

PARIS

December 29 – January 2, 1918

I got leave to go to Paris to replace my kit.

It was the fourth Christmas of the war. Everyone in Paris had lost a father, a brother, a son, or a friend. Over a million Frenchmen had died, and many more had been wounded. The German Army showed no signs of weakening, in fact, it was getting reinforcements from the Russian Front daily. Everyone knew the Germans were planning an offensive in the spring, already they were less than sixty miles away. One would have thought that Paris, the City of Lights, would be dressed in gloom.

Au contraire.

The French simply did not know how to get down in the mouth.

Paris was wild! Cafés were packed with French and English soldiers. People were singing in all the bars, banging away on pianos. Toasts were going up everywhere. *Vive la France! Vivent les anglais! Vivent les americains! A bás les Boches!* Theaters ran two shows a night, and always had an afternoon matinee. The shops were bedecked with all the latest fashions. If "gay Paree" were ever any gayer, I couldn't imagine how.

One errand stood between me and the delights of Paris. Most of my stuff was lost at La Vacquerie, so I needed to go to the American quartermaster to re-equip. Passing the Eiffel Tower and the Hotel des Invalides, I came to a large warehouse. A hand-painted sign read:

American Commissary

One hour later I emerged from that commissary, steaming mad, with no gear in hand.

First, I had to wait, and wait. Then the paperwork was wrong; the signature was below the line instead of on top of the line; they didn't have my size; could I come back in a week? It was enough to try the patience of Job. And this quartermaster fellow had the safest, easiest job in the army. He had never tried to sleep with a gas mask on, nor had he run across a field raked with machine gun fire. No shell splinter every threatened him, the only splinter he would ever get would be from the chair he was sitting on.

Several, slow, painful ways of torturing that quartermaster to death came to mind. But, it wouldn't replace my stuff, so I went to some nearby shops and just bought the necessary gear, to hell with the quartermaster. Prices were steep in those shops, and I emptied my pockets.

Well, nearly emptied my pockets. After all, I was in Paris, and I didn't want to pass up what might be my last opportunity for some good clean fun.

Paris, like London, was walkable, but its marvelous subway system—the Metro—served well when your feet got tired. The beauty of the French capital struck me at once, and stayed with me all day. One could see the city was built in the days of powerful kings when space and money were not spared. Everything seemed to proclaim *"La Gloire"* (the glory) of France.

For example, the Place de la Concorde had a great open space with a large obelisk in the center. In America, this would have been filled with skyscrapers, banks, shops—monuments to Mammon. Not so in France. Things in France had to proclaim greatness, immortality, beauty. Of what use were a few francs, more or less, when you could swell your chest with pride, hold your hand out with a sweeping gesture, and say, "Behold, the Place de la Concorde."

Atop a steep hill, the Church of Sacre Coeur was not just a church, it was an event. It sported bulbous cupolas, looking like a multi-headed Taj Majal. "You see," it seemed to be saying, "the great Khans that ruled India have nothing on us. I, too, can form feminine curves and alabaster roofs into a beautiful temple. But I serve no Khan, I serve France."

And the river Seine, curving through the center of Paris, was not an obstacle to be overcome with spans of steel and concrete. The Seine was adorned, draped with numerous little bridges, some dating back centuries. Like the Pont Neuf, either the oldest or among the oldest, was a graceful series of curves dancing across the water. I could feel myself becoming sentimental, almost maudlin as Paris swept past me. It was beautiful, as beautiful a city as stood on the face of the earth, and it carried me away.

Perhaps it was the contrast which sent me on this emotional journey, igniting me to think like a romantic poet, rather than a pragmatic, down-to-earth Midwesterner. One minute I'm in a trench, smelling of feces, bodies, and the lingering tang of poison gas; the next minute I'm strolling up the Champs Elysees, heading toward the Arc de Triomphe. At the Front, I saw actual soldiers—dirty, unkempt, more concerned with sleep and a meal than winning a medal. At the Arc de Triomphe, I saw brave soldiers, fearless soldiers, carved in marble. They were never tired, never hungry, they were always and forever fearless. They would never weaken, age, or die. If only we could all be like the soldiers on the Arc de Triomphe.

One sight summed up the whole Parisian, the whole French way of thinking—the Eiffel Tower. As tall as many a New York skyscraper, the Eiffel Tower consisted of mostly—AIR! Empty space! A filigree of iron coming together from four huge legs and pointing to the sky. A completely visible skeleton, but holding no tissue, no organs. (Yes, there was an impossibly expensive restaurant at the top, and there were observation platforms for tourists but the structure was basically empty.) From a distance, from close-up, and from the top of the Eiffel Tower itself, you saw beams and air, beams and air, mostly air. What function could this assemblage of framed air serve? One function, and one alone.

It bespoke *La Gloire*. It said, "I am France."

Walking back to the Hotel des Invalides I paused to look at Napoleon's tomb. It was an enormous mahogany crypt, with a curved and graceful lid. Simple and beautiful. I wondered if Napoleon would know how to break the trench war stalemate? What strategy would he implement? Maybe he would sneak around the Germans through Switzerland or Holland? Up to this point, the Great War had not produced much in the way of brilliant leadership, generals just kept throwing masses of men at machine guns and artillery, with predictable failure. Surely Napoleon would not have done that—not year after year.

Out on the street again, someone behind me shouted, "Ben! Ben Gallagher, you old reprobate!" Who in blazes would know me in Paris?

Ted Sweetser was running up to me. Ted had signed the medical tag of the first wounded man on that hospital train at Chichester. What a small world that we should meet in Paris.

"Ben, Ben," he started pumping my hand. "How are you? Just how the hell are you?" Ted was a big strapping fellow, with big meaty hands. He looked so . . . so . . . American.

"Great, Ted, great. What brings you here?" Thank God, a friendly face, a familiar face, an AMERICAN face.

"I deserted. Don't tell anyone, or they'll shoot me," he put his finger to his lip and looked to his left and right. Out of his pocket came his official leave papers. That Ted, always joking, for a split second, he had me going. I thought he actually *had* deserted.

"Let me see those, they're probably forged. Hmm." I gave it my best officious inspection. "Looks like a pretty good forgery at that. Still, though, they'd probably be better off shooting you, anyway." I handed his papers back.

"What's your story, Ben? How much time before you have to go back? Tomorrow, like me?" Ted asked.

"Yep. Tomorrow it is. Back to the lines to tend to the halt and lame."

"Well, then. That leaves us one full night in Paris, Ben." He clapped his hands together, looking like a kid in a candy store. "Got any money?"

"Some." Not enough to set the world on fire, that was certain.

"Then what are we waiting for?" Ted held his hand out, my self-appointed tour guide to Paris.

Ted filled me in on his adventures. He, too, had sweated out the Atlantic crossing. And he had crossed before the convoy escort system was fully in place. The Germans torpedoed one ship in his convoy. We were sitting in a café as he recounted the details.

"We couldn't stop to pick up survivors, there was the danger we'd get torpedoed too. You could here the guys shouting, could see them waving. Some oil spilled out from their ship and caught fire. You could hear the screams get real high pitched when the flames hit them." Ted paused for awhile, the experience playing out in his eyes. "I hope somebody used the wireless to call for a destroyer to pick those guys up. I know *some* of their lifeboats got lowered in time. You'd hate to think they just floated around out there, on those little lifeboats, until they died of thirst or starvation." Ted had a far-off look. He could see those men in the water, could hear them.

"Was it a troopship?" I asked.

"No, no. Some kind of cargo ship. Logs or something. Timber. So there weren't that many men on board, just the crew. Still, though. That's got to be, what 50 men or so."

Ted drank a little wine.

"Fifty men. They go through fifty men pretty fast in the trenches." Fifty men. There had been about fifty men in that railway cutting near La Vacquerie.

"Where are you stationed, Ted?"

"Ypres. Wipers, as the English call it." That was up in Belgium. The British line formed a bulge, or salient, in military terminology, at Ypres. This meant the Germans could fire artillery into the British lines from three different directions. Soldiers on the Somme thanked their lucky stars that they weren't at Ypres.

I helped myself to a little wine. The waiter served us some crepes. Cheesy, gooey delicious crepes. Stuffed full of onions, peppers, bacon. A welcome relief from the English cooking.

"*Merci.*" I pronounced it extra carefully, trying to impress Ted with my worldliness. Mare-see, that was how they pronounced it, mare-see. I even gargled the "r" a little, just like the French. A pretty good rendition, if I did say so myself.

The waiter looked right at me, "*Merci,*" he corrected. It sounded the same! Why was he correcting me?

I tried to pronounce it the way he did, "*Merci.*" Mare-see. Just what *he* had said.

He rolled his eyes and walked away, shaking his head. What was *his* beef? I had said "*Merci*" just exactly, absolutely exactly, to a tee like *he* had. Mare-see, accent on the second syllable and everything.

"Touchy bastards," Ted said.

"At least they can cook." The crepe was velvety smooth, delicious. They can have their high-falutin' language, just give me the crepes. "Say Ted, speaking of bastards . . . "

Ted jumped in before I could finish my sentence, "The English?"

"Exactly." At last. A sympathetic ear.

"My boy," Ted said, filling my wine glass to the top, "you and I have a lot of catching up to do."

"Here, here."

Clink! Overdid it, spilled a little. Nothing to do but pour some more.

Ted, too, had felt the frost of the English reception.

"They call us Johnny-come-latelies. Why didn't we jump in back in 1915 they ask all the time. I tell you, Ben, they have no sense of camaraderie at all. They all but tell me the job's about done, and it doesn't really matter much whether we're here or not. Well, let me tell you, Ben. I don't know what it's like where you are, but the job sure doesn't look about done to me. The Huns are some tough cookies."

He had a point. The Boche didn't look beaten to *me* when I was running out of La Vacquerie.

"How about the French, Ted? What do they think of us?" That wine was going down smooth. A red wine. Do you eat red wine with a crepe, oops, I mean, drink red crepe with a wine? Hmm. Better slow down on this stuff.

"You get a whole different feeling from the French," Ted said.

"And what's that? I haven't met many Frenchmen myself. A few right on Christmas Day, but I couldn't talk with them much. My French isn't too good." If I had much more wine, my English wouldn't be too good, either.

"I've met quite a few here, and let me tell you, Ben, they love us. The French are hoping against hope that we'll come over here and pull their chestnuts out of the fire. They know they can't beat the Germans themselves. They need us. One of their generals said, 'I'm waiting for the tanks and the Americans.'"

"That's good to hear," I said.

"You're damned right it is. I just wish a little of that attitude would rub off on the English." Ted was shaking his head, tired of the second-class treatment he'd gotten from them.

But we hadn't gotten second-class treatment from the French. Up went my glass, "*Vive la France!*"

My toast was meant just for Ted's ears, but the whole cafe raised their glasses, and shouted with one voice, "*Vive la France!* There were plenty of cheers to go around. *Vive l'Angleterre! Vive l'Amerique! Vivent les Allies!*"

The party started. A simple "*Vive la France*" had opened the door. Four French aviators came over to our table, their uniforms spectacular. Ted and I looked quite scruffy by comparison.

"*Vous etes americains, monsieurs?*" one asked. His uniform *must* have come from a tailor, it fit him like a glove. Not a wrinkle in it, not a loose thread.

"You are looking at the genuine article, *mon ami,*" Ted said, leaning back, hooking his left arm around the back of the chair.

The aviator looked at us puzzled.

"Ted, his English probably isn't that good. Let me try." Turning to the French pilots, I did my level best rudimentary French pronunciation. "*Oui, nous sommes americains*, (yes, we are Americans)." Then I thought of something. What was it General Pershing had said when the Americans first arrived, it was so perfect.

"Ted, what did General Pershing say when the first Americans arrived here, last July 4th?"

"They shall not pass?" Ted guessed.

"No, the French guy said that." Then it came to me. I stood and lifted my wine glass up to the French pilots.

"*Nous voici, Lafayette!* (Lafayette, we are here!)"

The place erupted. The shout and roar that went up from that café could have knocked over the Eiffel Tower.

Ted and I could not buy another drink the whole night. The French aviators showed us the town, while all along the way we gathered reinforcements. Champagne everywhere. Champagne at Maxim's, champagne at the Folies Bergere. Champagne from glasses, slippers, from a gendarme's hat (why he didn't arrest us I don't know).

The French pilots even introduced us to some of their cousins. And pretty cousins they were, at that. Fine, sweet girls who agreed that the arrival of the Americans was a good thing, a great thing. Such heroism deserved a warm, warm welcome. Ted and I agreed it was our patriotic duty to let them know we appreciated the welcome. France and America were, after all, allies, were we not?

These girls did not wear khaki uniforms—they had on lace. They had no lice on their bodies—they had perfume. They did not talk—they sang. They did not walk—they floated on air. They looked good, talked good, smelled good, were good. It was a heavenly thing to pass some time with these French women.

"Sammy, Sammy!" one of the mademoiselles said to me. Her dress may have been a bit immodest, her lipstick a tad overstated, but who was I to complain? Why was she calling me "Sammy?"

"Sammy?" I asked, to no one is particular. We were at the . . . Deux Cochons, no the Trois Pates . . . I didn't know where we were. Music was playing, people were singing, on a stage some women were dancing, kicking up their skirts. Wherever we were, it was fine by me.

Somewhere along the way we picked up an American aeroplane mechanic who worked in the Lafayette Escadrille (a group of American pilots who had volunteered to join the French Air Force before America entered the war). His French was near perfect so he helped translate this term Sammy.

"They call us Sammies, for Uncle Sam. Get it? Every American is 'Sammy.'"

Those girls could call me whatever they wanted.

We got them singing, or trying to sing what they called "The Sammies' Marching Song" or "Over There." Ooh la la, to hear them singing that song in their French accents. A man could just melt.

"What means 'Over Zair,' *cheri*?" my old friend with the immodest dress and shocking lipstick asked me.

I had wrestled with that one, and my brother Frank hadn't gotten back to me with the answer. "*Pour là*," or "*sur là*," just didn't seem right. Then I got it. Like a bolt of lightning out of the clear, blue sky, the answer came to me. The great translation dilemma, which I had struggled with for months, now was solved. Eureka!

"*Ma cherie*, 'Over There' *veut dire* 'Les Sammies s'en arrivent' (My dear, 'Over There' means 'Sammy's on the Way')." In my own small way, I felt like a linguist. I had translated the spirit of the expression "Over There."

We sang it and sang it. Sang it 'til we were hoarse. Sang it 'til the sun came up.

Some kind soul must have checked our papers at some point during the night, for neither Ted nor I were shot for desertion. In the morning the French pilots poured Ted onto a train for Belgium, and poured me onto a train for Amiens, and we both got back before our leaves ran out. Our French friends even made sure my package of new clothes made it on board. (It had completely slipped my mind in the course of the night.)

On board the train, as the haze cleared, I looked at my package. There was something extra tied to the top—a bottle of champagne with a card attached. It said,

A Sammy   (To Sammy

Merci   Thanks

La France   France)

Chapter 8

RAIDS

On the St-Quentin Front
January – February 1918

Abe Haskell sent me a letter. The Army censors got to it first.

January ———, 1918

Dear Ben,

My assignment changed again after I last saw you and I ended
up with the ——— Division up in ———. It's an ——— unit, so we're
a little farther back than the infantry, and we don't move around a
whole lot, so our quarters are relatively comfortable. Still, the rain up
here, my God, the rain! Mud everywhere. We put down duckboards
but they just get swallowed up. Lately, it's snowed a lot, though, so
it's not so much a question of mud as it is frozen mud.

I keep cotton in my ears a lot, because they fire those ——— all
the time, and my ears were starting to ring, even at night.

We haven't taken a lot of casualties. The mud seemed to
swallow up and muffle a lot of the German artillery fire. Now that the
ground's harder, though, we're seeing more shrapnel wounds.

I imagine you have rats there, like we do here? The first time
I saw one I nearly jumped out of my skin. They're big as cats.

Our rest area is near ———. There is a kind of a castle,
overlooking the ——— River. Supposedly, some beautiful countess or
princess lives there, and I'm sure it's only a matter of time before she
runs into me, falls in love, you know the rest. If that's the case, you
will make my apologies to Brenda and Ruth, won't you? Oh, and
Kathy, too (she works on the labor and delivery floor, I don't think
I'd mentioned her before).

Your Comrade-in-arms, and

Future count (or prince).
Abe

I wrote back.

February 12, 1918

Dear Abe,

I got your letter, thanks. The censors had chewed it up pretty
well. No doubt, they will do the same to this letter, but here goes.

My permanent assignment is the 2nd/5th Gloucester battalion
in the Somme sector near Amiens. Like most battalions in the British
Army, the Gloucester's been thinned, reinforced, thinned again, and
reinforced again, so there are very few unwounded veterans in the

battalion. Through it all, though, the British seem to keep up their spirits. They have a kind of gallows humor that is most refreshing.

We recently moved south, taking over some lines from the French (I imagine Mr. Censor crossed that line out for sure). It means we're covering more miles of line with the same amount of men, and we're a bit thin. I should hope Brother Hun, across No Man's Land, doesn't notice, but I suspect he does. I suggested we sing the Marseillaise at night and start cooking our bully beef with garlic, to throw off the Boche, but Headquarters has not acted on my suggestion.

Before the French left, they threw us a little party (wait 'til I tell you about the party in Paris—that will have to be a whole other letter). The Frenchies explained they had a kind of "live and let live" policy with the Germans. We don't shell you much, you don't shell us much. Everyone gets along. Keeps losses down.

During the takeover of the French lines, I got to know a few of them, their ways, their attitude toward the war, and their attitude towards us Americans.

I hate to say it, and I don't know what the censor will make of this, but I couldn't help but *like* the French more than the English.

They don't pack the front line with so many men, rather, they have more men farther back, to keep losses down. They keep a lot of machine guns around, and keep their famous "75's" (a field gun that can fire almost as rapidly as a rifle, and it doesn't kick back when it fires, so they don't have to re-aim it after each shot) nearby. The French want firepower, rather than manpower, to keep the Germans at bay. It seems like a smart policy.

The French give detailed and colorful descriptions on each part of the line when they hand it over to us—"*Bon secteur, pas dangereux* (good sector, not dangerous), *Mal içi, beaucoup des Boches* (Bad here, lots of Germans)." In case you don't understand French, they make sounds and do pantomime to stress the point. "*Lá-bas, brrrrrrr* (Over there, rat-tat-tat)" as they point out a hidden machine gun.

For lack of a better term, the French are simply more "fun" to be around. Here we are in a war zone, death in the air, the enemy nearby, yet they always seem ready to open another bottle of wine or raise a toast. If things go wrong, they just say, *"C'est la guerre."*

The French know how to run a war. If only they were more tidy! They tend to defecate and urinate anywhere they want to, rather than having specific areas for that purpose. It does not smell like French perfume in their old trenches!

Oh yes, one other thing the French do to reduce losses, they put up camouflage and fences everywhere, to keep the Germans from seeing them (the Germans occupy higher ground across No Man's Land).

The English politely listened to their French allies, then promptly ignored this policy of live and let live. In a few days, the Pax Gallica fell apart, as did a lot of the careful French camouflage, and now the Germans pick off our fellows every day.

When we are not in the line, and are far enough back to be safe from artillery fire, then life for me can be quite enjoyable, for the English treat their officers somewhat like royalty. (Maybe the Revolution wasn't such a good thing.) I have a man to take care of my needs (almost like a butler—imagine, a butler in a war zone—they call him a "batman"). Also, I have a horse at my disposal. And there's even a man to take care of my horse!

But just when I get used to this "country estate" lifestyle, we rotate back into the front line. No horse riding up there!

We are in the area that the Germans vacated during their planned retreat of 1917. (To shorten their lines, and get the best possible ground, the Germans built a strong series of trenches well to the rear of their front line. Then they completely devastated the intervening area, and pulled back to these newly prepared trenches, leaving a "scorched earth" for the British to occupy.) We are now in that "scorched earth. They occupy all the high ground, all the good vantage points, and we are literally "under the gun."

Curiously, at night, when our ration trucks come up, the Germans don't shell us. Their ration trucks come up at about the same time (one can hear them easily), and we don't shell them either. There seems to be a mutual understanding that no one should fight on an empty stomach.

But night time is raid time. And I don't envy our men out there in the forward listening posts.

Yours truly,
Ben

On a cold February night I was in the forward Aid Post. It was hard to sleep because No Man's Land was so narrow there, only 60 yards across. We were forever waiting for a German raid. Just the night before, a listening post in front of our line had been hit. Two Gloucesters were killed and two more disappeared, apparently taken prisoner.

A sentry was "standing to," just a few yards down the trench from the Aid Post.

There was nothing going on in the Aid Post, so I "stood to"—that is, stood on the firestep with my head projecting above the top of the parapet, so as to look out over No Man's Land. We wouldn't dare do such a thing during the day, for a sniper would drill us in the head, but at night you could. It was clear, and there was good visibility far to the left and far to the right of our position.

About two miles to our left, the drama of a trench raid played out. The wind direction was away from us so the entire episode was a mute light display.

From behind the German lines, artillery flickered in quick succession. Some of the shells' trajectory was visible as orange specks rising over No Man's Land dropped onto our lines. Colored shell bursts fell first on our front line, then lifted and went behind, to the support line. From the German front lines, slow mortar bombs formed a steeper arc as they went up, then down onto our line. Flares started to go up, red ones, from the British line.

"Help!" the flares said. "We're under attack!"

Tracers from the British line lashed out, then the flash of individual rifles. More flares went up, bright, white magnesium flares, to illuminate the German raiding party. Small flashes just in front of the British line, then in it. Grenades. Close in work. Men were at arm's length now.

A green flare went up, then two yellow ones. A German signal? A British deception? An accident? No more flashes for a minute. Men were at each other's throats now. It was clubs, bayonets, bare hands. Still no sound, the wind direction muffled all.

Tracers from a British machine gun, red bullets spitting out into the night. Now rifle flashes. The Germans must have finished the raid, and were going back across No Man's Land, a prisoner or two in hand.

Suddenly, the wind came around, right from the direction of the raid. The sound came on crystal clear, like a wireless the instant it was plugged in.

Poom. Poom! Poom! Poom! German mortars popped into the air, coming down near the source of the tracer bullets. Kawoomp! Kawoomp-woomp-woomp! The tracers stopped. Pow! Pow! Pop! Rifle fire. Tat-tat-tat-tat. The machine gun was back in business. Tat-tat-tat-tat. Pow! Woomp!

Then, nothing. The entire raid, from first shot to last shot, lasted just five minutes.

The sentry and I had turned our heads the whole time, and were still looking to the left, when the barbed wire jangled right in front of us.

We both jumped about three feet.

"Jesus Christ! The 'ole bloody German Army could 'ave snuck up on me!" The sentry was flogging himself for not paying attention to his section. He was right. I hadn't been paying any attention either, so mesmerizing was the trench raid light show.

"Halt! Password!" the sentry shouted.

More jangling and shuffling. It sounded pretty damn close.

"Halt, damn your eyes!" He pointed his rifle forward in the dark and grabbed a flare pistol. He was about to fire his flare when a muffled groan came from the area where the wire was jangling.

"Maybe it's one of ours," I said.

"And maybe it's one of theirs." He had his hand on the trigger of his flare gun. He was hesitating to fire. If it *was* one of ours, the flare would reveal him to Jerry.

Another groan.

"He sounds wounded," I said.

"Could be a Hun trick." The Germans were good at "dirty tricks," though the British didn't hesitate to use them either.

"Could be," I admitted. It sure sounded like a wounded man, though. If it was a Jerry imitating a wounded man, he was doing a pretty good job of it.

"Password! Password! Oh bloody hell." The sentry laid down his rifle, picked up a trench shovel, and got ready to crawl out toward the sound.

"Doc, if he's one of ours, I'll kiss ya. If he's one of theirs, I'll bash in his head with this, then I'll come back here and bash your head in." His eyes were wide open, white visible all around the edges. Sentry duty did that to you.

"That's all right with me." As he clambered up, I realized *I* was now the acting sentry, should anything happen to him. His rifle was leaning against the trench. I had no idea how to work the damn thing.

"Do be careful, won't you?" My voice admitted to a little anxiety. Just because Jerry had done one raid, two miles to our left, didn't preclude him from attacking here. And me the sentry, not even knowing how to work the rifle.

He went over the top of the parapet. A few minutes later, he came back, dragging a Tommy with him. They flopped into the trench. The wounded man had a dirty white bandage running under his chin and over the top of his head.

The sentry was soaked in sweat, in spite of the cold.

"One of ours, Doc. Here's your kiss." His eyes had relaxed, no more white around the edges.

"You can owe me."

I helped the wounded soldier into the Aid Post, and my assistant prepared some clean bandages for me.

"Let's take off this old thing and see what we've got," I said.

When I took off the dressing, his chin flopped down onto his chest—hanging on only by the tissue of his neck. His tongue was nearly sliced in two, and so swollen it nearly filled his whole mouth. He could not talk, of course.

Bandaging him as best I could, I sent him back by stretcher bearers to the Main Dressing Station. Surely his wound was fatal.

By some miracle he survived. A month later, he sent us back a letter, detailing the terrible events that led to his injury.

During a raid, he was struck in the face with a bayonet. His face mutilated, he was left for dead. But he was not the only one out in No Man's Land. A German stretcher bearer, from the same raiding party, had been shot in both legs and was also left for dead. The badly wounded German dragged himself over to the Englishman, saw he was still alive, and put a dressing around his jaw and head. Side by side, the two lay there in No Man's Land all that night, and all the next day. The following night, under cover of darkness, the Tommy crawled back to our trenches, where the plucky sentry pulled him in.

I was sitting with my medical orderly, one Oswald Bradley, as we read the letter.

"What happened to the German stretcher bearer?" Bradley asked.

"He didn't say."

It started to snow.

Our position, opposite the town of St-Quentin, was in open, rolling countryside. You could see for long distances on clear days if you dared raise your head.

Every building in every village, and every tree and natural barricade had been flattened by the Germans in their planned retreat of early 1917. There was nothing in the area to help in the construction of defenses. All the villages were completely destroyed and the Germans had us under observation from the high ground around St-Quentin. They apparently had excellent telescopes, optical range finders, and superb gun crews who knew their equipment. They were there to kill, and they were good at it.

While in the trenches, we kept up with news on the other fronts. Our Allies, the Italians, were having a tough go of it. The Germans had reinforced the Austrians and given the Italians a good shellacking at a place called Caporetto.

How could the Germans be in so many places at once, and be so effective? They had the Russians on the ropes and (another little known ally of ours) Rumania had disappeared without a trace. The French were locked into their trenches, and two years of British attacks had done nothing but fill cemeteries and hospitals.

The Gloucesters talked about "Wipers," (farther north, in Belgium) and how glad they were to be out of "the Salient," as it was called in official communiques. (This was the area Ted Sweetser was in.) The Somme front looked pretty dismal to me, but even the officers confided the conditions around Ypres were worse, where you were being shot at from three sides, and the mud was bottomless. There it took four, and sometimes six stretcher bearers to evacuate one man, and the stretcher bearers were being wounded or killed right along. The Dressing Stations, especially the advanced ones, were often under direct fire.

But our area, the Somme, was bad enough. German fire, directed with maddening accuracy from the high ground, supplied me with a steady stream of wounded. By now, I was frequently the lone doctor in the Aid Post, but less overwhelmed. (Quite unlike my attack of nerves when I was ordered forward at La Vacquerie.) Experience, the great teacher, had steadied me.

About a quarter of our wounded had been hit by bullets; the rest by shells and grenades, the infamous "potato-mashers." Head and neck wounds, upper arms, leg and thigh wounds were the most likely injuries.

I saw a few chest wounds, but mostly these men died before they got to the Aid Post. We plugged their wounds with gauze held on by adhesive strapping, gave them tetanus antitoxin and low doses of morphine so as not to suppress their respiration. (Morphine relieves pain, but has a dangerous side effect of slowing your breathing. A man with a chest wound already has a breathing problem, so we had to be very careful with our morphine doses.) We got them back to the Dressing Station as soon as possible.

On occasion some of the chest wound patients recovered. They did not all die, but later complications like empyema—pus and blood in the pleural space—occurred. (We had seen some of those at Graylingwell.)

Where arms or legs were blown off, we tried to stop the bleeding with large pressure dressings, after placing hemostats (clamps) on large arteries and veins.

Lieutenant Bernard J. Gallagher, M.D.

Ben Gallagher

"He'd say stuff like, 'It's too hard to explain,' or 'Unless you were there, you really couldn't understand.'"

Drawn by a grandson, Kim P. Gallagher, Ph.D.

GENERAL HEADQUARTERS
AMERICAN EXPEDITIONARY FORCES

Bernard J Gallagher   1st Lieutenant
(Name)   (Rank)

Attached   25th Battalion
(Organization)

The award of the____ Military Cross _____

by the____ British _____Government to you having been approved
by the Commander in Chief, you are authorized to accept and to wear such
decoration.

The award was made for the following services rendered:

CITATION

For meritorious services rendered the allied cause.

BY COMMAND OF GENERAL PERSHING:

OFFICIAL:
ROBERT C. DAVIS,   JAMES G. HARBORD,
Adjutant General.   Chief of Staff.

Ben Gallagher's Military Cross

"Bill and Peg were reeling. First, their father is revealed as a kind of Cyrano de Bergerac . . . then . . . a hero, complete with medal."

William B. Gallagher, personal collection

Ben Gallagher

Medical school graduate, 1916.

"Oh, Marie, forgot to tell you. I made A.O.A. when I graduated from medical school . . .
I think it's just a bunch of baloney."

Statue of Liberty

"Pray that Lady Liberty wil keep that torch lit for all the world to see."

William B. Gallagher, personal collection

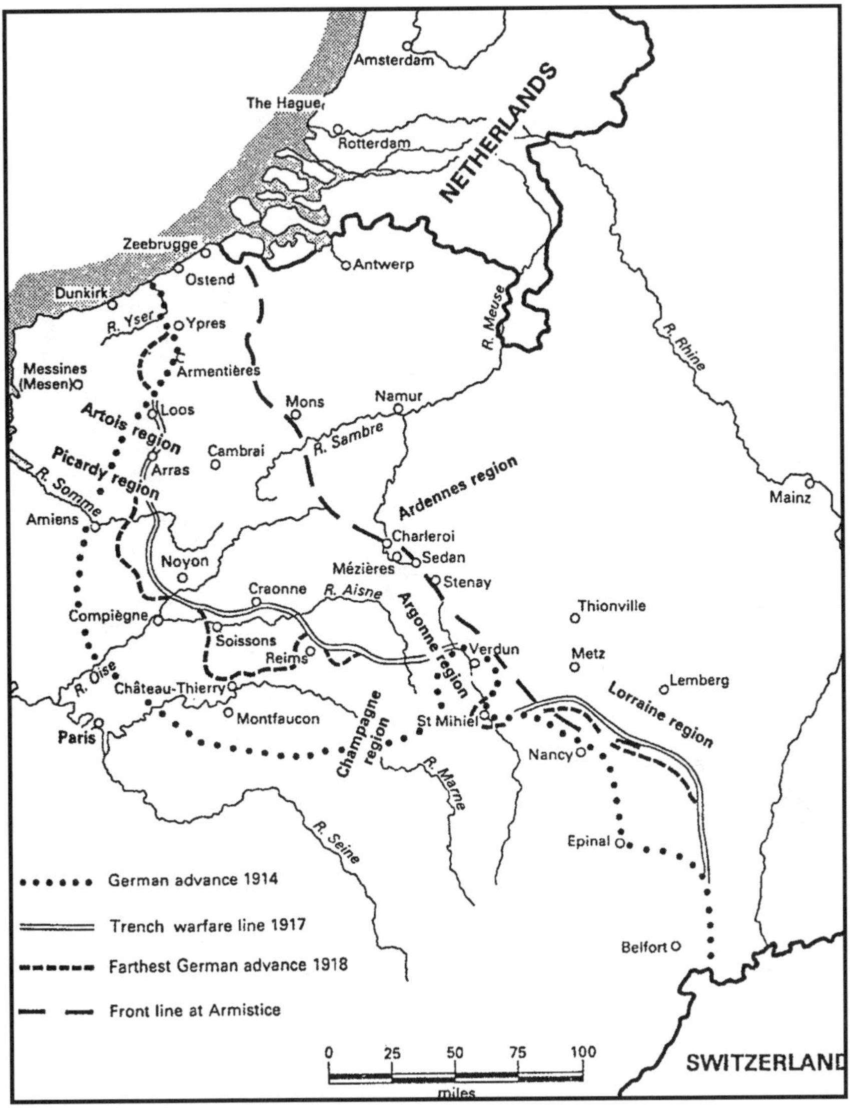
Amsterdam
The Hague
Rotterdam
NETHERLANDS
Zeebrugge
Ostend
Antwerp
Dunkirk
R. Yser
Ypres
R. Meuse
R. Rhine
Messines
(Mesen)
Armentières
Mons
Namur
Loos
Artois region
R. Sambre
Cambrai
Picardy region
Arras
R. Somme
Ardennes region
Mainz
Amiens
Charleroi
Sedan
Noyon
Mézières
Stenay
Craonne
R. Aisne
Argonne region
Thionville
Compiègne
Soissons
Reims
Verdun
Metz
R. Oise
Château-Thierry
Lemberg
Lorraine region
Montfaucon
St Mihiel
Paris
Champagne region
Nancy
R. Marne
R. Seine
Epinal
German advance 1914
Trench warfare line 1917
Farthest German advance 1918
Front line at Armistice
Belfort
0
25
50
75
100
miles
SWITZERLAND

The Western Front

". . . an unbroken line of trenches that goes from the North Sea . . . to Switzerland."

John Laffin, *A Western Front Companion: 1914–1918* (Allan Sutton Publishing Limited, Phoenix Mill, Far Thrupp, Stroud, Gloucestershire, 1994), p. 73

John Barden's Record from the 5th Minnesota Volunteer Infantry

"The regimental record says only, 'Killed in action. Was a good and faithful soldier.'"

Minnesota Historical Society: Minnesota History Center,
St. Paul, Minn.

Two Officers in the Mud

"We lose more men to wet feet than we do to hot lead."

Martin Gilbert, *The First World War: A Complete History*
(New York: Henry Holt and Co., 1994)

British Tank

"Maybe those new tanks will punch a hole in them."

John Laffin, *A Western Front Companion: 1914–1918* (Allan Sutton Publishing Limited, Phoenix Mill, Far Thrupp, Stroud, Gloucestershire, 1994), p. 165

Munitions Factory

"Whole factories must have been working round the clock just to supply . . . this area alone. What a waste of steel."

Lyn MacDonald, *1914–1918: Voices and Images of the Great War*
(London: Michael Joseph, 1988), p. 142

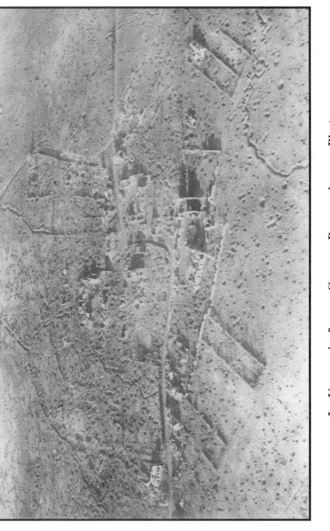

La Vacquerie, from a German Reconnaissance Photo

"At La Vacquerie, the sunken road gradually became less sunken, and we had to crouch lower and lower . . . No houses were intact."

Deutsche Kriegsarchiv, Stuttgart, Germany

Stretcher Bearers

" . . . a stretcher bearer . . . looked ready to drop. The veins in his arms bulging from the strain of carrying heavy stretchers down the crowded trenches."

British Soldiers Giving Water to Wounded German Prisoners

". . . the men didn't really hate 'Brother Hun' . . . the poor, freezing, sleepless, German fellow . . . was doing his job, as he understood it."

Martin Gilbert, *The First World War: A Complete History*
(New York: Henry Holt and Co., 1994)

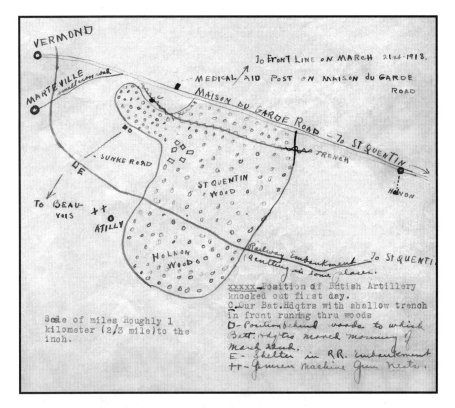

Ben Gallagher's hand-drawn map of the situation on March 21, 1918, the day of the great German assault. Scale: 1 kilometer to the inch. He later typed in some additional information.

"If the Oxfords cop it, we'll be in front of our front line."

Corporal Oswald Bradley

"Bradley proved invaluable, as always."

Evacuation of Wounded

"Finally, there was one cart left."

Lyn MacDonald, *1914–1918: Voices and Images of the Great War*
(London: Michael Joseph, 1988), p. 171

Marcelcave, March 30, 1918

In the center of the photograph, his back to the camera, is a man in a British coat. This could be (we are not certain) a picture of Ben Gallagher as he walks through the town trying to get help for his men.

Deutsche Kriegsarchiv, Stuttgart, Germany

Lieutenant William Tenney, St. Albans, Vermont

Sent us maple sugar lumps for years; suddenly the lumps stopped coming around 1936.

William B. Gallagher, personal communication

Minnesota Historical Society, Minnesota History Center,
St. Paul, Minn.

Lieutenant R. H. Jeffrey, M.D.

". . . at least I was among friends, and they were Americans."

A fellow prisoner of Ben Gallagher. On a trip to Allentown, Pennsylvania in 1950, Ben Gallagher tried to look him up. At a hospital there, someone said, "Yes. We had a Dr. Jeffrey. He died in 1940."

William Gallagher, personal communication

Gallagher (Bernard James and family) papers. Prison camp materials.
From the collection of the Minnesota Historical Society, Minnesota
History Center, St. Paul, Minn.

Lieutenant James R. Quigley

Adrian, Pennsylvania

"In the prisoner of war camp . . . the food was none too delicious, and the sleeping quarters were none to luxurious, but they sufficed."

Minnesota Historical Society, Minnesota History Center,
St. Paul, Minn.

"Lux," the Canteen Man

"For a bigger bribe, Lux would serve us the Kaiser's head on a silver platter."

Ben Gallagher with His "Class" of Russians

"Trying to teach Russians English was a terrible job."

William B. Gallagher, personal collection

**Russian Prisoners Taken in the Village of Villingen,
Germany on October 3, 1918**

*"Poor fellows, though. Once members of the Russian aristocracy, they were now in a bad way . . . . A
revolution had broken out in their country . . . They had no way of knowing what awaited them."*

Gallagher (Bernard James and family) papers. Prison camp materials.
From the collection of the Minnesota Historical Society,
Minnesota History Center, St. Paul, Minn.

Left to right:

R. H. Jeffrey, M.D.

(Seated) Dr. Hardesty—Was the master of ceremonies at the Fourth of July bash. Later became a professor at Johns Hopkins.

Willis—Aviator who escaped.

Isaacs—Sailor who escaped.

"[Isaacs' brother] got three home runs off me."

Guards at the Camp

"A guard, no matter how dedicated, has one shift to think about his work . . . but a prisoner never stops thinking of escape."

Gallagher (Bernard James and family) papers. Prison camp materials.
From the collection of the Minnesota Historical Society, Minnesota
History Center, St. Paul, Minn.

Willis—One of the Three Successful Escapees

"Willis was nothing if not confident."

Russian Prisoners

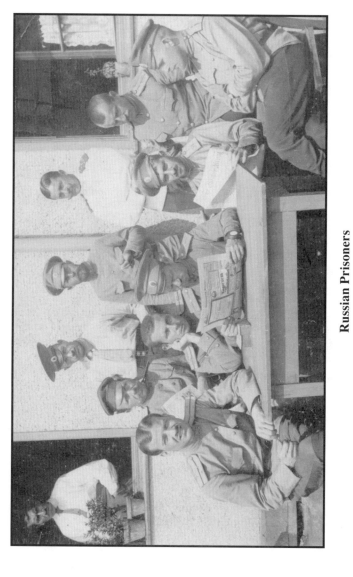

The man in the center reading the paper gave Ben Gallagher the two paintings.
"Four your helpink me English to speakink."

Gallagher (Bernard James and family) papers. Prison camp materials.
From the collection of the Minnesota Historical Society,
Minnesota History Center, St. Paul, Minn.

Ben Gallagher is second from right in second row. Photo was taken October 23, 1918.

"And there we were, prisoners, helpless behind the barbed wire, in a country that was going to wrack and ruin. What would happen to us?"

Gallagher (Bernard James and family) papers. Prison camp materials.
From the collection of the Minnesota Historical Society,
Minnesota History Center, St. Paul, Minn.

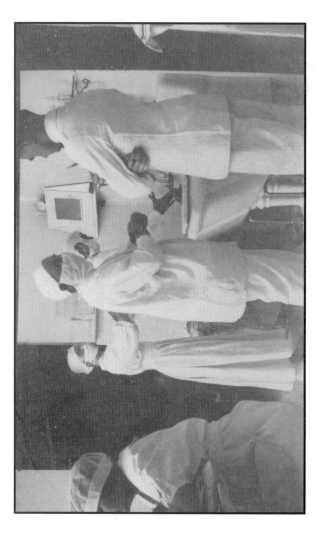

Ben Gallagher (at Right)

Taken in the scrub sink area of St. Mary's Hospital, as a Surgery Fellow at Mayo Clinic, 1919.

"What about after we got home?" Abe asked.

"Maybe I'll try for a Surgery Fellowship at Mayo Clinic."

George Cave

"Doctor Gallagher, am I going to die?"

Grave of Unknown Soldier

"By ones, and twos, and dozens, they died. Sometimes they died fast, in an instant. Sometimes they took longer."

Lyn MacDonald, *1914–1918: Voices and Images of the Great War*
(London: Michael Joseph, 1988), p. 171

Margaret Manahan

"Margaret Manahan captured him and never fired a shot."

Oswald Bradley on Holiday, Isle of Wight, 1963

"Leftenant Gallagher, it is my very considered opinion that we may better serve the British cause in another location," Bradley said, with icy calm.

Ben Gallagher's Children

"And I would tell my children about [George Cave], if I ever had children."

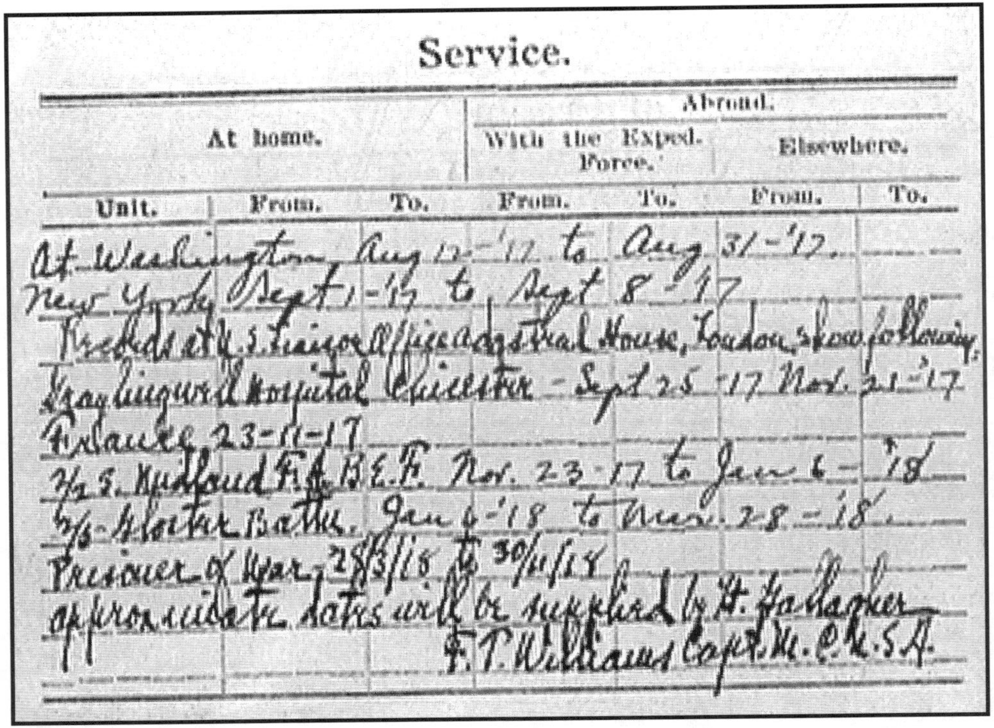

Service.

Unit.	At home. From.	At home. To.	Abroad. With the Exped. Force. From.	Abroad. With the Exped. Force. To.	Abroad. Elsewhere. From.	Abroad. Elsewhere. To.

At Washington Aug 12-'17 to Aug 31-'17.
New York Sept 1-17 to Sept 8-17
Records at U.S. Liaison Office, Central House, London, show following:
Hospital Chichester - Sept 25-17 Nov. 21-17
France 23-11-17
2/5 [illegible] B.E.F. Nov. 23-17 to Jan 6-18
[illegible] Jan 6-18 to Mar. 28-18.
Prisoner of War 28/3/18 to 30/11/18
approximate dates will be supplied by B. Gallagher
F. T. Williams Capt. M.C. U.S.A.

Record of Ben Gallagher's Service from His Personnel Officer's Record Book

"Congratulations men. You've just joined the British Army."

William B. Gallagher, personal collection

Ben Gallagher in 1950s

"I had fixed what I could fix, and saved who I could save. And that is what a doctor does."

At times we evacuated the men with hemostats still "clamped" on the vessels, the steel handles of these clamps jutting out of the wound.

Once, the stretcher bearers brought in a man bleeding from the groin. A shell splinter had flown between his legs. It had almost missed—but left him neatly castrated. "Doctor," the Tommy growled, "this is one Blighty I didn't want."

Shock and low blood pressure we saw all the time—the patients would be pale with clammy skin and dilated pupils. We treated this by placing a heater under the raised stretcher and draping blankets over the patient reaching to the floor. Back in the CCSs (Casualty Clearing Stations—the front-line hospitals) they were given intravenous fluids, either salt solution ("normal saline"), Ringers' lactate, or a gum acacia solution. I heard that blood transfusions were also being given with excellent results, the donor being a lightly wounded or gassed patient. A tube went from one man's arm (the donor) into the other man's arm (the recipient). The reward for blood donors was a week's leave in Blighty.

If there were only some way the wounded could get the intravenous fluid and even the blood earlier—perhaps in the Advanced Dressing Stations. I didn't think it would be practical in the Battalion Aid Posts. Other doctors agreed with me on this. We all hoped some clever fellow, some researcher, was looking into this problem and would come up with a better way to treat shock. If we could only treat it earlier, it seemed we would save more men.

The worst was to watch men dying, knowing that nothing could be done, yet trying to reassure them. Some wanted us to write letters home for them. This was a distraction one seldom had time for; sometimes I fobbed the job off on my assistant, Ozwald (Ozzie) Bradley, or a chaplain, if I could find one.

Some soldiers had heart disease and what often appeared to be pulmonary tuberculosis. I usually sent them "down the line," to the base, to be evacuated.

Strangely—after a few weeks—many of these fellows returned, sent "back to duty." They weren't considered "sick enough" by the base hospital doctors.

This war was not consuming only the healthy and fit.

We received orders from the Royal Army Medical Department—stern directives—not to make the diagnosis of shell shock anymore. (We had received the same directive at Chichester, months before, but apparently some doctors were still writing "shell shock.") There seemed to be some bureaucratic (whether medical or military, I did not know) objection to the very concept. But whatever you called it, shell shock, nervous disease not yet diagnosed; we saw it, plenty of it. Some soldiers complained of tiredness, irritability, dizziness, inability to concentrate, headaches . . . Others, who had been through a big battle, or prolonged shelling, or some traumatic trench raid (whether as raiders or raidees) would seem to be all right, then suddenly break down for no apparent reason. Some of these men gazed vacantly, with a loose-lipped, too ready smile. Others scowled, or sat apart, or crouched in corners.

We were ordered—in no uncertain terms—to cease putting "shell shock" on a patient tag, and write, instead, NYD(N) [Not Yet Diagnosed (Nervous)] or "neurasthenia." This was a slight variant of the instructions to write NDNYD (Nervous Disorder Not Yet Diagnosed) we got at Chichester.

I guess back at the base there would be specialists with training or experience in mental or nervous disorders to sort these patients out and treat them, mostly with rest and quiet, as we had done at Graylingwell.

I certainly didn't know what to do for them, and was only too glad to send them "down the line." The disease was not limited to enlisted men, by any stretch, for many officers developed these symptoms. It was referred to as "cracking up." But, surprisingly, two or three weeks later many of these men returned to duty in the line, much improved after a stay in a Rest Station at the base.

I had made good friends with another American, Mike Cahill, medical officer in the Oxford Battalion. (The Oxfords were in our Brigade, so I had frequent occasion to visit with Cahill.) He found out why we weren't to use the term "shell shock." "Shell shock" implied a war injury (a "W" would appear on the patient's record) and the government would eventually have to pay the soldier a pension. The alternative term, Not Yet Diagnosed (Neurasthenia), implied sickness (an "S" would appear on the patient's record) and the soldier would receive *no* pension. So the Royal Army Medical Corps told us to stop using the term "shell shock" in order to save the British government from paying pensions. Neither Cahill nor I liked that very much.

I wondered how the French and Germans handled the question of "shell shock?" Surely they had it, too. Actually, after La Vacqueirie, I wondered why everyone didn't go stark raving mad.

One had to be careful about drinking water. If it came from a trench or shell hole, you had to boil it, because it was usually polluted by a rotting corpse or the vestiges of a poison gas attack.

It was in these lines I first got "cooties," better known as body lice, a condition virtually universal among soldiers on both sides. The itching drove me crazy. I scratched myself bloody raw. Worst of all, the itching made it all but impossible to sleep. This lice infection gave me an acquaintance with trench fever, something I'd seen in Graylingwell Hospital. I had a fever, a headache; my shins ached miserably, to the point I couldn't even stand to put a blanket over them, just as the patients at Graylingwell had suffered. More fortunate was I than some, as the worst of it passed in a few days, but my legs continued to ache for a very long time. My British comrades blamed the infestation on the previous landlord of these trenches—the French.

The trenches we'd taken over from the French still had a lingering smell to them. They had no shit wallahs in their battalions, taking care of their business wherever. Our own shit wallahs had to do an *extensive* house cleaning. The Anglo-French alliance was on shaky ground, indeed, as far as the cleanup crew was concerned. There was extensive talk about letting the Germans capture the trenches, let *them* clean it up, then recapture them once they were good and flushed. Whatever that would have cost in lost lives was deemed worth it.

It was bitterly cold this fourth winter of "deadlock" in the trenches. Many soldiers were used to it, having already lived in trenches for a long time. To some it seemed their whole adult lives had been spent thus, mole-like below the surface of the earth. It was not a pleasant life for either side, for it was characterized by mud, the stench of decomposition, and feelings of almost unbearable strain and futility—strain, as a result of the conditions; futility, as a result of the utter lack of success which had attended all efforts to break through. The stalemate had existed now for three entire years, blocking the progress of nations, robbing their populations of happiness, and ending so many lives in futile and inconsequential agony.

Early in February I was sent to the town of Ham, nine miles behind the lines, for a week of training. Twelve medical officers, mostly Americans, (Cahill among them) were sent with me, and we welcomed the opportunity to get out of the line, get deloused, and live a normal life for awhile. Ham had been occupied by the Germans from 1914 to 1917, and was now an important British Army headquarters. For this reason, it received a lot of attention from the Hun flyers.

Since they had held the town for years, the Boche knew exactly where the British could be found—namely, in an officer's club, and in a movie theater, both near the rail station. These two locations might just as well have had large X's painted on their roofs. The Germans would wait until dinner time, then bomb the club. Then they'd return to their bases, load more bombs and fuel, and come back to bomb the theater at show time. Dinner and a movie. Why the British didn't move the officers' club, the theater, or at the very least change the hours, escaped me as folly. The British, in the indecipherable way of theirs, took the bombings as great sport.

In the club, when the air raid alarm sounded off, the men refused to go below into the cellar, perceiving a retreat as cowardly, or worse, not sporting. At the movie theater, the men would cheer like gleeful boys each time a bomb dropped closer. I cheered a little, too, so as not to appear a stuffed shirt, but my heart was not into it. For some reason, artillery fire, terrible though it was, never scared me too badly. But bombs, falling from a plane, frightened the living hell out of me.

One night a Boche aviator nearly got me. I was asleep in a dingy room over an old store when the roar of Boche engines woke me up. German planes made an irregular sound. "RRRRrrrrrrr RRRRrrrrrr RRRrrrr." The British planes made a constant "RRRRR" sound. I had heard bombs hitting the ground before, but this time I could clearly hear them closer than ever. As one screech got louder and louder, I was sure this particular egg was going to land right on my head. The bomb landed with a huge crash, and all the windows in my "home away from home" blew apart. The bomb had landed on my side of the street, a half block away, killing two people. How could the British treat these air raids as "sport"?

My last night in Ham, I was out in the street and German bombs started falling again. To see the terror-stricken French women and children running for shelter was pitiful to behold. There was nothing sporting about this—nothing sporting about it at all.

Chapter 9

BEWARE OF MACDUFF

Spring in Picardy
March 1918

I had now been with the British for four months, and knew them fairly well. Oswald was the quintessential enlisted man—hardy, tough, and optimistic in spite of all the failures and hardships. No matter what happened, Bradley would "carry on." There was so much contained in the term, "carry on."

Last stretcher's broken? Sling the man over your shoulder, and carry on. Ammo wallah buried in a trench cave-in? Get a shovel, dig him out, carry on. No more tourniquets? Use the wounded man's boot lace. Carry on. Carry on said it all. And the British enlisted man, whether going over the top, or scuppering a German night raid, or brewing you up a pot of that barbed-wire-dissolving tea, would always carry on.

The English officers, too, had an imperturbable "carry on" attitude about them. In the front line, these officers shared the same hardships as the men. Shells, mortar bombs, and aeroplane bombs landed on officers just as they did on men. (The awful screeching crescendo—eeeeeEEEEE!—as the bomb got closer and closer was horrifying to endure.) Snipers picked off officers as they did enlisted men. And the cold and damp, the monotonous diet, and boredom alternating with terror all took a medical toll on the officers as well.

Our commanding officer, Col. Collett, was a case in point. Poor health would force him to go back to England, and we would miss him sorely.

Shortly after the battle at La Vacquerie, the 2nd/4th Gloucesters were cannibalized, mixed in with the remnants of another battalion, and added to the depleted 2nd/5th Gloucesters. (Every army periodically reshuffled the deck this way. When the British did it, they sometimes kept more than one of the original battalion's designations. That left you with a bewildering hodgepodge of 2nd/4ths, 2nd/5ths, even 2nd/2nds.) My original C.O., Col. Barnsley, (the man who looked like a basset hound) got another assignment and I didn't see him again. Col. Collett became my new C.O. in mid-December, and the 2nd/5th Gloucester became my new unit.

Up until Col. Collett, I had always had a hard time getting on friendly terms with the English officers. Just as Ted Sweeter had told me in Paris, the English officers viewed me as a Johnny-come-lately, a fifth wheel. They had little interest, and plenty of disdain for their American cousins. This attitude chafed me. Although I respected them as brave men and good soldiers, I could not get to like them. Col. Collett was an exception.

"So, Gallagher, I've got to tell you, this American way of talking, I find it so lively," Collett said. He was short, had a slight frame, and coughed a lot. His hair was wispy. Only his eyes had any robustness and vigor to them. And he smiled. More than any other English officer, he smiled.

We were sitting in a dugout, rain pelting down outside, playing bridge. I didn't like bridge, was no good at bridge, knew the English were better than I at bridge, and secretly hoped for a dugout cave-in to put me out of my misery.

"Yeah?" I was wondering whether to bid spades, or go outside and throw myself on the German barbed wire.

"Yes, that's it, 'yeah.' What a term, 'yeah.' It says so much, conveys an attitude. Just like your 'OK.'" Collett was on fire. He loved "Americanisms."

I put down some spades, Major Day snorted in triumph.

"'OK,' 'OK.' There really isn't a good synonym for it." Collett was analyzing the term, digesting it. Meanwhile Major Day was digesting me at this bridge game. Collett went on, "Nothing has the flexibility of 'OK.' It says, 'All right, I understand,' or 'I agree with your suggestion,' or any number of things. He gave a disgusted look at Major Day and let him have it. Oh Major Day, would you quit gloating. Just pick up the cards and keep playing."

In addition to American expressions, Col. Collett had a great interest in the Civil War, and would often talk to me about Stonewall Jackson. We were in the same dugout, a few weeks later. This time we were playing poker, and it was Major Day's turn to suffer.

"You no doubt have read about the battle of Chancellorsville, haven't you, Gallagher?" Collett asked, sitting bolt upright on his chair. He sometimes seemed a little short of breath, and would sit straight up to breathe better. His ankles would also, all signs of a weak heart.

I was holding a full house, and Day was looking none to happy. The pot had worked its way up to a week's pay, and Day was wondering whether to call or not.

"Your bid, Major Day," I said with my best poker face. A smile was trying to sneak out, but I held it back, my lips quivering with the effort. There was a lot of money in that pot.

"Oh, a rat!" Day shouted, getting up.

"Never mind the rat, Major Day, Gallagher said it's time for you to make your bid, OK?" Collett beamed at his own clever use of "OK." The rat escaped. Day would not.

"Yes, Col. Collett, I've read quite a bit about Chancellorsville, Stonewall Jackson's swan song," I said. Jackson had worked with Robert E. Lee to defeat the Union Army at Chancellorsville, but the night after the battle, he'd been shot by his own men. In the dark, they mistook him for a Yankee.

"Pity he was killed there. Brilliant man. Splitting his forces right in front of a superior army, then smacking the Union Army where they least expected it. And to think, shot down by his very own men that night. Almost has the air of a Greek tragedy to it," Collett said.

"Tragic." My eyes were on the cards. I myself had never liked Stonewall Jackson much. A good general, yes, but I was from Minnesota. My favorite generals were all Union men.

In the poker game, Major Day decided to call, and coughed up another week's wages into the pot. I put down my cards, aces and eights, the dead man's hand. Day had two pair. He was the dead man today.

"Yes, Col. Collett," I gathered in the money, looked Day right in the face, "that was tragic."

On Saturday, March 16, we had a send-off for our dear Col. Collett. He had been much closer to the men than most English officers, and genuinely cared for their well being. It pained him to see his men suffer, and he knew many would be suffering soon, as the Bloody Moloch of war reached a fearsome crescendo. The boys put on a show for him, with great joking and lots of singing all around. His look, as he watched the frolicsome boys that day, could melt a heart of stone. But his health was failing, and he could no longer endure the rigors of trench life, so we bid him a fond farewell. Everyone was sorry to see Col. Collett go. I had lost a real friend.

Just a few days later, Bradley and I were talking in our Aid Post.

"Beware the Ides of March, Great Caesar," I told Oswald.

"The Ides of March have come," he came right back with the next line from Shakespeare's *Julius Caesar*.

"Ay, but have not gone," I finished it up.

That brought a laugh all around. It was March 15, and the German attack was expected soon. Why not hit us on the Ides of March? It was as good a day as any. But Bradley didn't think so.

"Jerry don't read Shakespeare, sir, he'd be more likely to hit us on old Bismarck's birthday or the Kaiser's, something like that."

Bradley was a burly fellow, handy when we had to lift patients onto carts or when we had to hold the patients down and splint their broken bones. He was rolling extra bandages, as was I. We would need extras of everything. Everybody knew the Germans were coming.

"Where do you think they'll hit, Corporal Bradley? Here?" I asked.

"Oh yes. They'll put a stunt up here, everywhere actually. Now that the Russkies have copped it, Jerry's got an extra million men or so. They'll put them all to good work." He set down one roll, and took up another.

"But the big hit will be up North. They'll head for the Channel ports, try to cut off our retreat to England." Bradley was sure of himself.

"Think we'll stop them?" Bradley had been in this war longer than I had, he should know.

"When haven't we?" Oswald said, answering my question with a question. Not too reassuring.

"Not as many of us here as I'd like. Lot of empty stretches of trench, it looks like to me," I said. No general was I but the trenches were thinly manned, anyone could see that.

"Well, the word out is we're not so much holding lines now as blobs. You know, a string of redoubts. Each one's packed with plenty of machine guns, plenty of ammo, just not so many men as before," Bradley said. Not so many men as before, not so many men as before. That was food for thought.

"Couldn't Jerry just go through the gaps between the blobs?" I asked.

"Wrong on two accounts, Doctor. First, the field of fire from those redoubts covers all the intervening spaces. We'll tear them to shreds. And second, Jerry's never aimed at a space before, they aim for the strong points, batter their heads against it." He nodded, satisfied with the explanation. I was not so sanguine. That's what the Germans had done *before*. Maybe he'd do something different this time.

Bradley finished wrapping his last roll.

"So don't you worry about old Brother Hun. He hasn't broken us yet, and he's not about to break us now. Tea?"

Tea again. I'd heard all of Bradley's arguments before, and the rest of the soldiers seemed to think the same. This attitude pervaded the Front. The preparations for our defense seemed half-hearted, at best. Support trenches were shallow. Barbed wire lines were thin and poorly maintained. There was a "business as usual" attitude.

On Sunday, March 17, we got a new C.O., Lieutenant Colonel Lawson, a cavalry officer from the British "West Point" of Aldershot. Young, efficient, and well trained, Lawson had been in France in the early weeks of the war. The Kaiser had called the English Army "contemptible" in those early days. In characteristic fashion, the British heard about his disparaging comment, and turned it around to their own advantage, renaming themselves the "Old Contemptibles." They then engaged in a fighting retreat from the city of Mons, and brought the initial German offensive of 1914 to a halt. These "contemptible" soldiers would bend and bend, but they would not break. And our man Lawson was one of them. He was a quiet, unassuming chap, but all efficiency. He would be with us hardly long enough to get acquainted before the storm broke and he would face the acid test. Our admiration and faith in him grew and grew.

Monday, March 18, we moved from the reserve line (located in the town of Ugny) to the support line (which happened to be in an area called Holnon Woods). The Oxford Battalion was in the front line. The Berkshire Battalion (nicknamed the "Bucks") was behind in the reserve line. This was the luck of the rotation. (No battalion stayed forever in the front line. We rotated in the following way: support → front, front → reserve, reserve → support.)

The next day we got word the Germans were going to attack on the morning of March 21. Apparently some German prisoners, taken in one of the night raids, had tipped us to the date. Everyone seemed completely confident that any attack the Germans might make on our front would be easily repulsed. Though the front line was expected to fold (I wondered how that sat with the Oxfords up there in the front line) we would whip them in our support line, or battle position, as it was called.

I was considerably less confident than my fellow British officers. My only experience with a German attack was in La Vacquerie, and they had banged us around pretty good then. The Aid Post was as prepared as it could be. We'd laid in extra splints and bandages, had double checked the anti-gas curtains at the entrance, and made sure the oxygen tanks were full (for resuscitation of poison gas victims). Looking around our support position, I wished we had done a little more spadework. The trenches seemed inadequate.

On the morning of March 20, Lieutenant Munday, our signal officer, and I were walking around our positions to get more familiar with the lay of the land, when we met General White, our brigade commander. He was all alone—rare to see a high staff officer alone and so close to the Front. General White had not thinned out. Fat and jolly, the war was agreeing with him. Cheerily, he said to us, "Well, boys, the Boche are going to attack here in the morning, and I hope he does, too, for he will get an awful drubbing."

Such breezy confidence spoke volumes for the British state of mind prior to the German offensive.

Later that same day, we were treated to a Shakespearean performance by an *American* no less.

Mike Cahill, an American medical officer with the Oxfords, had stopped by my Aid Post. His battalion had rotated up to the front line and I was in the support line. He had come back via a communication trench to pick up some supplies, and made a visit out of it. This Cahill was a character.

His father was an actor, his mother an actress. How he ended up in medicine remained a mystery, for Cahill was an actor himself. He knew Shakespeare *better than the English did*, and that was not an easy thing to do. Cahill had a Shakespearean line for every activity known to man.

—You'd knock on the door of his dugout, he'd say, "Open locks, whoever knocks!"

—A messenger would arrive, he'd say, "Thou comest to use thy tongue, thy story quickly."

—Rain would pour down on us, he'd say, "This foul night will drive us all to fools and madmen."

Our own profession came under the lash of his well-versed tongue. He told one soldier, "The doctor kill, and the fee bestow upon the foul disease."

Cahill could be a bit much, but he was no fool himself; he would tone down his "thou's" and "to be or not to be's" when we had had enough.

He was a great one for physical training, too, this Cahill. Push-ups, sit-ups, every day he did them. And sometimes he'd grasp the top of a dugout doorway and pull his weight up. A "Western Front chin-up" he called it.

No slouch at his medicine, either. Cahill knew his stuff. When he'd put down his Shakespeare for a while, we'd sometimes test each other on the most obscure medical facts. (Some day we would be returning to the States, and sooner or later we'd have to take our medical boards exam. Neither of us wanted to get too rusty.) Try as I might, I could not trip him up. I began to suspect that Cahill had a true photographic memory, though he denied the accusation.

"Oh, I've got a photographic memory all right," he said, "only the camera's broken, it won't take any pictures!"

Cahill was standing in our dugout, a fifteen by fifteen foot affair, with the usual dirt floor, rough board walls, and timbered roof. The heated trestle, oxygen tank and extra stretchers were pushed off to the side, to give Cahill more room to "strut and fret his hour upon the stage." He was a little shorter than I, so he could stand at full height without hitting his head. His booming voice—much deeper and lower than you'd expect of this man of medium build and stature—filled our little dugout. His vivid expression transformed our small cockpit into "the vasty fields of France" or Hamlet's castle or, in this case, the haunted cavern where the three witches spelled out Macbeth's future, and his doom.

"Double, double toil and trouble;
Fire burn; and cauldron bubble."

Cahill stood there, imitating the stirring motion of a witch brewing up trouble. In his other hand, he held a dog-eared book—*The Complete Works of Shakespeare*. He rarely looked down on it, so he must have had this memorized. What a prodigious mental feat to remember all those lines!

"By the pricking of my thumbs,
Something wicked this way comes: —"

Cahill *would* edit some, jumping down a half page or so at a time, hitting all the best lines, and leaving some behind.

"Whew! Break time. I'm thirsty," Cahill said, and sat down.

Break time? I'm thirsty? Did the witches say that? Oh no, *Cahill* was saying that, for himself. He could get you so entranced, you'd forget when he stepped out of character.

Ozzie Bradley, my medical assistant, handed Cahill a cup of coffee. (Cahill had some mystical connection with a coffee supplier, a secret he guarded with his life. His visits were doubly welcome, for he always brought a little coffee for me, too. A welcome relief from the endless tea it was.)

"So Ben," Cahill said, sniffing the heady aroma of real, live coffee, "those witches in Macbeth, they might have been talking to us."

Talking to us? Cahill could really stretch it with this Shakespeare stuff. But he provided some welcome relief from the boredom at the Front, and his coffee was a godsend.

"Well then, unhold your tongue and speak anon," I said.

Cahill's brow furrowed, he was leafing through his voluminous list of Shakespeare quotes. It was rare that someone could stump him.

"Where's that from?" he finally asked.

"The Tragedy of King Gallagher the Fourth," I said, "I made it up."

The dugout was cool, but not uncomfortably so. Spring was in the air, and the slightest hint of greenery and new life was trying to scent the air. But the usual stench of the trench overwhelmed it.

"Well," Cahill said, now leaning forward with his elbows on his knees, "the story of Macbeth is a lot of things—ambition, guilt, murder, revenge—all the usual stuff you see in Shakespeare. But there is something else in the story of Macbeth. Shakespeare might have been talking to us, right here, warning us about the German attack."

"How do you figure that, Mike?" I asked. A German plane came overhead "RRRRrrr RRRRRrrr." Then we heard a British plane come to greet it, "RRRRRRR." A dogfight might be in the making. Usually, that emptied the dugout and we watched the aerial duel. But Cahill had spun a web with his story, and we were trapped.

"The story of Macbeth applies to us, because we are playing the part of Macbeth, and Jerry is playing the part of MacDuff," Cahill said, in a low voice. "And the witches said, 'Beware Macduff.'"

Next to Cahill was a copy of the *Wipers Times*, an irreverent newspaper put together by the British soldiers themselves. "Real" newspapers reached us in the front line, but the *Wipers Times* was much more amusing. Jokes and phony ads abounded, for example:

—"Lice for sale, two cents per thousand" (as if we needed more lice).

—"The High Command has decreed that all mud be removed from the Western Front. Those not in compliance will be shot at dawn."

But hidden among all the humor was some truthful reporting, much more straightforward than the heavily censored "official press."

Russia had fallen, freeing up roughly a million German soldiers. And those soldiers were heading our way. These were not raw recruits, either, they were seasoned veterans. Germany was planning a huge offensive, and would launch it sometime in the spring, hoping to defeat the Allies before the Americans could arrive.

Almost a year had passed since America declared war on Germany, but the training, equipping, and transport of the American troops was taking a long time. Best estimates said it would be late summer or fall before there were enough Americans to make a difference. That left plenty of time for the Germans, with their million men reinforcements, to defeat us.

The naval blockade was supposed to be weakening the Germans, and the French and British were supposed to be "grinding them down," but they certainly didn't seem weakened to us. Besides, every time we tried to grind *them* down, they ground *us* down, too.

But the British seemed supremely confident about the upcoming battle. It took Cahill, another American, to sound a note of concern. He had just told us that the three witches in Macbeth had warned him to "Beware MacDuff". Cahill then likened us to Macbeth, and the Germans to MacDuff.

"How does that work, Leftenant?" Bradley asked. Bradley himself knew quite a bit of Shakespeare.

Cahill warmed to the task, using his hands to emphasize the points.

"Macbeth thinks himself perfectly safe; he has risen to power, taken over the throne, murdered most of his enemies, and is defending himself in the impenetrable castle of Dunsinane. And all of this rise to power has been predicted by the three witches."

"Yes, and . . . " Bradley wasn't buying it. "What does that have to do with us?"

Overhead, British and German planes were starting to tangle. "RRRRR! RRRrrrr! Tat-tat-tat-tat-tat! RRRR! Tat-tat-tat-tat." The sound faded away, no sound of an explosion or a crash. Both pilots must have missed. We stayed in the dugout, hearing out Cahill's tale.

"Because there is one fly in the ointment—MacDuff. 'Beware MacDuff' the witches said. So Macbeth, who felt completely safe, now has this sort of irresistible force coming at him. He's not sure when, or how, but he knows

MacDuff is on the way. And the witches' prophecies, which have all come true in the past, hang heavy on his shoulders. MacDuff is coming, and there's no stopping him."

I started to get it. MacDuff was the Germans, the irresistible force, and he was on his way. Bradley got it, too.

"So you're saying, Leftenant, that we're Macbeth, sitting in our castle," he gestured around the dirt and timber underground dugout, "and MacDuff is going to come along and do us in."

"In a sense, yes," Cahill said.

"Bah!" said Bradley. "All due respect, Leftenant, but you're daft. Jerry's not going to do *us* in, we're going to do *him* in."

Cahill had told me the British in his battalion thought the same. "We'll defeat the German assault this time, just as we've defeated them every time before." No one was making extra preparations. No one seemed to be "girding their loins" sufficiently. Cahill and I were quite nervous about this lackadaisical attitude, and he was using Shakespeare to make his point.

Cahill's hands were working, his head was going so fast his words could hardly keep up.

"OK, take one of the witches' predictions:

'No man borne of woman can harm Macbeth.'

Well, this is a stretch, I know, but they were telling him that the usual enemy, the average man, could do him no harm," Cahill said, a little exasperated that his point wasn't coming across.

Bradley said, "What the hell does that have to do with us? Are all the Germans over there in St.-Quentin born by Caesarean section?"

A couple other fellows in the dugout chuckled. One of them chimed in.

"No. But they're all bastards, I can tell you that!"

More laughter. Cahill looked down at the ground, disappointed he wasn't making his point. The Britishers weren't interested in his cockamamy theory. But I was.

"Go on, Mike," I said.

He lifted his head up, glad for the reprieve.

"It's not that they're born by Caesarean section, that's not the point. MacDuff was *different,* he was not the *usual* man, so the *usual* defense didn't work. Haven't you noticed anything *different* about the Germans?"

The laughing in the room died down, even Bradley's broad grin slackened a little.

The British soldiers *had* noticed something different. Cahill was starting to make sense.

Bradley's interest was piqued.

"So you're saying we're facing a different Jerry, is that it, Leftenant Cahill?" Bradley asked.

"You tell me," Cahill said.

An enlisted man, who had come in to see the show, spoke up.

"'E's puttin' up quite a few raids, 'e is. That's one thing."

A man next to him said, "And 'e ain't lettin' us get too many o' his lads when we's the one puts on a raid. Seems a bit secretive, ol' Fritzie does."

"Saw the oddest thing, the other day," the first one said. "We finally gets a hand on one o' their officers. Young fellow, tough-lookin' though."

Bradley was writing off all these concerns as tripe. A few more raids, a little more secrecy, what's so different about that?

"So what did you see on this officer, that put such a fright in you, lad?" Bradley asked.

"Leather patches on his knees," the enlisted man said, "like the kind you'd use if you was crawlin' around in the dark. Now I've never seen that before. Why would Jerry give his men leather patches on them knees?"

Cahill broke in. "Maybe this isn't the same Jerry we've been seeing. Maybe they've come up with something new."

New? On the Western Front? Infantry came straight at the strong points, the machine guns. If you shot them down fast enough, you held them off. If not, you were overwhelmed. But knee patches? For crawling around? What would they crawl around? We had a solid line of trenches—wait, we *used* to have a solid line of trenches. Now there were gaps.

Gaps you could crawl through, on your knees.

"Did this German fellow tell you anything?" I asked.

The man shook his head, "Didn't let on much. Just asked to be moved as far back as soon as possible. Seemed 'e didn't want to be in our lines when the big show started."

Cahill nodded, but he was not gloating. He himself would be in the front line when the big show started.

"Wasn't one of the predictions something about a forest moving, or something?" the second enlisted man asked.

"Yes, there was:

> 'Macbeth shall never vanquisht be, until
> Great Birnam wood to high Dunsinane hill
> Shall come against him.'"

"In effect, MacDuff's army camouflaged themselves with tree branches. When they moved, the woods seemed to move," Cahill filled in, not even glancing at his Shakespeare book. He really did have a phenomenal memory.

"Well," the enlisted man said, "I don't want to put too much faith in this witch's business, but . . . "

The dugout suddenly darkened, this, at mid-day. We all got a start.

"Grub wallah, interested in some eats, gentlemen?" A big man with a bulky container stood in the doorway to our dugout, blocking out the light and throwing us in darkness. All this talk of witches had spooked us. We looked at each other, a little embarrassed.

"Sure, set it down!" Bradley shouted, irritated that the grub wallah had interrupted a good story.

"Well, as I was saying," the enlisted man said, pleased *he* was now the storyteller, "I've got a brother, Dick, in the Royal Flying Corps. He was flying reconnaissance, and he was over some woods, right behind St-Quentin, straight across from our own lines. You wouldn't *believe* what he saw."

The dugout grew silent.

"So Dick is over these woods. It's spring, you know, and the trees are starting to green up a little, so he can't see too much. Dick drops down a little lower to 'ave a look-see," the enlisted man said.

Bradley started divvying up the grub wallah's container of food. Creamed peas, bully beef, and cheese.

The enlisted man went on, "Jerry doesn't like Dick snooping around, so 'e's puttin' up plenty of Archie. 'Thick enough to walk on,' me brother says, 'Thick enough to walk on it is."

I had seen the ugly black puffs from German "Archie" (anti-aircraft fire). It was a miracle that most planes seemed to fly right through it, unscathed. A frightful thing it must be, though, to have it exploding all round you in one of those flimsy fabric-and-wire aeroplanes. And those pilots had no parachutes!

"What did your brother see?" the low voice of Cahill, the actor-at-heart.

"He fired a burst of machine gun fire into the woods, to see if anything was in there. Thought he might stir things up a little, get some Jerry to break from cover," the enlisted man said.

"And . . .?" I was on the edge of my seat.

"The woods *moved*. The 'ole bleedin' woods moved. Those weren't trees 'e was lookin' at, they was guns. Guns with camouflage on 'em. And guns wasn't all 'e saw."

The enlisted man was rivetting us with his story.

"'E saw somethin' else. His machine gun burst made the men in that 'woods' turn to look, or duck for cover. The sun was out that day, and it glinted off their bayonets." The enlisted man looked sober as he gave this description. Whatever his brother saw, it would be coming our way soon. "A river of steel, that's what 'e called it, a river of steel. 'E didn't think there was that many Jerries left in the 'ole world." The man pointed towards St-Quentin, "There's a river of steel, boys, and it's right over there." He turned to Cahill. "I think our cousin, Leftenant Cahill here, may be right. We are not looking at the same Jerry assault we've seen before. All those raids, the funny knee patches, all those guns, all those men behind St-Quentin. I think Macbeth's in for a rough time of it."

That night everything was quiet and serene along our front. I did not undress before laying down on my cot, mostly because no one else did. Everyone knew there would be no time to dress in the morning.

Just before Cahill left, to rejoin the Oxfords in the front line, he finished his Shakespeare presentation with a flourish. It was the last scene in Macbeth. MacDuff had caught up with Macbeth and they were squaring off for the final duel. Macbeth, who felt himself invulnerable to attack ("No man born of woman can harm Macbeth") had just been informed that he *was* vulnerable ("MacDuff was from his mother's womb untimely ripped"). The parallel to our situation was clear, at least to Cahill and me. The British felt their defense was invulnerable, but we suspected this not to be the case.

Cahill was now going forward to the very frontmost line on the day before the largest offensive in history. He stood up before us, on his little imaginary stage in our fifteen-by-fifteen-foot dugout. He pretended to pull a sword out of a scabbard.

Cahill said, "Lay on MacDuff, and damn'd be him that first cries 'Hold enough!'"

He charged out of our dugout door and disappeared.

Chapter 10

CHAOS AND CONFUSION

March 21, 1918—The Maison de Garde Road

Aid Post in No Man's Land

No witches visited me that night, no goblins, no specters. For the first time in a long time, though, I thought about Robson, my friend who'd died outside La Vacquerie. He knew what it was like to be dead. Would I find out tomorrow? Would Cahill, in the front line, find out tomorrow? It was morbid, to think about it, so I refocused on practical things—how many stretcher bearers were available, would that sticky valve on the oxygen tank function properly, should I send Bradley back to pick up more irrigating solution? These day-to-day thoughts helped salve my overheated imaginings, and I was soon asleep.

"Sleep, death's counterfeit," Cahill would call it.

In spite of Cahill's dire predictions, and the knowledge the fight of my life was to start in the morning, I never slept better than I did that night.

I was awakened by a din that seemed to shake the earth from its very foundation. The cot nearly tipped me out. Beneath me the ground felt more liquid than solid, moving left and right, up and down at the same time. Everything shook so much, I had trouble lacing my boots. The fight was on. All was businesslike and orderly. These British had faced attacks in fixed trench lines many times over the years. They knew the lay of the land, knew what to do.

Outside, it was like the Final Judgement Day.

German and British guns were firing for miles on either side, up and down the lines. So numerous were the reports and explosions, you couldn't make out an individual noise, just the constant, unending roar. I opened my mouth, hoping in some way to equalize the pressure in my middle ear and prevent my eardrums from breaking.

Visibility was limited to a few yards by the thickest fog I had ever seen outside of London. Yellow explosions flared up all over. Some made a soft "poofing" sound. Men appeared for an instant in front of me, then just as quickly disappeared into the foggy soup. One soldier ran by carrying a bedroll, then another with a Lewis gun, almost colliding with me, then another, stumbling, holding his hand over his left eye, blood streaming through his fingers. Each image flickered past, then disappeared, like a kinetoscope.

The fog felt cool but tasted funny. More "poof" "poof" explosions, softer than the high explosive kind. I stepped on a dead rat, then stepped on two more. That was odd. Rats usually survived the worst bombardment—except when the bombardment was poison gas.

Exploding gunpowder had an acid smell as well as taste, and I could taste that powdery, gritty flavor getting stronger and stronger. These explosives must have had extra strong charges, because the taste became overpowering, nauseating. My vision narrowed to a tunnel, my legs started to buckle. I breathed hard, nothing came into my lungs. The earth was moving toward me, up. It wasn't just gunpowder I was smelling, and it wasn't just fog I was seeing. It was poison gas. That gas had killed the rats, and it was killing me.

God Almighty, I couldn't breathe in anything. Anything! My diaphragm pulled in, but the stinging, burning gas made my vocal cords spasm shut. My belly went out, my chest caved in—just like Giancomo had done so long ago. He had choked to death on his own blood, and now I was choking to death on this god damn gas.

My vocal cords opened a little, letting air in—poison air. The burning sensation was deep inside my chest now. A sickly feeling came over me too, waves of nausea, soon I'd be breathing in poison gas plus my own vomit. The sounds of artillery got soft, then silent. White mist started turning gray, then black. I was reliving Giancomo's last struggle, I was redying Giancomo's death.

Bam! My head hit the ground, but it didn't hurt. Hands flailed, hit the ground, my helmet, my jacket, my mask.

MY MASK! GET THAT FUCKING MASK ON!

The straps, the straps, which one goes behind? To hell with it. Shove it on your face, breathe. BREATHE!

I put it on backwards first, breathed in another mouthful of poison gas, now *everything* was black, I tried to suck on the eyepiece, the canister, anything.

My hands fumbled as if in mittens. TURN IT AROUND, TURN IT AROUND!

Mu-AAAAAAAAH! A breath of pure air. I swallowed hard, fighting off another wave of nausea. Don't vomit *in* your mask, you'll die for sure.

The mist went from black to gray, to yellowish, to white. Sounds of artillery came back. Boom! BOOM! Poof! Another breath, then another. I held my breath for a second and rearranged the straps around my head. More deep breaths. The nausea passed, and my hands started working again. Now, for the first time, I noticed that my eyes were burning and tearing. I pulled the straps on extra tight.

Jesus Christ, Jesus Christ Almighty, I had just about died. The battle was three minutes old and I had almost killed myself with carelessness. It was my own fault, I should have known to put my mask on, I had just forgotten in all the excitement. The dead rats should have tipped me off. It was a terrible nuisance to have a gas mask on, for you could hardly see or hear anything. Working was almost impossible.

Oswald Bradley, two other medical assistants, and I ran to our Aid Post, a little sheet iron shelter dug into the side of the Maison de Garde Road. It was a peculiar situation, for our Aid Post was actually in front of the Gloucesters' defensive position. But these positions were, after all, our second line of defense, so I was not sitting out in No Man's Land, rather, I was between the front-line Oxfords and the second line Gloucesters. This curious location proved useful, at first.

As feared, the front-line Oxfords, under a Colonel Bennet, suffered most of the casualties that first day. Their Aid Post, with my friend Cahill, was captured early on in the fighting. That left only me to treat both the Oxfords and the Gloucesters. Immediately, the wounded Oxfords began streaming back to me, limping, holding arms as still as they could, covering seared eyes, wheezing. We gave them oxygen, placed bandages and splints, and sent them back. Evacuation got more and more difficult as the day progressed.

The Ambulance Company had an Advanced Dressing Station about a mile down the road at Marteville, and they sent ambulance cars up the heavily shelled road without hesitation. One ambulance right in front of our shelter lost its roof to a German shell, but remarkably no one inside was hurt. In the afternoon, another ambulance, packed with men, suffered a direct hit. Nothing was left of the wounded men, or its driver; just a hole in the ground and a scattering of limbs and entrails. After that, no more motorcars came up.

A heavy mist, mixed with poison gas hung in the air, making it impossible to see more than a few feet. The gas masks made work cumbersome. All day long the front-line battalions put up a wonderful fight, until the number killed and wounded almost equaled the number of men in the line. A wounded officer from the Oxfords brought back some disturbing accounts of the fighting.

I was wrapping up his right hand, his thumb was gone.

"Jerry's got a different stunt up, Doc, ooh, careful there, that stings a bit." Cahill's words came back to me. "This is a different Jerry, a different enemy. They're not going to do things the same this time."

"Sorry," I said. The officer was trying to pull his hand away, involuntarily, but I held it firm. The whole conversation was muffled by our gas masks.

"I've been here since '15, you know. I've seen a few things. Oh, God, Doc. Think I might pry a little morphine out of you? That does hurt a fright." His face was two large circular eye discs and a breathing canister. He looked like a monster, we all did with our gas masks on.

"Bradley, Bradley here! Grab me a morphine tablet." We had dropped both anti-gas curtains at the entrance to the Aid Post. In spite of my brush with death, I was willing to risk anything to get out of those god damned gas masks. I took mine off and took a hesitant little breath. No choking sensation. Another little deeper breath—still OK. The curtains were working, thank God.

Bradley gave the officer a morphine tablet and a sip from a canteen. Everyone followed my lead, took off their gas masks, and heaved a sigh of relief.

"Buck up, Captain, that'll kick in before too long." Bradley was his usual unflappable self.

"Thanks ever so much."

Bradley asked the officer what was different about today's attacks. I wondered if he were thinking about Cahill's words, too.

"More guns. More than I've ever seen. More gas, more everything. We can't see 'em, either. They seem to be avoiding us. We're in our redoubt, ready to let them have it. A few come sniffing around, then, they go to ground. Pretty soon, flares to left and right. Later on flares behind us. *Behind us?* Before you know it. They're shooting at us front and back. None of the boys are scarpering, though. Bloody good stunt Jerry's got going, if I do say so. Ooo, ow, ow! How soon before that morphine does the trick, Doc?" He was trying to pull the hand away from me again.

"Give it time." I was done. "Back you go, down that road to Marteville, you can't stay here all day."

"I can't go back up there, Leftenant? Who'll take care of my company?" He had a lost look. Leave his company? Just for this scratch?

Bradley spoke up, "Don't you worry about those boys, they'll carry on all right. You get on back, like the Leftenant says now."Already, the bandage was soaked through with blood. The officer left, resigned to his fate, unhappy about leaving his men.

"So much for the Blob Theory," I said. The British system, strong points with intervening gaps (the Blob Theory of defense), had played right into the German attack plan. Now we knew why the Germans had leather knee patches. They *were* crawling through the gaps in our line. And to think, they had already snapped up Cahill. That river of steel, that forest of guns, was heading right down our throat.

Even at this moment of highest danger, the British soldiers were *still* coming up with new slang words I hadn't heard before.

"What does 'scarpering' mean, Corporal Bradley?" I asked.

"Retreating. Getting the hell out. Don't you worry about those Oxfords, they won't scarper on us. They'll stick," Bradley said.

Other soldiers came in with stories similar to the Captain's.

"He's sneaking around us like a thief in the night."

"Brother Hun's keeping his head low."

"I thought they were our chaps, shooting at us by mistake from the rear."

"Where did the Boche get all those guns?"

Bradley looked like he was wounded himself, covered in other men's blood, but he never frowned, never complained. Still, it did not keep him from making some salient observations.

"You know, Doctor, we're in front of our Gloucesters. If the Oxfords cop it, we'll be in *front* of our front line," he said, with perfect composure.

I finished splinting a man's arm. It didn't look good, his fingers were all purple, maybe I had tied it on too tight. I loosened it a little.

"That would not be particularly good, Corporal Bradley. I should rather dislike that." The fingers got a little more color in them, good. The *front* of the front line. Bradley was right. We would be in front of the front line, if the Oxfords were annihilated. And so far, they were getting good and annihilated.

To restore the line, the Bucks, in reserve, were ordered up in the afternoon to counterattack. *That* should get things back to normal. I didn't relish the prospect of being in the very front of the British Army, armed only with splints, bandages, and a poorly functioning oxygen tank.

The Bucks marched right up through us, a fine body of men, with Colonel Dimmer, their commanding officer, riding in front on his horse. He seemed an easy target, and rather out of place on a modern battlefield. Brave as a lion he was, having already won the Victoria Cross. The Gloucesters cheered them on.

"Hit them for six, Bucks!"

"Let ol' Jerry taste some British steel, Bucks, have at 'em."

"Smash 'em up, Bucks!"

The Bucks waved back.

"If I see Kaiser Willy, I'll kick 'im in the arse for ya, Gloster boys!" They were smiling and confident, those Bucks.

German machine guns opened up, well behind our front line redoubts, and heavy German artillery blasted the Bucks just after they passed through us. Jerry started firing from all around. In less than an hour, those Bucks who got back, got back wounded. Colonel Dimmer had been shot dead off his horse. Mixed among the Bucks were more soldiers from the front line Oxfords. Towards evening we could hear the guttural sounds of German on both sides of the Aid Post. I remembered what John Leeds had said, back in Chichester, "There's no mistaking the sound of German."

Our three line defense system had broken. The Oxfords, in the first line, had virtually disappeared, and the Bucks, in the third line, had gotten blown apart in the counterattack. That left just one line, us, the Gloucesters. And my Aid Post on the Maison de Garde Road was IN FRONT of our line. I manned the only Aid Post in the world in No Man's Land. Oswald and I didn't sleep much that night, but we managed to bandage and evacuate the last man from our Aid Post before daylight.

During those last few hours, the fighting quieted down. Everyone needed a breather, and it was "all quiet on the Potomac." For no particular reason, I thought about Abe Haskell that night. I might not get another chance to write him soon. I might not get another chance to write him, period.

The Sunken Road   March 22, 1918

At daybreak, the forest of German guns opened up, and shells started dropping everywhere, again.

Bradley looked up the crest of the hill in front of us. He had to duck, our men were starting to fire over our heads at the Germans.

"Leftenant Gallagher, it is my very considered opinion that we may better serve the British cause in another location," Bradley said, with icy calm. A few more minutes in the Aid Post, and we would be dead or captured.

Heavy fog made it hard to see, but there were gray lumps moving around. They were starting to fire their rifles at our lines, that is, right over our heads. Our Gloucester line was firing too, right over our heads.

"Corporal Bradley, you may have a point there," I admitted.

We dashed across the field to the Gloucester trench line, shouting, "Don't shoot!" all the way. Good luck, or poor English marksmanship attended us, for we made it all in one piece.

This defensive position was a half-hearted affair, slapped together as if the British never thought they would need it. "You consider yourself invulnerable, just like Macbeth did." The ghost of Cahill was present in everything I saw. We moved our way down the trench to Battalion Headquarters, a little sheet iron shelter, with a large door opening to the east, meaning, the door faced the enemy. Colonel Lawson, in command of the Glosters (short for Gloucesters) for all of three days, was there, surrounded by other officers and messengers. Within minutes the air sounded like the neighborhood of a beehive, German rifles and machine guns began rattling at our position—four men in the doorway fell into the shelter, two dead, and two badly wounded.

We grabbed the wounded and prepared to scarper, in the direction of the woods. For the first time, I saw British soldiers crack. Many seemed to feel they were in a hopeless situation, they dropped their guns, and ran like hell for the cover of the woods. Then something extraordinary, unreal, "stuff of legends" happened right before my eyes. Colonel Lawson turned around, drew his pistol, walked back out in front of the trench, in full view of the enemy, and ordered his men to stick to their positions. Lawson's own fearlessness restored the men's courage, and the men did stick—many of them, poor fellows, never to get away.

We proceeded to the back of the woods, and immediately sent a message to Brigade Headquarters via two homing pigeons. (I wasn't convinced those birds did much good.) The nervous system of British command, the extensive telephone lines, had been smashed to pieces by the German artillery. Our men still held the trench in front of the woods, but the clever Germans were not coming straight on there. Instead, they laid a few machine guns in front of that line, continuing to sweep the parapet, keeping the men pinned down. Then the Germans began to work their way around either side of the woods, threatening to surround us. (Cahill's ghost again. This was a "new Jerry" we were fighting.) We knew where Jerry was, could follow his progress, because he continued sending up flares, some kind of signal to his own men to prevent his artillery from hitting him. These Germans appeared to have a good system for prying us loose from our positions. It was like playing chess with someone who clearly outclassed you, an opponent who read all your moves.

Colonel Lawson sent word back to the troops to retreat without delay, to avoid encirclement. He could have saved his breath, the men had already come to the conclusion it was time to retreat. Lawson directed the medical assistants and me to go on to a large abandoned railroad embankment about a mile back. There, we would find several old artillery shelters, and could set up an Aid Post, while the Colonel found another refuge for Battalion Headquarters.

A kind of sunken road led to this railroad embankment. As we walked down this road we heard an approaching sound, getting louder, the irregular RRRrrr of German aeroplanes. Three Boche planes had spied us and flew overhead. They came fast, at treetop level, firing their machine guns as they passed. Then they were gone, I thought. I looked back over my shoulder and was thunderstruck to see one of them circling, bearing down again toward the sunken road like an immense eagle.

There was something intensely personal about this turn of events. For months, I had been a kind of "group" target within the British lines. But here, walking along this sunken road, one man in a flying machine had spotted us, and he was putting us in the cross hairs of his machine guns. The biplane was red, with large black crosses on the wings. His head, flying cap, and goggles were plain to see as he straightened out his machine, coming in for the kill. To kill me.

He was coming toward us, only a few rods away, flying so low along the line of the road that his wings were only just above the banks of the sunken road.

His machine guns were spitting lead all around; I did not know what was best to do. There was not so much as a blade of grass to hide behind—was it best to lie flat, stand up straight, run, dodge or what? During the tense few seconds that followed I think I tried all of these, and as the singing lead tore up the dirt inches from my head or feet, the particular procedure was changed. The roar of the engine by then was almost upon us and strange to say I forgot any fear of getting hit by a bullet in my certainty that one of the propeller blades would hit me in the head as it went by.

Suddenly, he veered to the right, disappearing over the crest of the road. Where was he? As luck would have it, he had descended so low that when he turned for another go-around, his wheels touched the ground, forcing a landing. Not so much a crash landing, as an accidental landing. Some of our nearby soldiers jumped the pilot, and took him prisoner. They had to hustle him off in a jiffy, for we were in full retreat by now.

We reached the railroad embankment without further incident, and could see the enemy had penetrated deeply on either side of us. In a few minutes, Colonel Lawson and Captain Gray arrived. Just a few hundred yards away, a machine gun was sputtering wildly, the bullets twang-anging over our heads, and across the embankment. A gun directly *behind* us *had* to be one of ours, so the Colonel sent my orderly to "tell the damn fool to quit firing at us." Well, that "damned fool" turned out to be German, my orderly found out, none too soon, almost at the expense of his life. How were they getting around us so fast?

Efficient, these Germans. Pry us out of a line, lay a machine gun across our line of retreat, then mow us down in the open field. It was like coaxing a clam to open up, avoiding the hard shell, then snatching the soft, indefensible inside.

Colonel Lawson was more than a little worried about that machine gun, so he started scouting along a winding ravine, out of sight. In a few minutes a runner came to our shelter, shot through the arm. He was breathless and pale, blood running down his bicep and forearm, as he handed me a note from Lawson which read, "For God's sake get out of there right away, the place is surrounded." On the note he had diagramed a map of escape for us—backward across the open for 300 yards, to a small clump of trees, beyond which the ground sloped away again, affording some shelter. He had circled the clump of trees, as if to tell us, "get to the trees and you're home free."

I looked at the runner straight in the eyes. "Can you make it to the trees?"

He was still panting heavily from the run, hadn't registered the pain of his wound yet. The bullet had passed through the meaty part of his upper arm, but had not apparently broken the bone. It would hurt plenty, but he should be able to move.

"It's run with you or shake hands with Jerry, Doc, I'll take my chances with you," he said.

"Bradley?" I motioned towards the wounded man with my head. Bradley picked up my meaning.

"He's just a little slip of a thing, Leftenant. If he trips over his own feet, I'll pick him up and pop him in my vest pocket. Don't you worry about him,"

Bradley said. "Now, Leftenant, 'stand not upon the order of your going, but by all means go.'"

The time had come to run. And to run with dispatch.

The Germans had watched where the runner had entered the railway embankment, and they were waiting for their quarry to reappear.

We broke from the embankment and ran as if our lives depended on it—they *did* depend on it. There were six of us, and we ran Indian file. Bullets were no longer going twaa-aang overhead, they were going sssSSSss! right past my head. Dirt and grass were kicking up, too. I worried terribly that I'd step in a hole or trip on some odd piece of barbed wire laying around. ssSSss! ssSSss! Three hundred yards, those trees looked a long way off. Halfway to the trees was a patch of weeds. The first man running dove behind these weeds, we all piled in behind him. There was an almost imperceptible rise in the ground there, we all flattened behind it. We were halfway to the trees, under the flimsiest of cover, the German machine gunner knew right where we were. He couldn't see us, but he tore up the ground all around us, which was well dug up but not irrigated with any fresh American or British blood, I was glad to say. A minute or so passed, and he stopped firing. We waited, knowing he was waiting, too. Germans were going into the woods off to the right and left, so we couldn't stay where we were much longer. The morning fog had lifted, so the machine gunner had perfect visibility. Safety lay in that clump of trees 150 yards straight ahead, and death lay in the machine gun, 200 yards to our left.

We got our breath, then took off running with the devil on our tail. The second we appeared a stream of bullets began whizzing past. ssSSss! sssSSss! The man in front of me fell. He was hit in the arm, but dropped as if hit in the leg. I grabbed him by the good arm, he arose and we ran on. We made it to the woods in nothing flat. Twigs and branches snapped off the trees as the machine gun tried one last time to get us. But we were safe. Safe.

A few hundred yards in, the ground gradually rose again, to a crest revealing another open field. There, in shallow holes called "scrapes" (there were no trenches) were the remnants of the Brigade, all jumbled together—Scotsmen in their kilties, Glosters who'd just crossed that same field with me, and many fellows I didn't recognize. These men were covering our retreat with no artillery, few machine guns, mostly just rifles. A blind man could see they could not hold long. Each man in the field must have known it was a lost cause, but they were sticking there, so we could get away.

We all wandered back toward Beauvois—a village with another shallow line of defensive trenches. Darkness was approaching, and we hoped for a respite, but the Germans had somehow moved up their artillery, and began breaking shrapnel over our heads. Jerry seemed to know our every movement, probably from the prying eyes of all their planes. We marveled at the Germans' ability to get their guns up so quickly and greet us with this barrage. Their transport must be marvelous.

In Beauvois, I saw General White again. Just two days before, he had cheerfully predicted that "the Boche will get an awful drubbing." He himself had gotten drubbed. Now he was heading to the rear, face bathed in blood from a shrapnel wound, riding his horse with all the dignity of a king. The hackneyed expression "bloodied but unbowed" came to mind. In this case, it was quite literally true.

By dark, the German infantry had pulled up to within a hundred yards of our crude line and dug in. You could hear their spadework and distinguish snatches of their conversation. It was frightening to actually understand some of what they were saying. My high school German lessons had not been in vain, though I never imagined being close enough to the enemy to be able to use it. I didn't relish the thought of talking to the Boche.

By now all was chaos and confusion with the British. After two days of fighting, they were five miles back, a huge loss. From 1915 to 1917, armies had fought many months to advance just a few hundred yards. Now, in two days, the Germans had forced the British completely out of their trenches. Our division had suffered devastating losses, and we had no fixed lines, no redoubts, little artillery, and few, if any reserves. Nor did we knew who was covering our flanks. Facing this tattered division was a seemingly invincible horde of Germans. Their planes were forever pouncing on us, and reporting our position to their artillery. The artillery, in turn, moved forward quickly, and rained steel upon us in every field, road, and village. German infantry moved around us like water streaming past a rock. We'd make a stand in the woods, they'd go around the woods; we'd make a line in a field, then they'd go through the woods on either side. An intelligent, deadly, multi-headed monster, the German Army. The German soldier knew his business.

The road leading west from Beauvois, away from the Germans, was packed with straggling men looking for any pretext to keep moving to the rear. Officers were trying to call men out, stem the retreat, put men in the defensive line at Beauvois, but most of the men paid little, or no attention. To make matters worse, the British class system—officers representing the upper class, enlisted men the lower class—was breaking down under the severe strain of the retreat. In the orderly, structured world of the trenches, the officers maintained a kind of vaunted status, remaining somewhat aloof of the "rabble." Their authority was absolute, and woe to the enlisted man who crossed an officer. But the German offensive had smashed the accepted order. Men were separated from their regular officers, all accountability was lost. So the men started ignoring orders to get into the line—they just kept heading west.

The Casualty Clearing Station, (the most well-equipped of the medical treatment areas) had pulled up and left, leaving me the only medical service available. Setting up my own little area, I collected wounded men by the side of the road and improvised what treatment I could. I borrowed field dressings from knapsacks, tied bandages on with boot laces, and scrounged up a little bread and butter for the men from a destroyed quartermaster storehouse.

Some artillery wagons were passing by, "Hold up there a minute," I shouted to an artilleryman, "where's your commanding officer?"

"Uh," he looked back up the road, "he's uh, now that you mention it, I haven't seen him for quite a while." He didn't look eager to help me.

"OK, well, listen. You've got room on top of your wagon there for these three men on stretchers, do you see them over there?" I pointed to three men on the ground. Two couldn't walk because their legs were broken, one had lost his leg entirely.

"You will strap them to the top of your wagon, and hand them off to the first ambulance you see," I said. That was an order, not a request.

"Well, we're not really . . . " he looked up the road again, hoping his commanding officer would appear, hoping I would disappear.

"I said, *Corporal*, you will strap these men to the top of your wagon and deliver them to the first ambulance you see. I am a lieutenant and that is an order, now carry on." If he chose to resist my order, there was nothing I could do. It was like a poker game, and I was bluffing.

They loaded up the men and headed west. They hadn't called my bluff.

Lieutenant Gray, our adjutant, came along and told us the entire British Army was withdrawing, under cover of darkness, behind the Somme River. The plan was to cross at Voyennes, blow up the bridge, and dig in for defense on the other side. Our shallow defensive line at Beauvois was to be abandoned.

My battalion, the Glosters, had left their position in front of Beauvois and gone back by a different road with Colonel Lawson. Captain Gray and I had become separated from these men, so we headed back to the Somme by a different route. Gray was a former literature professor, and looked the part, bespectacled and owlish. In spite of this mild exterior, he had a reputation as a crack shot with a pistol, and had supposedly killed quite a few Germans. He himself never talked about it.

Captain Gray asked me if I knew anything about the lay of the land here. He emphasized that we both had a vested interest in getting across that bridge before it was blown up.

"Oh yes, Captain Gray. I was billeted here in reserve, even had a horse at my disposal, so I got to look around here quite a bit."

"So you think your Yankee ingenuity can get us back in one piece." He was grilling me, as if for an exam on Chaucer.

"You can count on it," I said, confidently. This professor wasn't going to intimidate *me*. Like the back of my hand I knew this place. Tonight, *I* would be the teacher, *he* the student. Night had fallen, but I was no longer the rank amateur, stumbling around like I had done outside La Vacquerie.

"Do you have a map, Lieutenant Gallagher?" Gray asked. Hah! A map.

"Don't need one," I tapped my temple, "the map's right in here." A doubting Thomas, he was. All the better.

Near the ruined village of Foreste, we arrived at a crossroads. I started down the road to the right. Captain Gray hesitated.

"The road to the left seems to go downhill, the kind of thing you'd expect if we were heading down to a river, and we are *supposed* to be going to a river. Are you sure we should be going right, Gallagher?" he asked.

"Look, I know these roads. I've ridden on them. I'm telling you, we go right." I looked up the road. "See those fellows up there, they'll tell us we're going the right way." These English officers, I thought, know-it-alls. Well I might be an American, but I knew a thing or two.

As we got closer, we could see four soldiers standing around, blowing into their hands to warm them up. They looked like they were taking their ease after a tough day's fighting. Their conversation became audible.

"*Später ist Jurgen gefallen, aber ich glaube er ist nur verwundet, nicht getötet.*"

"*Wirklich?*"

"*Ja. Stimmt. Ich hab' ihm gesehen, nicht so schlecht.*"

Captain Gray and I turned around, ever so slowly. We walked a good way down the road before I said anything.

"The left road does, in hindsight, seem to be the better choice, Captain Gray."

A Child's Gift   March 23–24, 1918

By daybreak, Gray and I had made it across the Somme and into the town of Mesmil. Fifteen minutes after we crossed the bridge, a thunderous explosion rattled the town and broke what few windows remained.

"Do you think we could have cut it any closer, Gallagher?" Gray asked, professorial glasses boring into me.

I leaped into a doorway, debris from the bridge was starting to fall into the street and I didn't want part of it to land on me. Gray jumped in the doorway, too.

"You could say that, yes," I said, steaming. At least Gray could have yelled at me, rubbed it in a little. But no, the whole night he had given me the silent treatment. He couldn't even *laugh* about it. We could have died, admittedly, when I led us right towards those Germans, but, it *was* kind of funny.

A rivet from the bridge came smashing into the concrete and bounced up. I was looking down at the time and the steel brim of my helmet was facing toward the ricocheting rivet.

Clang!

The force of the rivet dented my helmet and knocked me down. Stars danced in front of my eyes for a minute. Gray bent down and picked up the rivet.

"Yes, indeed, Gallagher. We did cut it close." He put the rivet in his pocket. "I'll keep this as a souvenir of your Yankee ingenuity." His lips started to curl up, just a little, just the faintest hint of a smile. Hallelujah! He *had* a sense of humor.

We got hold of a map from a passing artillery officer. Gray looked it over with a practiced eye.

"Mesmil. Mesmil. Here it is," he pointed to it on the map, using his souvenir rivet. "And here's where we started out last night." The rivet traced the route we took.

"Let's see, Lieutenant. Looks like your Yankee ingenuity took us on a twenty-one-mile hike to net out ten miles."

I scowled at the map, ever distrustful of cartographers.

French civilians were all astir, collecting what they could into a pitiful collection of wheelbarrows and carts, and heading west, as far away as possible from the Germans. Most of these people had fled the Boche before. (Americans, so far removed from the war's reality, had no concept of this, of fleeing before an enemy, scooping up children, a few mementos, some food, and venturing to God knows where, on dangerous, crowded roads.)

Gray and I set our bearings for Voyennes, but learned our Gloster Battalion had gone elsewhere. Navigating in daylight was much easier, and we ultimately found our comrades along the road to Billancourt. During our trek, Gray even loosened up a little, and almost told a joke, but he caught himself in the nick of time. When we caught up with the Glosters, we were shocked to see how few were left.

Of the original strength of 1,000 men, only about 250 remained. Having been with them for three months, I recognized many of the men, and missed many others. Our transport people finally caught up with us, and gave us a fairly good feed. It was our first good eat in three days.

All was quiet here. Later, in the afternoon, we received orders to move up to the Somme Canal at Breuil—that meant moving forward. After retreating for three days, doing whatever we could to get *away* from the Germans, it rattled me to move toward them again. But no one hesitated as we went forward.

We arrived at the Somme Canal around 10 P.M. British outposts were on the opposite side. The bridges were still intact, but had dynamite charges beneath them, ready to blow if needed. We slept the sleep of the dead that night, having gone two days with only occasional naps.

By morning's light we could see our protective "moat" of the Somme Canal was only a few yards wide. Slow moving and shallow, it was littered with debris: a man could wade across it easily. I had been hoping for something a little more substantial, a Rhine River perhaps, or a Mississippi during spring flooding. The village of Billancourt was across the canal, a stone's throw away. All day long a dispirited procession of wounded British kept coming over the bridge, through our position.

Civilians were packing and fleeing from Breuil and Billancourt, getting help from some poilus. There were no young men among the civilians, only old people and children. No doubt all the young men had been distilled out and sent off to the war long ago. Most the of the young women, too, had left these small villages, going to work in big city factories.

While walking down the road leading westward from Breuil, I happened upon an elderly lady and two small children. She was a thin, frail woman, pushing a wheelbarrow piled high with framed pictures, bedding linens, cookware, and toys. I helped her push it down the road a short way toward a setting sun, west, away from the Boche. When I left her, she started pushing it herself. It was so heavy, I knew she'd have to leave it behind sooner or later. The sight broke my heart, this kind of thing was happening over and over again in this part of France.

About a hundred yards away from her, I heard a high-pitched voice behind me.

"*Monsieur, monsieur le soldat! Anglais! Anglais!*"

It was one of the children with the elderly lady. He was shouting, "Mr. Soldier. Englishman!" He came up to me, I got down on one knee. (I wanted to be at his level, not look so much like a grown-up, look more like a kid.)

"*Monsieur le soldat. Merci beaucoup pour nous aider.* (Mr. Soldier. Thank you for helping us)."

"*De rien, de rien.* (You're welcome). *C'est mon plaisir* (It's my pleasure)."

"*Je voudrais vous donner quelque chose de'autre,*" he wanted to give me something, I couldn't quite make out the whole sentence.

"*Fait pas, fait pas* (You don't have to)."

"*Non, non. J'insiste. Ce n'est rien.* (I insist, it's nothing)."

He reached in his pocket and pulled out something wrapped in an old newspaper. Then he turned and ran back to the old woman with her cart. Tearing the paper away I saw the present was a tin soldier, painted horizon blue—the same color the poilus wore.

The wine cellars at Breuil were well supplied with champagne, and some of the poilus seemed more interested in liberating champagne from the cellars than in helping their countrymen. (The French Army was now sending reinforcements north to support the British, so we started seeing poilus more often.) As I passed one poilu on the village street, he tossed me a bottle.

"*Vive le roi George!* (Long live King George!)" he shouted. No use explaining to him I was American, not English. "*Vive la France!*" I replied in kind. That earned me another bottle of champagne. (Through all these years of war and privation, the average French household *still* held a tremendous amount of champagne. It seemed a priority to them.)

Famished for a drink, I popped the cork and drank half the bottle straight down. Nothing ever tasted so good before, or since. My new found poilu friend popped the next bottle. Before too long, I began to feel quite the fighting cock myself.

"Those Germans aren't so tough," I said, to anyone who was listening. They'd pushed us around long enough, God damn it, let's give them a piece of our mind. It was *high time* I got out on that canal bridge and let the Hun know just what I thought of him. I weaved my way toward the bridge, which was guarded by our Gloucester boys.

"Those Germans ain't so darn tough, huh?" I said, walking out onto the bridge.

Our men guarding the canal bridge looked like they agreed with my observation, though none were inclined to leave their trenches and join me.

"Yeah! Not so damn tough by a long shot!" I reiterated, to good effect.

The acoustics at our end of the bridge seemed inadequate to the task, so I stepped out to the middle of the bridge, just so the Boche would have no trouble hearing me.

"Uh, sir. I'm not sure you should be going out there," a guard warned me.

A shell landed in the canal, throwing up a spray of water.

"Missed! Nice shot, *Dummkopf! Ha ha! Deutschland kaputt!*" I shook my fist at them. That would put the fear of God in them, it would. "*Deutschland kaputt!*" Something caught my eye. "Oh look, there's two of the bastards now! Get a load of this, you sons-of-bitches!"

In the distance, on the far side of Billancourt, a pair of German cavalrymen appeared. They stopped. One of them pulled out a pair of binoculars, looking at the bridge. He lowered them, adjusted the focus, and looked up again. His comrade reached over and took the binoculars for himself.

I hope they enjoyed what I was showing them.

Encounter with a French Doctor   March 25, 1918

My fearsome display did not stem the German advance one iota, and may have actually encouraged certain elements among them, for they entered Billancourt that same afternoon. Snipers across the canal started making life unpleasant, one almost getting Col. Lawson as he entered Battalion Headquarters. My Aid Post was in a cellar across the street. Our troops were dug in along the water's edge, and now constituted the front line of the British Army.

Judging from the shell fire that began to come down on us, one would have thought the *entire* British Army was positioned in Breuil. Our numbers were so few by now, though, that enemy artillery rounds had a hard time finding anybody, and we took few casualties. There is a certain advantage to being "few and far between."

The bombardment that day was a nerve-wracking ordeal. Hour after hour, the shells sang, roared, blew up. Dust from crumbling buildings created an artificial haze which choked the men. The enemy made no move to cross the canal, content to hold us in position while their artillery pounded us. Sitting beneath this fire, I started to get an insight into the nature of shell shock (or NDNYD, or neurasthenia, or whatever the hell you were supposed to call it). There was no opportunity to return fire, or "get back" at the enemy. You just sat there, under the constant bombardment, your nerves wearing away, until you finally felt like snapping.

Late in the afternoon a rumor flared that the Germans had crossed the canal at Moyencourt, a mile to our right, and the men began to retreat. Major Day (he was in temporary charge, Lawson having gone to Brigade Headquarters) came to me in desperation, "For God's sake, Leftenant, help me get these men back. If we must leave this position, let us leave in order, not like a mob." I did what I could, and the Major bucked the men up a bit, and got them to return to their positions.

At dusk our patrols confirmed we were getting surrounded, we had only one direction to retreat—the road to Cressy, the same one the old woman had pushed her cart down. No one contested the decision to leave—we were all shot to pieces mentally, and just wanted to get out fast.

As we raced back toward Cressy, the Germans raked us with gun fire. Once again, they had pinned us down, outflanked us, and were now mowing us down as we retreated. It was maddening, we were dancing to their tune over and over again. Darkness provided *some* cover, but a few of our men fell nonetheless, some with a loud "Ow!"; some silently crumbling, like balloons losing air. During this retreat, many men from rear guard units sacrificed themselves so that others could get away. Good and faithful soldiers, all.

It would be impossible to recount or describe, to anyone who has not been a witness, the demoralizing effect of a big retreat. No telephones, no trenches, no hot meals, no plan. Few officers, few men. The daily loss of so many familiar faces. We were constantly being caught in a bottle and having to escape through the narrow neck of the bottle. From a medical standpoint, the retreat posed enormous problems—no ambulances and no way to contact them. Irrigating solution, to clean wounds, was hard to find and too heavy to carry. Bandages we had, but every time we ran from another position we had to leave some of them behind. And my supply of tetanus antitoxin was going fast. Lockjaw would appear soon, then full blown tetanus, a slow horrible death.

Bradley was a great help. Never a complaint. Never seemed to get tired. Carried as much as he could each time we left another post. He kept the precious tetanus antitoxin on him at all times.

We were trudging along some road nearing Cressy, shortly after the machine guns had raked us over.

"Corporal Bradley, we appear to be heading *away* from Berlin," I said. Joking in the face of disaster was part of "keeping a stiff upper lip"—so essential an element of the British character.

Bradley readjusted his heavy knapsack.

"That, sir, is a correct statement." Bradley's wit was as dry as the Sahara, and I loved him for it.

"So our blob defense didn't seem to hold back Jerry," I said. Cahill had been so right. The British thought themselves invulnerable in their trenches, and now the whole world was turned upside down.

"Sir, Napoleon hit it on the head when he said, 'God is on the side with the biggest battalions.' Right now, the Hun has the biggest battalions, and God sure seems to be on his side."

At the side of the road, in a ditch, I spotted the old lady's tipped over cart.

Bradley went on, "Nothing could have held Jerry back. No blob, no redoubt, no trench line, nothing. Only one thing could have stopped the Hun."

Overhead, in the dark, an aeroplane engine. RRRrrrr RRRrrr. At least he couldn't see us.

Bradley finished his thought, "More Brits. Only more Brits could have stopped them." He turned to me. "Or some Yanks."

The whole crowded road lit up in a white glare. A magnesium flare on a parachute floated down from the German plane. A few seconds passed, enough time for the German artillery to adjust their aim.

Eeeeeip! Whomp, whomp, whomp! Colored explosions broke over our heads, and metal fragments tore into the road. Everyone dove for the ditches.

Crump, crump, crump! The flare winked out, but the barrage continued. The Germans didn't need to see us anymore—they knew where we were and had the range. In five minutes the explosions came, without let up. I curled up, tighter and tighter. Shrapnel from air bursts made a fffft! sound. Crawling back to the old lady's tipped over cart, I slid underneath it. Her body was not underneath it, thank God, nor were the bodies of the children.

Glass crashed above me. Shrapnel must have hit one of her pictures. Something burned my left forearm. I reached to pick it off.

"Ow!" A hot piece of metal had come through the cart. Its passage through all the stuff had slowed the shrapnel down enough so the metal just rested on my arm, never penetrating the skin. The metal was as hot as a freshly baked potato, singeing my fingertips as I pulled it off. The barrage stopped. After a minute, I crawled out from under the cart. Standing before me was the unsinkable Bradley.

"Did I fail to mention that more *Frenchmen* would help too?" Bradley said, a smile breaking across his face.

I stood up, brushed myself off. My ears were ringing.

"Frenchmen? That's pretty high praise coming from an Englishman." Even *calling* them Frenchman was a compliment, usually he called them "frogs."

"Take a look," he pointed to a line of trenches just outside Cressy. It was dark, but I could see the unmistakable outline of the poilu helmet. From the light of a burning truck, you could see the horizon blue uniforms, the French!

We were overjoyed to see the French dug in. Someone now stood between us and trouble. I could have kissed them (they actually *did* kiss, once on each cheek, every now and then, I wasn't exactly sure when). Looking for a little medical camaraderie, I located the French Aid Station, *Poste de Secours*, in French. A Red Cross sign hung at an angle over a doorway. It looked more like a red "X". A French medical assistant ushered me into his Aid Post. A short man with sleeves rolled up was splinting a soldier's ankle. The soldier kept hissing in with each wrapping.

"Formidable, mon ami. Tu serás chez toi," he snapped his fingers, *"comme ça.* (Courage, my friend, you'll be home just like that)."

"Excusez moi, monsieur le docteur (Pardon me, Doctor)."

The doctor turned around: thin mustache, trim build, every inch the Frenchman.

"Oui, monsieur? (Yes, sir?)" he said.

"Je suis americain (I'm American), *est-ce que . . .* (and I . . .)?"

My French was petering out.

"Un Sammy! (A Sammy!)" he shouted.

He welcomed me, pulled up a chair, gave me a big kiss on either cheek and produced a bottle of wine from somewhere. My French was not up to snuff, and he spoke little English, so the following conversation was actually in German.

"You don't appear ready to evacuate," I asked him, looking around. Nothing was packed and ready to go.

"No," he said, swirling the wine around in the glass, savoring the bouquet. As he sniffed, his eyes closed and his head went up a little. This man did not have a care in the world.

"That line of yours out front doesn't look like it can hold off the Germans very long," I said, trying to make eye contact with him, but his eyes were still closed.

"No, it can't. It will crumble in no time at all." Now he opened his eyes and looked at me, smiling. "More wine?"

"Thanks." I held out my cup. Maybe I hadn't heard him right, or maybe I was translating wrong. He said his line would crumble, but he wasn't preparing to move. "What, exactly, will you do when that happens?" I asked.

"I will stay here with my men." He was serving the wine up as if we were sitting in a Parisian café, all he lacked was the towel over his arm. This man had nerves of steel. The Aid Post we were sitting in had about a dozen patients in it. None of them looked like they could move. There were a half dozen stretcher bearers.

"You will stay *here?*" I repeated.

"Yes." He looked at the wine bottle, it was just under half full. "Look, you might as well drink a little more of this wine. I would hate for the Boche to get it. They drink that sickly sweet Rhine wine." He spat on the floor. "Wine, they call it! It's grape juice. Unfit even to feed to the pigs. So, please, drink up. This is fine Burgundy. A little young," he shrugged his shoulders, "but still, good. The Boche, they would never appreciate it."

I obliged.

"Still, Doctor. You may not *just* get captured," I hesitated to say the obvious.

"Oh, I know that." He waved his hand dismissively, as if death were just a minor inconvenience. "But I cannot leave my men to the tender mercies of the Boche. I will stay with them." He broke into French. *"C'est la guerre!"* (A rough translation would be: thus is war; that's the way war is; what's to be done? *C'est la guerre* was used for any and all reasons. The French said it all the time.)

What had the Germans done so far in the war? —torpedoed hospital ships, massacred civilians in Belgium, and pioneered the use of poison gas. I had heard stories the Germans weren't slowing down to round up too many prisoners either, especially in a town. Quicker to toss a grenade in the cellar, or shoot a flamethrower down the stairs, then move on. Speed. Speed. Pause in the middle of a successful attack, to attend to twelve badly wounded enemy soldiers? Better to kill them and move on. Who would ever find out? Dead men tell no tales.

"You're *sure* of that, Doctor?" I asked again.

This Aid Post was small. One grenade could kill everyone in it. The explosion would tear apart the closely-packed men, and shrapnel would bounce off the walls until it found something soft to sink into. I had seen a dugout that had suffered such a fate, once. Nothing left but smudges of bodies along the walls. And if a flamethrower poked its nozzle through the door . . .

"You know, Doctor," the Frenchman said to me, picking up on my concern for him, "one must not worry about such trifles. If God, in his infinite mercy, chooses to take me up in his arms tomorrow, it will at least spare me one thing."

"What is that?"

"Perhaps it would be worse to survive. They would force me to drink German wine for the rest of the war." He emptied the Burgundy into both our glasses, threw the bottle in the corner, and raised his glass.

"*Vive la France!*"

A Letter to Mom   March 26, 1918

We marched ten miles back to the town of Roye, arriving there at 3:00 A.M., March 26. Fatigue dogged my every step—I had never been so tired. On one occasion, when we stopped for a few moments' rest, I went to sleep standing up. When everyone started marching off, I stood in the road dead asleep, chin on my chest. Bradley had to come back and shake me awake.

About 5:00 A.M. we got orders to march back on the road leading northwest toward Amiens. (Amiens was the largest city in the Somme area, a major rail center and marshalling area for the British Army. It was an obvious target of the German advance.) This road we marched on was the main thoroughfare for the Amiens area, dating back to Roman days. The scene along that road beggared description. Our Gloster battalion was swallowed up in the exodus. It seemed the whole British Army, transport, guns and all, was marching back along this ancient Roman trail. French civilians, with their overburdened carts, jammed the route. By the side of the road lay litter of all descriptions—household goods, artillery pieces, rifles, clothes, broken wagons, and here and there a body. One wondered if Napoleon's retreat from Moscow looked any worse.

Progress was slow due to the congestion. When one wagon stopped, everything else stopped, accordion-fashion, then it took a long time to get going again.

In one village, a young Frenchman approached me trying to give away his young calf. With a significant motion across his throat, he indicated what the Boche would do, so we might as well have the calf. Better "*les Anglais*" (the English) get a meal than "*les salés Boches*" (the dirty Huns).

At Meziers we stopped to rest. We handed a transport company the calf, to do with as they pleased, and they gave us a good meal. (Curiously, none of our men could find it in themselves to kill the calf, though they had no qualms about killing Germans.) The men were extremely weary and footsore, with terrible blisters. Armies were *supposed* to be able to march, but years in the trenches, with little movement, had softened the men's feet. They had only used their feet for marching to or from the lines, standing in their posts, or occasionally dashing across No Man's Land in a raid, but they had done no sustained marching for a long time. Ambulances were nearby, and many men could have asked to be sent back, so severe were their blisters, but nary a single man asked to be relieved. Every single one of those Glosters stuck it out.

During a rest stop, I inspected their feet, wondering how to help them with their blisters. There was no ointment around, and the only effective treatment was rest, but that was not an option. A helpless feeling was coming over me. Who came to my rescue? The men themselves. The privates and corporals—enlisted men who endured all and overcame all—shrugged off the blisters, the retreat, the Germans. And they did it all with their unbreakable humor and good spirits.

"Never you mind these blisters, Leftenant, I'll toughen 'em up in no time," one man said. (He must have been new, for his face looked unfamiliar. But he carried on like a veteran.)

"Don't you worry about old Tommy here, Doc, we can keep marchin'; we can retreat all the way to the Bay of Biscay, if we have to. We'll turn it around," another said, with a big grin.

"Jerry's got us on the run now, but you just wait, we'll give him a nasty knock, you'll see." This man I recognized, he had been guarding the bridge in Breuil when I showed the Germans a piece of my . . . mind.

"The Hun might have won this one, but we'll win the last one," he went on.

"That's right. We always win the last battle. All that matters is the score at the end of the test match, doesn't matter who's ahead half-way through." All this came from men with bloody feet, no transport, few officers, few weapons, little food, less rest, and in full retreat from the unstoppable juggernaut of the German Army.

These Tommies were a tough lot.

Rumors flew. The French were counterattacking, then they weren't, then they were again. The Germans had a new poison gas. The Americans had finally arrived. In our weariness and fatigue, we believed anything and everything, we grasped at straws.

We hoped to stay for the night and rest, but were ordered back down the road again, toward the Germans to defend the great Roman road between the villages of Hangest and Le Quesnel. We had *just* escaped the lion's closing jaws, and were about to get the rest we needed, when we had to turn around, double back three miles, and man another hopeless position. If we stood and fought here, it would be like the disastrous fight at Breuil all over again: a hastily prepared position with too few men to adequately defend it, a heavy German artillery bombardment, the Germans would out flank us, then we would dash through another field, with men getting gunned down all around. Every other time, we had escaped the trap by the narrowest of margins, but this time we might not get out.

Time to write Mother.

I sat down beside the roadside, with a pad of paper on my knee, a pencil in my hand. Not wanting to worry Mother, I took a bit of author's liberty.

March 26, 1918

Dear Mom,

If fresh air and exercise are good for you, then I must certainly be in fine shape, for I am getting plenty of both, lately. My British comrades are good fellows, and do their own mothers proud every day, so brave they are. Not that you really need to be so brave, as my job is comparatively safe. Give my best to everyone in Waseca.

Let Sister Marie Francis know that I attend Sunday Mass at each occasion that presents itself.

Love,
Ben

To ease my father's mind, I scratched a note to the American Express Company in Paris, requesting them to cable my father the following:

Dad Stop Safe and Well Stop Love to All Stop Ben.

Between the two correspondences, I hoped one would reach my folks. What with the disorganized state of the mails, I couldn't be sure if anything would get through, but it was worth a try. Our chaplain took the letters and headed back to the transport lines. I didn't know when, or if, there would be a chance to contact my family again.

We went forward.

Thick as Bees   March 27, 1918

March 27 was quiet on our section of the Roman road. (We were defending the road between the towns of Le Quesnel and Hangest.) No Germans were in sight, but their artillery boomed closer and closer all day long. Colonel Lawson sent Major Day forward to scout our situation. As I had nothing to do, I got hold of a horse and rode forward with the Major. Sitting up atop a horse made me feel a little conspicuous, but the danger seemed remote, as we could see no Germans.

We rode three or four miles forward to the village of Bouchoir, left our horses at the western end and walked to the eastern end of town. A few shells were landing near some scattered outposts of our men. Our positions seemed so weak that a strong gust of wind could have pushed them aside. What we saw next coming up the road was no gust of wind.

For almost a week now, an almost invisible enemy had plagued us. Heavy fog hid the Germans the first few days. Their attacks were stealthy, with men jumping from shell hole to shell hole in small groups. Most of the time all we saw of the Germans was the twinkling of their machine guns as they cut us down crossing another field. So, Major Day and I were amazed at what we saw on that road.

Germans! Thousands of them, packed together so tightly they seemed to form a solid gray mass twisting all the way to the horizon. Wagons and artillery pieces poked up here and there. There was no end to them. Thick as bees they marched along in broad daylight with no attempt at concealment.

Riding back a mile or so to an English battery, we arrived with the horses in a lather.

Day jumped off his mount.

"Quick, man, who's the C.O. here?" Day was in a lather, too.

An enlisted man took the reins of the horse and pointed to a man walking up to us. He had a big mustache that made him look like a walrus. He introduced himself.

"Captain Davon. How may I help you Major . . . "

"Day. Major Day," he held out his hand and shook Davon's.

"Captain Davon, listen, about two miles due east of here, in a straight line between those two houses," Day held his arm straight, pointing between two farmhouses, "there must be a whole division of Germans walking right up the road."

"Oh," Davon looked toward the two houses. "That's rather close."

Day's voice went up a notch, "They are out there, Captain, jamming the road. You've got to fire on them. Now!"

"Oh, I'm afraid that's rather out of the question." Davon's voice was incredible. He turned down the request to fire his guns as if he had turned down a social engagement.

"What?" I asked, irritated. By now, I was off my horse, too. It was not my place to order around artillery units, but I was so tired, so worn down by all this retreating, that my fuse was cut pretty short. Davon looked at me, surprised a medical officer should behave so brazenly.

"Well, you see, sir, I'm afraid I've got no map of this area, no grid coordinates. So I'm afraid I can't just blast away like it's a holiday or something," Davon said, his palms up, as if to say he were completely helpless. Holiday, he said! Holiday! When those Germans marched between those two farmhouses, he'd be celebrating a holiday all right. THE END OF THE WORLD, that holiday!

Major Day was stomping around waving his hands. "You don't *NEED* a map. I'm telling you, point your guns over those farmhouses, shoot two miles, and you can't miss. There are an ocean of them out there, and they are coming this way. Now shoot damn you! Fire those guns!"

Davon looked shocked. He wasn't about to take orders from a raving lunatic infantry officer and his doctor sidekick.

"Calm down, please. You'll upset the men." Davon tilted his head toward the right, towards his men. The men were just sitting by their guns, dog tired. They weren't even preparing to withdraw.

"Would you like a little tea before you go?" Davon asked, completely unruffled.

Day looked at Davon, unbelieving.

I snapped. "Tea? Tea! Tea at a time like this? The whole God-damned German Army is about to land in your lap, and now it's time for tea. Well la dee da!" My arms were going, I was walking around in circles, stomping my feet, my face reddening, my voice rising with each word.

Day tried to calm me down, but to no avail. He put a hand on my shoulder, but I shrugged it off. The artillerymen by their guns had perked up a little bit, happy to have some entertainment.

"You damned Englishmen and your tea, I swear! Tea in the morning, tea at night. Tea and biscuits. Tea and jam. Tea, tea, tea, tea, tea! Tea to celebrate a victory or console a defeat. And now we're about to get swallowed alive, like Jonah in the whale, so it's time for tea." I was not finished, was NOT finished, and I would have my say. Day was pulling me back to my horse, apologizing for me, getting me up on the horse, leading me away. Nothing could shut me up.

"I swear to God, when the Judgement Day comes, when the Four Horsemen of the Apocalypse appear from the depths of hell, you will offer them each a cup of that God-damned tea!"

By now, we were riding away, Day leading my horse by the reins. He seemed angry at me, but he didn't speak for some time.

"A word of advice, Gallagher." We were trotting now, going through pretty green countryside, a cool breeze on us. Day had returned the reins to me. The Germans were well behind us, the artillery unit was behind us, and I had finally gotten a hold of myself. By now, of course I was embarrassed by my outburst. All those days without sleep had worn me to a frazzle, but I had no right to yell like that. And I hadn't just yelled at the artillery officer. I had insulted tea itself! Tea, the lifeblood of the British Army, of the whole British Empire. I would be persona non grata for a while.

"Yes, Major Day." Mine was the voice of the chastised child.

"Let's not make a spectacle of ourselves," Day said. In his eyes, I had committed the only unforgivable offence a British officer could commit. I had failed to keep a stiff upper lip.

That night around 10:00 P.M., we were relieved by the French, and ordered to go back somewhere near Amiens for reorganization. Our three battalion brigades had nearly disappeared: the Glosters now numbered 250 men; the Oxfords 80, and the Bucks about 100. Most of our casualties came on March 21–22. We lost a few men to shell fire in Breuil, and a few more to machine gun fire while evacuating that town.

What became of our wounded during these days? Those able to walk, or men fortunate enough to be carried to ambulances, got away. Those too badly wounded to move simply lay where they fell, to be overrun and, we hoped, cared for by the enemy. We hoped and prayed for our lost men. Many were dead, we knew, but a lot of them *must* be alive. Alive and in a German hospital.

The conversation with the French doctor haunted me. Like a captain going down with his ship, the French physician would not leave his men, even if it meant losing his own life. And he had been perfectly calm. This Frenchman, and the French in general, seemed more humanitarian than the British in the question of what to do with the wounded during a retreat. (I had been with the British for a long time now, and had adopted many of their ways, but I couldn't stop thinking about that French doctor. Capture? Death? *C'est la guerre!* he would say. What would I say?)

As for myself, I had come a long way since that day in the emergency ward at Minneapolis City Hospital. By now I could splint, tie off, bandage, and clean out almost anything in no time. Maxwell's infusion of confidence in Chichester, plus that first day by La Vacquerie, working like a madman alongside Craig in that dugout, had made me grow immensely. Then four more months of front-line work, taking care of everything from infected feet to a chest full of shrapnel, had turned me into a real battalion medical officer.

After the French relieved us, we marched back to Mezieres, arriving at midnight, only to stand around shivering for hours. "Where do we go from here?" was the question of the hour.

In pitch darkness our question was answered. A number of motor lorries came up, with their usual hooded lamps, and we piled aboard, bound, it was rumored, for Villier-Brettoneux for some rest. I was happy to get a ride, until one of the soldiers took me aside and explained that trucks were not necessarily a good thing.

"Lorries often mean a quick trip to a nasty job, sir," he said. "Me, I'd rather walk."

We drove all night, lurching along gutted roads in total blackness, moving slowly, hardly faster than a walk, sometimes stopping for 15 or 30 minutes at a stretch. Somewhere, after stopping awhile, we turned right. It was not yet dawn when we pulled up in the square of a small village and unloaded.

The name of the town was Marcelcave.

Over the Top and Lots o' Luck   March 28, 1918

The entire 61st Division, about 1,000 strong, was positioned around the city of Marcelcave. These 1,000 men represented a pitiful remnant of the roughly 10,000 men in the Division just one week before. (Just as our Brigade lost about 90 percent of their men, so had our Division.) French civilians had abandoned Marcelcave in a hurry, leaving foodstuffs of every kind in their houses, which our hungry men ate up.

At the north end of the village was a wide and deep railway cutting—a ready-made trench for our men to occupy.

The Germans were pursuing more slowly, but they had already reached the next village back, La Motte. Geographically, it was a mile or so off to the northeast, with a rising slope between us. Low grass grew on the slope, no trees, no bushes, no cover of any kind. About noon, Jerry began to shell Marcelcave and the railway cutting very heavily, continually raking the top of the cutting with machine gun fire. Our men kept low in the cutting, pinned down. The Germans weren't stupid enough to charge across an open field toward us.

Word came to our division to attack the German-held village that afternoon. The news came as a shock. Attack? Could that be right? With ninety percent of our men lost, and at a time when we needed every last soldier to hold a position, we were going to attack? Attack across an open field? Surely Colonel Lawson would not send his men out of the protected railway cutting and up that slope. It would be suicide. Perhaps the men would balk, refuse the orders, or maybe just make a show of it then jump right back under cover. But to attempt to cross that completely open field in broad daylight? It was beyond the power of men to do it, or even attempt it!

The 61st Division WAS going to attempt it. The men knew the score, and they were going over the top, without a second's hesitation. In the scheme of things, they had to know that this tiny counterattack, just a thousand men, was not going to stop or even slow this enormous German offensive. But, "theirs not to reason why, theirs but to do and die."

Promptly at 3:00 P.M. an officer shouted, "Over the top and lots o' luck," and blew his whistle. Our men advanced slowly, keeping as close to the ground as possible, stopping every hundred yards or so for a rest. About halfway up the hill, the entire enemy village opened up. Earth and grass flew up, all the men hit the ground at once. Some laid still, some rolled around, but most started feverishly scraping little mounds of dirt in front of their heads. A few actually returned fire.

Once in a while, a man would jerk crazily, as if a puppet on a string. Some men found a crease in the field and crawled back under its protection to the railway cutting. Officers shouted, "Fall back!" It was as one-sided an affair as a firing squad, and lasted just a few minutes. What a waste! What a waste of men!

Within minutes the wounded started coming in to the railway cutting. Wounded who could walk were sent west; those who could not were sent back with me to my cellar Aid Post in Marcelcave. The cellar was a sturdy structure, under a half-wrecked timber house. In front of this house was a courtyard, containing a well. Twelve or fifteen steps led down to the Aid Post which measured about 30 feet by 25 feet. We could fit over a dozen men in it. It had no furniture, except for some old boxes to sit on. A number of shelves, long enough to hold a stretcher, were along the walls. The cellar looked like a front-line dugout, except the walls had nicer boards. It looked more "civilian."

We needed ambulances desperately, but I didn't know where they were, or how to send for them. With the heavy shelling of the area, it was doubtful any could get through anyway.

After the failed attack, Colonel Lawson and Major Day left the railway cutting and moved into Marcelcave where they set up a Battalion Headquarters in some cellar about a block away from my Aid Post. Lawson seemed completely unruffled by the disastrous assault, and assured me we would hold the railway cutting, and the village, for the night, at least. My optimism did not match his.

I resolved to evacuate as many men as possible. Every man who could possibly walk was sent westward. Many were weak from loss of blood and said they couldn't make it, until I called their attention to the enemy machine guns even now starting to work their way around our right and left flanks. That put the fear of God in them, and they limped out.

We had no supplies but what we carried on our backs. Luckily, we came across an abandoned Dressing Station in another cellar, and liberated what remained of its bandages, splints, blankets, and instruments. Bradley proved invaluable, as always.

A lot of men could not walk due to fractured limbs, gunshot wounds to the abdomen, and mutilating wounds of all description. For these, we ransacked the neighboring courtyards for carts, wagons, and wheelbarrows. Those men with minor wounds pushed those with severe wounds towards the west, and safety.

I worked like a machine—treating men, loading them onto carts, all the while amidst shellfire, and the ominous progression of German machine guns, farther and farther in our rear. Finally, there was one cart left. Bradley and I loaded it with a man shot through the hip. That left 18 men still in the cellar. None of them could push the cart, they were all too badly wounded. My other assistants had already gone to the west, pushing carts themselves.

"Corporal Bradley, push this cart yourself," I said. Shells were digesting the town. eeeEEEYIP! Kaboom! Glass shattered about a block away, and timbers shot up into the air.

"Yes, sir," Bradley said. He looked around, saw there were no more carts, no more assistants. eeeeEEYIP!-YIP!-YIP! Kaboom! Boom! Boom! An entire, intact window frame rose up over the courtyard, and landed next to the well, smashing to peices. We both turned our eyes away, fearing the glass. There was a moment's quiet afterwards.

"One thing. Leave that knapsack, the one with the tetanus antitoxin. And see if you can find where the motor ambulances are," I said.

Bradley put down the knapsack, placed his hands on the cart, but hesitated for a moment.

"Carry on, Oswald. That is an order."

Bradley pushed the cart off to the west, his silhouette disappearing with the setting sun. Dusk was coming on. I sat down in the doorway of the cellar, far enough back to be protected from any more flying window frames. The German shelling lifted from my immediate area and moved north, towards the railway cutting. My eyes closed for, what I thought was just a second, but I must have dozed for a few minutes. When I opened my eyes, it was dark in Marcelcave.

The Cellars of Marcelcave   March 28, 1918

I was about to descend into the cellar when the German shellfire stopped. This was of considerable significance, for why should they raise their artillery unless they were about to enter the village? To the west, Verry lights (flares to indicate the German positions) went up. Marcelcave was surrounded. A sprint over to the railway cutting, revealed a few rifles, some abandoned back packs, a fluttering copy of the *London Times*, and one headless corpse, but no living soldiers. The battalion had scarpered, had retreated, and no one had told me. I was alone.

It is said that "once to every man and nation comes the moment to decide." This surely was my moment and like a flash from a clear sky it was upon me. Could I get away in the gathering darkness? Should I run away to save myself from capture, or worse, and abandon the men who were crying to me for help? The answer came fast and easy, I had never made a decision I was so sure was right.

The moment had arrived, life or death, freedom or captivity. I had chosen the only way possible that would allow me to look my friends in the face again, if indeed I should live to see my friends again. I would stay. No more could I leave those men than I could cut off my own hand.

I went into the cellar and lit a candle for light. Eighteen wounded men lay all about, with bandages, splints, rifles, and knapsacks scattered across the floor. I did what I could for the men, giving each a little water, trying to prop them in a comfortable position.

One soldier was having a terrible time breathing. His clothes were not torn, nor were there any bloodstains. I helped him sit, finally propping him up onto a box, it was the only way he could seem to draw enough air into his lungs. He could finally breathe well enough to talk.

"It's my side, my ribs," he gasped.

His rib cage had a bumpy, crackly feel to it. His ribs were broken, and air was leaking out of his lungs, under his skin, giving it a crunchy feeling—"subcutaneous emphysema," in medical parlance.

"Mortar, Doc." He caught his breath. "Right in front . . . felt like . . . thunderclap." He could only say a few syllables at a time.

"All right. We'll bind you up. Hold tight," I said.

Some gauze lay on the floor, I picked it up, stood behind the soldier, and started winding the gauze around his chest. We were both now facing the stairway that led to the outside courtyard.

A distant popping sound started drifting down the stairs.

"Sounds like . . . Jerry, Doc."

A short burst of machine gun fire, a little closer now. But it was a Lewis gun, a British gun—one of ours!

"Sounds like one of ours out there," I said, hoping by some miracle our men had re-entered the town.

"No, Doc . . . it's Jerry . . . he likes our . . . Lewis guns."

It was a British gun all right, but held in German hands. Jerry did like our air-cooled Lewis gun, it was lighter than their water-cooled machine guns.

Ka-whump! Ka-whump!

The cellar shook. The sounds were getting closer.

"Grenades . . . in the . . . the cellars . . . mopping up." The soldier's gasping staccato was getting more tense, I could feel his nervousness. There was no way to escape from this cellar, there was just the stairway, and Jerry was getting close to the stairway.

Ka-whump! Ffffff-hwooooosh! What was that sound?

The soldier stiffened, tried to get off the box, tried to get away from the stairway.

"Hold still! I'm almost done, here," I said.

He turned around, all the way, looking at me. Just turning around had exhausted him. He tried to say something, but was too short of breath. He inhaled as hard as he could, tried to speak again, formed his lips, but again ran out of steam. Gathering himself, he took one long deep breath in.

"Flamethrower." His eyes read terror. This man had endured artillery, mortars, and machine guns. But a flaming death in a closed room, burned alive . . .

Ka-whomp! The cellar shook again, dust floated down. That sounded like the building next door.

Fffff-hwoosh! Crackling sounds followed the hwooshing sound. The cellar next door had just gotten incinerated.

Outside our cellar, boots crunched on the broken masonry and bricks. A surprisingly high-pitched voice was shouting orders, and more boots came crunching up to the entrance to our cellar.

"*Nächste! Hier. Bereit? Schnell. Flammenwerfer!* (Next one, over here, ready? Quick. Flamethrower!)"

There was a click, clicking sound, then a loud ffff!

"*Verwundeten hier! Schiessen Sie nicht. Wir ergeben uns!* (Wounded here, don't shoot, we give up!)" I shouted. God don't do it. Don't do it. Don't burn these men alive. Don't burn me alive.

Ffffffffff! That had to be the primer, or the trigger mechanism on the flamethrower. In a split second, yellow flames would come shooting down the stairs and hit me right in the chest. How fast does it take you to die when you are drowning in flames?

"*Halt!*"

Click, click. The ffff sound stopped.

The wounded soldier let out a sigh, a short sigh, but a sigh.

"Glad you . . . speak Ger . . . German, Doc."

He had wet his pants. My own mouth was warm and salty, for I had bitten the inside of my cheek so hard it was bleeding.

The first thing we saw was a pistol. Whoever was coming down the stairs was taking no chances, crouching low and going down pistol first. Next came his boots—covered in brick dust, then his face. It was a baby face, not a whisker on it. The coal-scuttle helmet over that baby face looked rather out of place. As the rest of him appeared, I noticed his pants had leather knee pads on them, and one of them had torn open. Underneath, he had a skinned knee. It looked like he had tried to slide into second base on a playground.

He looked around, then shouted "*Kommt doch herunter!* (You guys come on down here!)"

Four men with bayonets came down the stairs. They were older than their officer. Their faces were drawn—all business. The flamethrower man didn't appear. The young officer with the pistol took in the room, with a glance.

"*Sprechen Sie Deutsch?* (Do you speak German?)" he asked.

"Ein bischen (A little).*"*

"Arzt? (Doctor?)*"* he said.

"Ja (Yes).*"*

He was decent; this boy non-com. He told me to stay there and care for the men, ambulances would come up soon and take them away. As he was heading out of the cellar, he stopped, then turned around.

"Sein Deutsch ist gut, Herr Leutnant, aber sein Accent ist ganz anders. Sind Sie Engländer? (Your German is good, but your accent is quite different. Are you an Englishman?)*"*

"Nein, Amerikaner (No, American).*"* He raised his eyebrows.

So that was it. I was captured, they hadn't killed me. *Perhaps* my speaking German helped. It's hard to kill a man who speaks your own tongue.

In a few minutes, some other German officers came along.

"You are the American?" one asked me in English. Word must have gotten out there was an American and the Germans' curiosity was piqued.

"Yes."

He turned to his fellow officers, explaining the whole situation. He spoke so fast I couldn't follow along. They nodded vigorously at this amazing "find" and all regarded me with wonder, but no one showed any antagonism. I felt not unlike a rare and curious specimen at the zoo.

"How interesting that you here are. We heard that an American was here come and we wanted to see if that true was." The German was translating literally. (In the German language, the verb tends to come at the end of the sentence.) It came across as stilted and funny sounding.

One of his comrades whispered something to him.

"Oh yes. Please to stay here. Outside is dangerous. British shells soon will be here falling. Soon the ambulances will come."

They saluted me and left the cellar.

That night and the whole next day passed without any relief.

My second night, I found myself holding a 1/4 grain morphine tablet to my lips. In my other hand, I had a canteen cap of water—oh, to sleep, to rest. It had been over 24 hours since my capture, and I was still in the cellar. And I had not slept. Two men with belly wounds and one with a crushed pelvis had died.

No ambulances had come up, the British shellfire had been too heavy. That same shellfire had driven the wounded men, and me, nearly mad. It was endless.

Ker-whump. Ker-whump. Ker-WHUMP, Ker-WHUMP, KER-WHUMP, KER-WHUMP, KER-whump, KER-whump, ker-whump. Up and down the street the shells fell, in maddeningly methodical British fashion. Like a giant's footsteps, up and down each and every street in Marcelcave. One could tell exactly when the pattern of shells would walk over one's head. Then hunks of ceiling would rain down, the steps would fill with debris, and the shells would walk away again. I had to unbury the men, with my bare hands, by myself. All the other men were too wounded to help.

A few German *Sanitäter* (medical orderlies) had helped me round up some potatoes and water earlier that day. The Germans warned me that the English had probably poisoned the wells, but I told them we didn't poison wells, and drew water freely from the one in the courtyard.

"*Sehen Sie? Kein Gift. Schmeckt gut!* (See? No poison, tastes good!)" I said to them, as I drank the water. They seemed disappointed when I didn't keel over dead.

Later, a shell hit that very same well, smashing it to pieces, putting us in a terrible bind. Each man now got only a tiny sip of water, no more than the cap of a canteen. Of course, there was no water for cleaning the men, let alone flushing out their dirty wounds. The specter of tetanus arose.

I had gotten about halfway around the room, injecting each man with the precious anti-tetanus medicine, when a beam came loose from the ceiling and landed on my knapsack, smashing the precious vials Bradley had left me. The men toward the back, about eight of them, didn't get any of the tetanus antitoxin.

Everyone was filthy and covered with lice. The poor wounded men couldn't even get up to relieve themselves, so they lay in their own urine and feces. It had been a terrible twenty-four hours, the worst in my life, and now I was looking at a morphine tablet to offer me a little relief. It was wrong, of course, for a doctor to take morphine, but I desperately needed rest. Maybe just a couple hours' sleep. And this morphine tablet would do it. Just one tablet. Just this once. As the tablet was about to cross my lips, an unseen force seemed to say, "There is always a first time," and I put the morphine tablet back in the bottle.

Ka-pow!

I jumped, the bottle flew into the air. It fell to the ground and broke into a million pieces. Someone had fired a rifle right there in the cellar. Picking up a candle, I went to the back of the cellar, from where the shot had come.

"'E couldn't take it, sir. Couldn't take it no more," one soldier told me.

Propped up against the wall was the man with the broken ribs, the one with the subcutaneous emphysema who had so much trouble breathing. The top half of his head was off, a rifle lying in what had been his mouth. He hadn't been able to reach the trigger with his finger, so he had used a bayonet to push the trigger. Brains, hair, and blood had splattered the wall, the ceiling, and nearby men.

"I don't suppose you'd be having any more of those morphine tablets, would you sir. I don't know that I can take too much more myself either."

I held the candle to the man who'd just spoken. His hands and feet had been blown off, and there was shrapnel in the rest of his body.

"What's your name, son?" I asked.

"Cave, George Cave, sir." He managed a smile, in spite of his terrible wounds.

"I'll get us out of here, George," I promised. George had been in the back of the cellar. He had received no tetanus antitoxin.

"Don't worry, I'll get us out of here."

A machine gun detachment. Curious the Germans should send us a machine gun detachment to help evacuate the wounded. One never thought of machine gunners as angels of mercy, but they were angels of mercy to us. And I certainly had gone through hell to get those angels.

Very frustrated, the morning after the suicide, I marched right through the middle of occupied Marcelcave—in full British uniform—hoping to get "recaptured." The town was swarming with German soldiers, but I had such a determined look on my face that they parted like the Red Sea. Nobody shot at me, but something finally clicked with one of their Landsers (privates), and he shoved a rifle at me.

"*Hände hoch!* (Hands up!)" he said. That was how Germans said "surrender!"

He looked proud, he had captured an officer.

"*Ich muss mit deinem Oberst sprechen, jetzt gleich!* (I must speak to your officer, right now!)" I said, in no uncertain terms. I would out-Prussian these damn Prussians. He marched me away, but on our way, we ran into three drunken enlisted men, one of them seemed none too friendly.

"*Engländer?*" he asked (English?). "*Und ein Offizier* (And an officer)." There was a sneering, mocking tone in his voice.

With this, he reached for his bayonet and pretended to unsheathe it, then mimicked a stabbing motion into my chest. The other two enlisted men apologized and pulled him away. All three of them were drunk as lords. Come to think of it, *most* of the Germans in the town looked drunk. Maybe French wine would stop the Germans, rather than English guns.

"*Entschuldigen Sie bitte*, (Excuse me, please)" my captor said sheepishly, and took me on to some sort of headquarters. The officer there looked plenty busy, but I got his attention by putting on my outraged Prussian act.

Ich bin Artzt and ich habe viele Verwundeten in diesen Kellern. Sie gehören im Krankenhaus oder Lazarett! (I am a doctor and have several wounded men. They belong in a hospital or Field Dressing Station!) "*Sie müssen meine Männer rausnehmen!* (You must get my men out). *Oder ich ein Bericht schreibe* (Or I will write a report). *Das ist ein Befehl!* (That is an order!)"

An order and a threat to write him up—that was enough to unnerve any German. He gave me just what I needed.

He assigned a machine gun officer and eight of his men to help us. We found more carts, and wheeled vehicles in nearby buildings, and started loading up the wounded men. Another man in the cellar had died in the interim (his spinal cord had been severed at the level of his shoulders, he never had a chance). British shells were dropping, marching up and down the streets again. The German officer, a young fellow who looked very much like Abe Haskell, was absolutely fearless, calmly loading my men on carts, all the while smiling. The closer a shell hit, the "louder" he smiled.

We finally got all the surviving men out, leaving five bodies in the cellar. Before I parted company with this brave machine gun officer, I had to ask him, "*Wohin jetzt?* (Where to now?)"

"*Für Sie, Feldlazarett, und Sicherheit* (For you, a Field Hospital, and safety). *Für mich, wer weiss?* (For me, who knows?)"

He smiled.

At last, we were out of the cellars of Marcelcave.

The machine gun crew pulled my wounded men out of Marcelcave and took them to an old factory, about 1/4 mile away, which served as a German Dressing Station, *Verbandplatz*, in German. Here, we met a most curious fellow. A big man with white hair. He greeted us at the entrance to the Verbandplatz and said, *"Ich bin ein Rheinländer, ein guter Mann* (I am a Rhinelander, a good man)." He said this with considerable vehemence, seeming to feel that his goodness and his being from the Rhineland were inextricably linked.

"Lass mich helfen, Ich bin ein Rheinländer, ein guter Mann (Let me help, I am a Rhinelander, a good man)." He never tired of saying it. This giant of a man was as strong as an ox, and carried our wounded men as gently as he would a baby—reassuring each and every man that he was a Rhinelander, a good man. He was as strong as an ox, all right, and not much smarter.

Once the men were all tucked away, he heated us up a bunch of bully beef and potatoes.

"Ein bisschen Rosé auch, Herr Doktor? (A little Rosé, too, Doctor?)" It surprised me that Rosé was in his vocabulary, but who was I to argue?

"Natürlich (Sure)." I'd have given him a tip if I had so much as a farthing in my pocket.

He fed all my men, and gave them some wine to drink. Then he washed them off as best he could, not hesitating for a minute to clean off even their bodily waste.

"Ich bin ein Rheinländer, ein guter Mann (I am a Rhinelander, a good man)."

He *was* a good man.

A drizzling rain had now set in. Our good man from the Rhineland set up a fire in a pot-bellied stove, which got us good and warm for the first time in two days. There were a lot of German stretcher bearers in this *Verbandplatz* and they had plenty of bully beef and other canned food the English must have left behind. They had lots of French wine, too, and most of them looked very cheery. My theory about the French wine slowing down the Germans did not seem entirely farfetched. There were bottles everywhere. This wine, plus the phenomenal success of their offensive, had "bucked up" all the Germans quite a bit. It was hard to blame them. They were certainly "ahead" in the game.

But I remembered what those tough Tommies said by the side of the road, when I was inspecting their blisters a few days before.

"We always win the last battle."

After a short time, a horse ambulance came to evacuate four of my wounded men as well as myself. My other wounded men were also now being cared for, I felt I had done my duty. My conscience could rest easy. I had been a good and faithful soldier.

It came as a surprise that the Germans had only horse ambulances. Looking around, one saw no motor vehicles at all. Certainly they must have some! How could they have made this tremendous advance on horses alone? How could they have moved up their artillery so quickly? This was a great puzzle to me.

The men were loaded up, filling the back of the ambulance, leaving no room for me to ride. The front seat of the ambulance had a driver and his assistant, so it looked like I'd be walking. But this assistant, who must have been sixty years old, saw the officer's bar on my shoulder, and climbed down off the wagon.

"*Bitte, bitte* (please, please)," he said, indicating that I should take his place on the wagon.

Of course, I didn't want to do so, he was 30 years my senior. I shook my head.

"*Bitte, bitte, Herr Doktor. Sie sind Offizier. Sie müssen fahren* (Please, please, Doctor. You are an officer, you must ride)," he insisted.

"*Nein, nein, ich kann spazieren gehen* (No, no, I can walk)," I said. Common courtesy says a young man should walk.

"*Sie sind Offizier, ich nicht. Sie fahren, ich marschiere. Keine Frage darüber* (You are an officer, I am not. You ride, I march. No question about it)." He got down off the wagon, making it crystal clear that *he* was going to walk, and *I* was going to ride. His sense of duty would not allow it otherwise.

Ours wasn't the only side with good and faithful soldiers.

Chapter 11

FELDLAZARETT

March 31 – April 16, 1918

"*Achtung!*"

Every German within earshot snapped to attention, even the wounded men stiffened.

"*Herr Major Landenburg, darf ich Ihnen Herr Doktor Gallagher präsentieren* (Major Landenburg, may I present Doctor Gallagher)." My "guard," a *Sanitäter*, introduced me to the chief of the field hospital. We shook hands.

"*Das ist alles. Danke. Hilf jetzt darüber, ins Operationstheater* (That's all, thanks, go over there and lend a hand in the operating room)." Major Landenburg stood at my height, had his hair cropped very short. His eyes were gray. Deep lines etched his face. He looked like he had seen a lot in his day.

Landenburg held his hand forward, bidding me to join him in a tour of the Feldlazarett, the field hospital that would be home to me for a few weeks. There were no beds in the place. Men were jammed like sardines on the dirt floor. The place stank of excrement, necrotic tissue, death. It looked little better than the cellar I'd just left in Marcelcave. At least it was above ground and had some windows to let in light and fresh air. A former French army barracks, it had been completely stripped of furniture. Four walls, a roof, and a curtain at one end of the barracks. That was it.

"Herr Doctor Gallagher," Landenburg started out, "is it all right if we talk in English?" His accent was good. Curiously, in spite of his near perfect English, he kept calling me *Herr* Doctor, mixing the German and English. It must have been a reflex, using the term "Herr" in front of "doctor."

"Of course."

"Good, good. Practice make you the master, no, how do you say that again?" Landenburg asked. He was looking up in the air, searching for the phrase.

"Practice makes perfect."

"Yes, that's it, practice makes perfect. A lovely language, English." We started down the middle aisle of the Feldlazarett. (Aisle was the wrong term, it was merely the unoccupied stretch of dirt between two long lines of wounded men.) "Do you read Shakespeare, Herr Dr. Gallagher? I've always enjoyed him."

We passed the curtain at the end of the barracks. The "operating room" was on the other side. An amputation was going on, and you could hear the "zzz zzz" of the saw going through bone. Landenburg pulled back the curtain, revealing four *Sanitäter* holding a man down.

"*Scheisse, Scheisse!* (Shit, shit!)" he shouted. "*Lieber Gott! Scheisse!* (God Almighty! Shit!)" He was twisting around, trying to get away. The *Sanitäter* held him fast, while the surgeon shouted at him.

"*Bald ist es bereit. Ruhe!* (Soon we'll be done. Quiet!)" Zzz! Zzz! Zzz—crack! The saw had snapped. "*Scheisse!*" Now it was the surgeon saying "shit!" The man's femur, the large bone in his thigh, was not quite cut all the way through. The surgeon started to twist it, to snap it off like a green twig. Landenburg drew back the curtain. The wounded man stopped saying "*Scheisse!*"

and started screaming. Someone must have stuffed a rag in his mouth for the screaming got muffled all of a sudden.

Crack! The femur snapped.

By now, I had forgotten Landenburg's question about Shakespeare. "Major Landenburg, that man is wide awake. Don't you have any . . . "

"A little ethyl chloride. That's all. We've only *ein bisschen*—I'm sorry—a little. We save it for the worst cases." Landenburg was pointing out that they had very little anaesthetic gas, so most of the men had to endure their operations wide awake, just like this man. It struck me then that armies always seem to be short of medicines, but they are never short of bullets.

"Isn't an amputation a worst case?" I asked. I kept hoping the poor man behind the curtain would pass out, but his pitiful, muffled cries kept coming. Just then, a second voice joined in. *"Fick! Fick! Scheisskopf hat mir gebissen!* (Fuck, fuck, this shithead just *bit* me!)" One of the *Sanitäters* shouted, and ran out from behind the curtain, his finger bleeding. Bravo to the wounded man, tormenting his tormentors!

Landenburg shrugged. "At least it's a fast case, Herr Doctor Gallagher. If a man yells loud enough and long enough, he gets some anaesthetic." The *Sanitäter* squeezed past us, dripping blood from his finger. "I guess if he *bites* enough people, we'll give *him* some anaesthetic, too. We do what we can." I was not really in a position to criticize. In the dugout near La Vacquerie, with Dr. Craig, I had done some amputations without anaesthetics. God, the pain on those men's faces.

He showed me around the rest of the hospital. For bandages, they had a kind of flimsy crepe paper that fell apart as soon as it got wet, so it was useless. All the men were infested with lice, and scratched constantly. Pus and maggots drained from wounds everywhere.

"Your men will get the same treatment as ours, Herr Doctor Gallagher. As you are seeing, it's not much. I am a little embarrassed by all this," he admitted. "We usually run a tight boat . . . "

"A tight ship," I corrected.

"A tight ship, yes. We usually run a tight ship, but this advance of ours has outrun our supplies. So here we are, at the end of our, our . . .," he was searching again.

"Rope," I helped.

"Yes, our rope."

So this was a Feldlazarett, the German equivalent of our Casualty Clearing Station. Whereas our Casualty Clearing Station was a *real* hospital, capable of *treating* men, this Feldlazarett was a warehouse, a dumping ground. Of course, I had not seen any of our Casualty Clearing Stations since the battle began. They, too, might be in sorry shape. What surprised me then, was how an *advance* could cause as much confusion and disruption, as a *retreat*.

Landenburg had said he was at the end of his rope. From everything I had seen, the Germans *were* at the end of their rope. Outside the hospital I saw their transport. Whereas the British had good horses and motorcars galore, the Germans had only little Russian ponies, ready to drop in their tracks. Wagons squealed for lack of grease, tires rattled for want of rubber. And here in their field hospital, they lacked the most basic supplies. Did they even have enough food to keep going?

"Would you like some lunch?" Landenburg asked.

"Yes, please."

We would see.

Sitting down in a nearby tent, I looked over the lunch—barley soup and a hunk of rock-hard black bread. This was the food that fueled the tremendous German offensive.

"*Bon appetít!* as the French say," Landenburg said, as he dipped his bread in the soup. One couldn't help but like the man. He was cut from the same stuff as the unflappable British officers.

"Herr Doctor Gallagher, I have never heard an accent quite like yours. You pronounce your 'r's' differently than any Englishman I have ever met," Landenburg said.

"I'm American."

He didn't skip a beat. "I thought as much." He chewed on the bread—it took a lot of chewing. "Where are you from, exactly?"

"Minnesota." Not one Englishman had known where Minnesota was. Why should a German?

"Minnesota. That is where the Mayo Clinic is located, by Rochester, is it not?" How did he know that?

"Yes, it is. The Mayo Clinic isn't far from my hometown."

"When you get back there, please tell the doctors I have translated many of their articles from English into German for our medical journals," Landenburg said.

"I will do that," I said.

The brotherhood of medicine—crossing borders, oceans, languages, even crossing over battle lines. Yet there *were* some caveats to this brotherhood. The English had developed the all-important tetanus antitoxin in 1915. Had they "shared" this discovery with the German doctors? No. Not that the German doctors were "without sin." Development of newer, deadlier poison gases required experts—medical experts. Germany's doctors came forward. Pulmonary specialists helped design gases to scald the lungs, to make a man drown in his own secretions. Eye specialists helped formulate the best gas to destroy the delicate tissue of the cornea, and blind a man for life. Skin specialists gave their expertise on the development of a gas to peel the skin off a man the way skin falls off a boiled chicken. And once the German doctors had done this, the Allied doctors pitched in to develop poison gases of their own. The brotherhood of murder.

But right now, Landenburg and I were simple field hospital doctors. And we were breaking bread together. One of the cooks pulled a big white bone out of the soup. The bone was so large, it must have come from a horse. He threw it outside the tent into the mud. A passing soldier picked it up, mud and all, broke it into two, and sucked the marrow out of the broken ends.

Major Landenburg saw the whole scene, too.

"He must have been a rather hungry fellow," Landenburg observed, dryly.

That soldier, sucking the marrow out of that bone, told me something. He told me something important, something I needed to hear. They were running out of steam, the Germans, you could feel it. First, the sorry state of their transport, second, the drunkenness, third the food. I had seen a lot of hungry Brits, and I had been hungry a few times myself, but no one ever sucked the marrow out of a muddy horse bone. And during our whole retreat, I thought only *we* were taking casualties. Not so. There were a lot of wounded Germans in that Feldlazarett, and more coming in all the time. Most of them were hit by artillery. I hadn't realized how deadly accurate the British artillery was.

Landenburg and I ate in silence for a few minutes.

"Do you know something, Herr Dr. Gallagher, I have nephews myself, fighting for the British!" Landenburg said.

"Really?" That reminded me of the stories of our Civil War, where brother had fought brother.

"Yes," he went on. "My brother settled on the Isle of Wight and married an Englishwoman. His sons are fighting for the King. And here I am, fighting for the Kaiser. And to think, the Kaiser and the King of England are cousins themselves! What was it Shakespeare said, oh, what was it, he said it so well, oh yes, 'What a tangled web we weave.' But tell me, Herr Dr. Gallagher, why should you, an American, enter this tangled web?" He asked it in a spirit of curiosity, not rancor.

"Well, Dr. Landenburg, your country has been sinking American ships for years, killing American sailors," I said.

"Oh come now, Dr. Gallagher, surely you know we were sinking only ammunition ships," he said, dismissing my whole argument. This glib explanation of his surprised the hell out of me. This, from an intelligent, educated man? What had the German government been telling their people?

"The *Lusitania* was a passenger ship, Dr. Landenburg," I reminded him.

"It was full of ammunition, that's why so many passengers died." Another pat explanation, it seemed Landenburg never questioned anything he heard.

"That's ridiculous," I said. My veneer of congeniality was disappearing fast. I didn't know whether to blame Dr. Landenburg, for believing the lies, or to blame the Prussian government, for feeding him the lies.

"No. I read about it. Besides, if your ships were truly neutral, why didn't they come to Germany? Why didn't they run through the English blockade?" Landenburg asked.

"The *English* never sank our ships. *You* did."

We were getting nowhere on this issue. I took a different tack, bringing up the German intrigues with Mexico.

"What about the Zimmerman telegram, Major Landenburg, what about that? Germany tried to get Mexico to fight America, in exchange for German aid. And you would have returned Texas, New Mexico, and Arizona to the Mexicans." You wanted to take land away from us, sovereign territory, no different than us trying to take Bavaria away from you."

That whole episode had steamed me, and the rest of America, too. Not that we had a lot to fear from Mexico. (Mexico was still embroiled in revolution and rebellion. Their army couldn't even control their *own* people, let alone invade America). But the *gall* of the Germans, to try to incite our neighbors against us, *that* was infuriating.

"Oh that, the Zimmerman telegram. A British forgery. Their spies invented the whole thing to get you to enter the war," Landenburg said. He waved his hand dismissively, as if the whole thing were a schoolboy prank, unworthy of further discussion.

I was not going to convince Major Landenburg of anything, but was determined to go down trying. We had been right to enter this war, THEY had started it.

"But your very own Foreign Minister Zimmerman *admitted* he sent the telegram. He said it was authentic!" How could Landenburg wiggle out of that?

"Zimmerman must have been mistaken. Anyway, are you really so scared of Mexico? Does America fear that Pancho Villa might go back to Texas and rob a few banks?" Pancho Villa—that was a sore point, he had me there. "There *must* be a better reason. Tell me, Herr Doctor Gallagher, why are you here? Why did you leave Minnesota and go to war?" Landenburg asked.

"Well, Major Landenburg, let me put it this way." I spoke in German to emphasize the point. "*Wenn mein Vaterland nach Krieg geht, auch gehe ich!* (When my country goes to war, so do I!)"

He nodded approvingly. "Faithfulness to the Fatherland. That's a good reason, Herr Dr. Gallagher. I'd never thought of America as being a 'Fatherland,' but, of course, to you it *is* a Fatherland. Just as much as Germany is *my* Fatherland," Landenburg said.

"Well, Herr Doctor Gallagher, it stands to reason that *you* think you are doing the right thing, and *I* think that I am doing the right thing. Each of us is a patriot who sees his country as just, and the enemy as unjust. All your clever arguments will not turn me into an American, and all my clever arguments will not turn you into a German. I suspect if I had been born in Minnesota, and you had been born in Berlin, we would be turning the arguments around." He was a clever fellow, this Landenburg, it was a shame we were on opposite sides.

He drank a glass of water down.

"But, Herr Doctor Gallagher," he pointed outside, there was a rumble of artillery, "unfortunately, it is not a war of words we are fighting. It is a war of bullets and bombs." He stood up. "Let us go back to the hospital and do what we can for the men. You and I are doctors, and it is our job to save people, not kill them. In that, we are on the same side, are we not?"

"That we are," I agreed.

When we got back to the hospital, a short, handsome blond-haired man in à resplendent leather flying jacket was visiting the wounded men. He bent over them and shook each one's hand, saying a word or two. Around his neck hung a medal on a ribbon.

Major Landenburg pointed to the man. "Baron von Richtofen. His aerodrome is nearby. I believe the British airmen find him bothersome."

My jaw must have dropped to the ground. This was Baron von Richtofen, the Red Baron, Germany's top pilot. There had always been such an air of romance and mystique about air combat. In the trenches, we even found it entertaining to watch the occasional dogfights. And here he was—the premier ace of the war, the best dogfighter the world had ever produced.

"You see that medal he's wearing? Germany's highest decoration, the *Pour le Merite*. Curious, isn't it? Our highest medal having a French name," Landenburg explained.

I did not meet Richtofen personally, but I felt somewhat giddy being near him. The feeling was similar to seeing the Queen of England pass by when I was in London. What is it that makes us feel so queer in the presence of famous people?

Later that very afternoon, the Baron and his "flying circus" took off from their aerodrome and engaged in a dogfight with the British, right over the hospital. Two English planes caught fire. Then, as we watched, the pilots crawled out of their burning cockpits and jumped, falling hundreds of feet, their clothes smoking as they fell. They hit the ground with the most nauseating thud. All the romance and mystique of air combat ended then and there for me. It was murder, pure and simple. Murder in the air, no different than murder on the ground. I could never understand why pilots weren't given parachutes. Of all the idiocy I saw in the war, that had to be the worst—no parachutes for pilots—an automatic death sentence if they were shot down. What must have gone through their minds, up there, hundreds or thousands of feet in the air, as their planes plummeted to earth? On the ground, death tended to be unpredictable—a bullet or shell hit you, and down you went. But to be sitting in a cockpit, in a sickening free fall, knowing in a minute or two you would be smashed to a pulp—it was too awful to contemplate.

Two weeks later, Richtofen himself would get shot down and killed.

About fifty British soldiers were under my care in the Feldlazarett, among them, George Cave. He had been in the Marcelcave cellar with me, next to the man who'd shot himself.

Like all the others, he was laying on the ground with one thin, lice-ridden blanket covering him. He was about thirty feet away from the "operating room," well within earshot of that awful place. It was a rainy day, gray outside, gray inside. But George didn't look gray, he never did. In spite of his awful wounds, and the filth in this so-called hospital, George Cave's face still carried the fresh-scrubbed look of youth. He reminded me of a medical student arriving at the hospital for his very first day on the wards—looking like his mother had just washed and washed his face until it was pink from the rubbing.

"Afternoon, George, let's see how we're getting along," I said, in my best "ward" talk, even though this was more of a charnel house than a ward.

These were my rounds, when I dropped in on the patients and was supposed to "do" something for them, and "monitor" their progress. Of course, with no good bandages, no medicines, no beds, and precious little water, there was little I could "do" and little progress to "monitor."

But I could talk to patients, help them pass the time, I could do that.

Peeling off Cave's dressings (the flimsy crepe paper) unleashed a swarm of maggots on the stumps of his fingers. The same thing happened when the dressings came off the stumps of his feet. The temptation was automatic and overwhelming to brush the nauseating creatures out of the wounds, to clear out the swarming mass of pearly white larvae, but I didn't do it. Maggots eat only dead flesh, not live flesh, so they were "cleaning out" the wounds for me. Once the maggots were done, the wound that remained was pink and debrided. It was awful, a medieval way of treating a patient, but such were the conditions.

"Awful lot of the little beasties, eh?" George regarded the maggots with the detached air of a naturalist, much as you might look at a butterfly in a collection.

"That there are, George." I put more crepe paper dressing on the wounds, but the dressings soaked and fell apart in an instant, the maggots protruding through and continuing their mad, frantic wiggling.

"Pushing and shoving. Pushing and shoving. All for food, I guess." George continued the observations on his own personal menagerie. "They look like the piglets, at me uncle's farm, all pushing and shoving to get at their Mum's teat."

He was right. I had never looked at maggots with anything other than loathing before. But George, now somewhat of an expert on their ways, had opened my eyes a bit. What were maggots but small animals, looking for a bite to eat, looking to carve out their own little place in the sun?

"Well, George, I must admit, you shed a whole new light on this subject." I continued to regard the maggots with a newfound respect—though they still made me want to vomit.

"Not a lot else to do 'ere, Doctor. Not a 'ole 'ell of a lot else to do." His eyes took in the Feldlazarett. It would have been nice to have a grammaphone in here. Surely the Germans must have captured one somewhere during this advance. Some music would help to treat that most undertreated of maladies—boredom.

"I'll talk to Major Landenburg, George, see if we can't liven this place up for you a little bit." Liven! What a term to use, *liven*. Dead men were carried out of this place every day, sometimes every hour, and I wanted to liven the place up!

"If you could roll a piano in here, Doc, I'd do my best to tickle the ivories." George held up his mangled hands and moved around his finger stumps. "Of course, I might 'ave a little trouble reaching a full octave, with me fingers a little short." He lifted up his leg, his nearly footless leg, "And don't ask me to work the pedals." He grinned.

I couldn't believe what I just heard. George, torn to pieces, making light of his own mutilation. He was in terrible pain (he hadn't gotten morphine for many hours). Maggots swarmed in his open wounds, lice burrowed under his skin, he lay on the cold ground in a cold enemy field hospital, and he was still able to summon up some humor, and humor at his own expense. If ever a man embodied all that was good and true about England, George Cave was that man.

From that day on, I made it a point to get to know George a little better. It was a bit of a luxury, allowing myself to make friends with him, but the maggots were cleaning out his wounds well, no gas gangrene had set in, and it looked like George might survive after all. His fingers, all amputated about halfway down, *did* look like they could reach a few notes on the piano. Something told me that if *anybody* in the world could play with half-fingers, George Cave was that man.

But George wasn't just interested in George, he wanted to learn about me, too.

"So, a doctor, bet you 'ad to burn the midnight oil a few times before you sat for your tests, eh?" he asked.

The British did not "take" tests, they "sat for" tests.

"Yes, I had to crack a book or two along the way," I was looking over George's finger stumps. Our friends the maggots had left and the wounds were starting to close themselves up with pink, healthy-looking tissue. His feet, though, still had a thriving colony of wrigglers. George's sundry shrapnel wounds in his body all looked about the same—not getting worse at least.

"Did you ever cheat, on a test, I mean?" George asked, a mischievous look in his eye.

"Nope, never did, Mr. Cave." I was putting on the stern schoolmaster. "Did you, pray tell, ever let your eyes wander over to your neighbor's desk?"

Overhead, a steady RRRRRR! sound started up. English planes, an air raid. People started to run in a panic. But the RRRR! faded, and no bombs fell.

George was averting his head, not to dodge any bombs, but to avoid my "I-think-you-may-have-cheated-on-your-exam" stare.

"Doc, I've got a confession to make. I did cheat, but just once." His schoolboy frown was starting to turn upside down, into a smile. "God damn if I didn't suffer for it!"

"Did you get caught?" I asked.

"No, worse than that." He was shaking his head, wearing a Cheshire grin, "I had the right answer written down. Then, what do I do? I look at the next desk over, see what my neighbor's written, and I changed me answer. Change it to a wrong answer! Serves me right, I guess," he laughed.

The bread they served us was made of dried ground turnips and sawdust. A paste was provided made of mashed turnips. One of the enlisted men called this "Hindenburg butter." Occasionally we had a kind of stew of horsemeat and dried "vegetables" which were predominately nettles. The soldiers were sent out periodically on nettle-picking expeditions. I heard someone refer to the dried vegetables as "barbed wire entanglements." No one gained weight on the Feldlazarett diet.

Most of the Germans treated me with respect and courtesy. But three incidents stood out during my stay at the Feldlazarett that were not so pleasant.

The first was the German reaction to British bombing. As a hospital, we were not a "legitimate" target, but the Germans had a large field gun nearby (that sure helped the wounded men sleep). Several troop tents, supplies, and other "legitimately bombable" targets were also within a hundred yards of the Feldlazarett. (From all I had seen in the war so far, the concept of legitimate didn't really apply, though. Neither side paid any attention to the Red Cross if it interfered with the progress of the battle.) So, whether it was "right" or not, the British bombed the area every night, and sometimes during the day. One night the sickening "eeeeEEEEE Ka-boom!" occurred right next door, portions of the bomb passing into the Feldlazarett and wounding several Germans. But for the tragedy of the wounded men (I helped in their treatment) it was almost comical to see the consternation of the Germans in the air raid. They ran around like chickens with their heads cut off looking for shelter, but there was none to be found. Each time a bomb fell the Germans looked at me like it was my fault. Their attitude was in vast contrast to the British—who cheered during the air raids when I was in the town of Ham—and the French—who would no doubt have drunk some wine and said, "C'est la guerre."

The second unpleasant occurrence was with a chaplain, of all people. There were three chaplains in the Feldlazarett, and two were fine. When any of our men were buried, as many of them were, the chaplains attended the service. The cemetery, or Friedhof in German, was right alongside the old Roman road that led to Amiens, the very road I had retreated on. The chaplains took pains to keep the Friedhof neat and respectful. They would hold a brief service over the grave, the clergymen genuinely touched by the tragedy of all these needless deaths. They were good men, these chaplains, all but one.

The third chaplain was a red-faced Prussian with a "Hindenburg" scowl. When he learned I was an American he flew into a rage.

"Warum kommt Amerika in den Krieg? (Why has America entered the war?)" he shouted at me.

Debating the fine points of submarine warfare, intrigue with Mexico, and so on were useless, so I went with my simplest explanation, the one I had used with Major Landenburg.

"Wenn mein Vaterland nach Krieg geht, auch gehe ich (When my fatherland goes to war, so do I)," I said.

"Dein Vaterland! Amerika? (Your fatherland, America?)"(Many Germans had this same response. Major Landenburg had been the only one to accept that countries other than Germany could be a "Fatherland.")

The chaplain bellowed, ranted, raved, and waved his hands around, a real display, then he walked away. Later, when he learned I was a doctor taking care of the British wounded, he seemed a little ashamed and tried to be sociable, but after that I pretended not to see him when he came around. It seemed odd to get abuse from a chaplain.

And I had one more bad encounter, this, with a German doctor.

We were debriding the infected leg stumps of a German infantryman. He had been hit by a shell and had the bad luck to lay unattended for twenty-four hours before help arrived. The German doctor was cleaning out one leg, cutting away dead tissue, and I was cleaning the other.

"Sie verlieren (You're losing)," he said, with a snippy attitude in his voice.

I first thought he was referring to the leg, as if we were engaged in some gruesome race to see who could clean out a stump faster. Then I caught on, he was saying we were losing the war.

"Wir vorwärts, Sie rennen (We're going forward, you're running.)" He was rubbing my face in it, playing the gloating, overbearing winner. But he was counting his chickens before they were hatched. Paris had not yet fallen, nor, for that matter, had Amiens. The Tommies and French were slowing them down, and it was only a matter of time before the Americans arrived.

Visions of those blistered Tommies by the side of the road came back to me. Tired, footsore, hungry, battered, on the run. But unbeaten.

"*Bald sind wir in Paris. Allies kaputt* (Soon we'll be in Paris. The Allies are finished)," the German doctor said, heckling me. He thought the war was won, but he hadn't seen those Gloucester boys of mine. Not one of them asked for an ambulance. They all stuck with the battalion.

"*Ja, ja, Deutschland is zu stark für die Engländern, und die Franzosen* (Yes, yes, Germany is too strong for the English and the French). *Und die Russen sind auch kaputt* (And the Russians are done for also)," he said.

Let him say what he wanted, I remembered the icy cool of the French doctor, shrugging off his coming capture, or death with an airy, "*C'est la guerre.*"

"*Und Amerika. Ha! Wo sind die berühmten Amerikaner?* (And America, ha! Where are the famous Americans?)" Now he was getting personal.

So he wanted to know about the Americans, the famous Americans. I thought of the send off party in Minnesota, the faces on everyone in the hospital as we sang "Over There,"—Abe standing on the *Orduna*, saying, "If you never wanted to fight before . . . now you did"—the Missouri engineers with their Boy Scout hats, the one who had picked off the German guard and called it a "lucky shot." I knew plenty about Americans.

"*Was sagst du davon, mein Freund?* (What do you say about that, my friend?)" he threw down the gauntlet. The look on his face—the smugness, the certainty. Well, I knew some Tommies, some poilus, and a hell of a lot of Americans who were going to wipe that look off his face soon.

I finished cleaning the soldier's stump, placed one of the flimsy bandages on it, and wrapped it up as best I could. Bringing my head up, I looked the other doctor right in the eyes.

"*Sprichst du English?* (Do you speak English?)" I asked.

"*Nein* (No)." Even this one word answer came out as pure arrogance.

"*Dann hier is deine erste Übung* (Then here is your first lesson)."

I sang for him—as good a way as any to learn a language.

> "The Yanks are coming,
> The Yanks are coming
> And we won't come back 'til it's over, Over There."

I translated it for him, "*Und was das bedeutet, Herr Oberartz, ist—Wir kommen* (And what that means, Doctor, is—We are coming). *Vergisst du das nicht* (And don't you forget it)."

Some British soldiers died, then others came in, I continued to care for about 50 of them. The supply situation remained deplorable, there wasn't much I could do for anyone. Water was still scarce. I couldn't even clean their wounds. All the men were lousy, including me. The one way I *could* help was with pain relief. Though short of everything, the Germans had plenty of injectable morphine, so I went around at night and gave the men a shot of the painkiller. For many, it was the only way to get any sleep.

On April 14, I was making my usual nighttime rounds with morphine. I knew one poor fellow who would need a strong dose of it, my friend George Cave, the man who joked about playing a piano with his blown off fingers.

Lice and scabies tortured him, but he could not scratch himself, for he had no fingers. He could not roll over when he had to relieve himself, so we were forever trying to clean him off. Through all of this, though, he never complained, and he continued to crack the occasional joke. Tonight, he looked grayer, sicker.

"Evening, George, how are you doing?" I asked.

"Oh, nothing new here. Same old Georgie."

He wiggled around a little, trying to scratch himself against the ground.

"Here's a little something to take the edge off, George." I injected his thigh with the morphine.

"Thanks, awfully. You know, Dr. Gallagher, the oddest thing 'appened today when I was trying to eat some soup," he said.

"What's that, George?"

"Had a devil of a time getting my mouth open. Seems as stiff as a rusty 'inge, it does," he said.

Lockjaw, the beginnings of tetanus. The thought came so fast and loud, George might have heard me think it. He had been at the back of the cellar in Marcelcave, and had received no tetanus antitoxin.

"Doctor Gallagher, am I going to die?" He asked it as a point of information, as you might ask whether it was raining outside, or whether dinner would be served on time.

"Of course, it's impossible to say for sure, George, but I will say this, you are rather badly wounded." For months now I had been talking to badly wounded men, dying men, and avoiding the statement, "You are going to die." But most men could tell what I was thinking. And George Cave could tell what I was thinking.

"Well," he was perfectly calm, "I suppose it would be better if I did, the way I'm all torn about." No jokes now. Time was short.

It was getting dark outside. Artillery flashes flickered through the windows of the Feldlazarett. George Cave would not see the sun rise.

"Could you write my Mum? It's easy to remember, but maybe you should write it down.

Mrs. George Cave
Rock Ferry, Cheshire, England"

I wrote it down.

"No street address?" I asked.

"The postman's my cousin. He'll get it to her."

"I'll write." I tucked the slip of paper in my field journal (a kind of diary I carried with me).

George started to get sleepy from the morphine. I came back an hour later and gave him a second shot. Three more times I came back that night, injecting him each time. The muscular contractures were creeping upon him now, twisting his body, turning his face into an awful leer, his breathing labored, but the morphine at least kept him somewhat sleepy and unaware.

The next morning George Cave was buried by the roadside.

Chapter 12

FRENCH COOKIES

April 16–29, 1918

George Cave's grave had a wooden cross above it:

Fürs Vaterland Gefallen
(Died for his country)

Rudyard Kipling, I think it was, spoke of "A small corner of a foreign field that is forever England." George had made this corner "forever England."

I looked at his grave as we were marched past, a few other English prisoners and I. We had a guard, who spoke no English, escorting us farther back, starting us on the long journey to a prisoner-of-war camp, somewhere. With us was a German quartermaster named Michael Baptist. His English was excellent.

Baptist spoke up, "Did you know him?"

"Yes, I knew him." I knew George Cave. I knew a hundred George Caves, a thousand George Caves. But his name wasn't always George Cave. Sometimes his name was Robson. Sometimes he wasn't buried in this cemetery, he was in a convoy with Ted Sweetser, jumping off a sinking ship into the icy Atlantic, only to be covered with burning oil. Sometimes he wore a German uniform, and laid out in No Man's Land with both legs shot, and put a bandage around a wounded Tommy's jaw. I knew George Cave all right. He disintegrated in front of me during a barrage, fell next to me crossing a field, and died a dozen times in my Aid Post. I saw George Cave sprawled on a road, buried in a trench, and laid up on a parapet. I knew George Cave.

Baptist didn't say anything for a few miles. When we sat down for a rest, he passed around a canteen.

"You're the American, I hear," he said.

I took a swig of water. "That's right."

"So what are you doing here? Why should you want to leave America and come here, to fight for the British?" Baptist asked.

Out came the old arguments about submarine attacks, plots with Mexico.

"Oh, all those ships we sank. We had to! A man in my regiment has a brother at Supreme Command. He told me about the *Lusitania*, you know, the secret poison gas you had on board," he said. Here we go again, more lies fed to the German people.

"What secret gas?" I asked.

"You know, the poison gas that goes right through our gas masks. You made it in America and were shipping it to England, hidden aboard a passenger ship. But we sank it first," Baptist said, unaware of the patent stupidity of such a story.

"What?" I asked. Germany had given us Beethoven and Goethe—great minds, geniuses! And now it was giving us dummies, who believed the most fantastic lies.

"Don't play a game with me," Baptist said.

"There was no secret poison gas on the *Lusitania*. If there was, why wouldn't we just send another shipment?" I said. Put all the "secret gas" on one ship, and never make any more? A *child* could see the error of that reasoning.

"Well, I don't know, but my friend's brother said that all the poison gas went to the bottom of the sea," Baptist concluded, unwilling to hear any more discussion about the *Lusitania*.

The fact he believed such a preposterous story told me a lot about the German state of mind. They believed anything they were told. Germans did not seem to question their own propaganda or think for themselves. If someone higher in the chain of command said it, then it was so. In America, by contrast, we tended to question our political figures. It was the basis of the two-party system of democracy. Not so in Germany. If their national leaders said something, the Germans swallowed it hook, line and sinker. They thought and acted like sheep.

"OK. What about your agreement with Mexico?" I just couldn't let it go. "What about that? You were trying to get Mexico to go to war with us, weren't you?"

Baptist recapped his canteen. The guard got us up and moving down the road again.

"Of course we were. We need *some* Allies, don't we?" That made me madder than ever, I was not going to drop this debate. *Some* German *somewhere* had to admit they were wrong.

"What about your treaty with Belgium? Didn't you have a treaty with them? Don't you honor your agreements?" I was driving home the point. There was something extra aggravating about hearing the German arguments spoken with almost flawless English.

Baptist explained, "Military necessity, that was. France about to attack us, Russia mobilizing, England's powerful fleet just over the horizon. We *had* to do it. It was a military necessity. If a lion is chasing you, and your neighbor has a garden with a sign that says 'No . . . Crossing.'"

"Trespassing," I corrected. Thank God, Baptist had finally made a mistake in his otherwise perfect English.

"Yes, that's the word. Trespassing. If your neighbor has this sign, 'No Trespassing,' but a lion is going to eat you, well, then you go across the garden. That is a military necessity. And that is because we crossed Belgium," Baptist said.

"*Why* we crossed Belgium," I corrected, yet again. Triumph! Another grammatical error.

"Yes, that is why we crossed Belgium," Baptist said. It was hopeless. The Germans had an excuse, a rationalization, for every single action they had taken. They really thought they were right.

Baptist took my address in the States; why did he want that? I suspected he was like many other Germans I'd talked to, wanting to move to America after the war. If Baptist thought I'd sponsor him, he could go to hell!

The road we were on was packed with soldiers, artillery and wagons, all moving toward the Front. Here and there, couriers and wagons of wounded men moved toward the rear. The surrounding landscape was the usual monotonous flat, to gently rolling hills, torn up by warfare. Greenery was fighting its own war, though, and was winning in a few places! Try as we might to convert France into a sterile wasteland, there was grass peeping through by the roadside, and some of the battered trees were throwing out some green buds. Nature was repairing herself.

The Germans still appeared optimistic about the progress of their enterprise. Passing soldiers were laughing and smiling. News was a little hard to get, but if they had captured Amiens, we would have heard about it. No such report came through. The Allies seemed to be holding.

We marched back another 15 miles, to a train station in Peronne. Baptist took leave of us. All day we sat around in this station, along with several hundred other British and French soldiers, waiting for a train to Cambrai. Though the German guards had plenty of barley soup, they gave us none—no food, and no water. As luck would have it, a persistent German corporal admired my leather puttees (leggings), so to stave off my hunger I bartered the pair for a bowl of soup and some bread. Those leggings were worth at least ten dollars, but I thought the exchange well worth it. I could only pity my fellow prisoners, who got nothing.

They piled us into wooden boxcars. For some unknown reason, I was separated, and put into a crowded car with French soldiers. We traveled all night, in darkness. There were no blankets, so we huddled together for warmth. The man lying beside me on the cold floor spoke up.

"*J'ai entendu dire que vous êtes americain,*" he said.

I didn't quite catch it all, but I heard the word for American.

"*Oui, je suis americain* (Yes, I'm American)."

That caused a little stir in the boxcar. These Frenchmen hadn't met many Americans.

"Parlez v*ous français?* (Do you speak French?)" he asked.

"*Pas beaucoup* (Not much)," I said.

"*Je parle mieux la langue des Boches* (I speak the language of the Boche better)." The Frenchmen liked that and a ripple of laughter went through the boxcar. Anyone who called the Germans "Boche" was a good fellow.

We shifted into German. It struck me as odd that whenever I spoke to the French, I spoke German. Whenever I spoke to the Germans, I spoke English, and the people I understood the least were the English themselves.

"You are a doctor?" he asked.

"Yes. Ben Gallagher, nice to meet you."

"Theodore. Theodore Demonchaux. Charmed." His face, like all other faces in the boxcar, was a shadow.

"Are you a doctor too, Theodore? I noticed the Red Cross on your sleeve." It was about the only thing I could make out in the darkness. A little moonlight had entered the boxcar through some cracks in the boards.

"No. I'm a stretcher bearer, *brancardier* we say in French." All this spoken in German with a French accent. The language sounded more melodious when a Frenchman spoke it, less guttural.

"What were you before the war?" I asked.

"A priest."

"A priest?" Sister Marie Francis would love to hear this story.

"Yes. A lot of us put down the cloth, and took up this one," he ran his fingers under the Red Cross armband.

Clickety-clack. Clickety-clack. The train rumbled along, swaying from side to side.

"Father, could I have you hear my confession?" I asked.

"Confession? Of course. I can't imagine you have much to confess, but I will be glad to hear it. I am still a priest!" he said, with a great enthusiasm. He seemed eager to take up his old "profession."

He heard my confession and gave me absolution.

"I am a little out of practice, my son. Say your prayers with extra zeal. My absolution may not have the same 'oomph' that it used to. I should hate for you to go to Purgatory on my account," he said. A shaft of moonlight allowed me to see him smiling, chuckling at his own little joke. We were in a prison car, going to an uncertain future. We had received no food, no water, and no blankets. All of us were filthy and covered with vermin. And this priest was right in there with us, suffering our same agonies, giving me the holy Sacraments, and keeping a sense of humor, too. If ever a priest were Christ's vicar on earth, this French priest was that vicar.

In the town of Le Cateau, the train jolted to a stop. We were ordered off the car and marched through the town. The French people of this town had been under the conqueror's boot for four years now, but their spirit was magnificent. They cheered us lustily as we marched up the street. French people ran out from the sidewalk trying to give us food, because I suppose we looked hungry, but the German guards wouldn't allow it. Once through the center of town, the Germans separated the officers from the enlisted men. We officers were billeted in a kind of office, and the men were sent to a factory. My friend the priest went off with the enlisted men.

We finally were given some food, and even some water to wash ourselves, along with iron cots and clean blankets. I was housed with two English doctors, an English infantry officer, and a Frenchman, who'd been assigned to interpret for the British.

This Frenchman, Guy Le Brun (his first name was pronounced *Gee*), was the first one I'd met who spoke English well. He spoke it near perfectly, complete with slang and swear words.

"My governess was English, that's all she spoke to me," he explained one day, as we were washing our socks in a basin.

(Governess, I thought, pretty heady stuff, maybe this Guy guy had been some kind of royalty.)

The English officers acted quite aloof to Guy, not engaging him in conversation much. The old English-French animosity was palpable. That put Guy and me on common ground, for the English were none too friendly to me either. So the Frenchman and I took to talking, and if the Englishmen didn't like it, then that was just too bad. Guy Le Brun was jowly and whiskered. Years of *speaking* English had made him *look* English, if that was possible.

We sat side by side on one of our squeaky iron cots, he pulling one leg up holding his knee with his hands.

"*Ou est-ce que vous est . . . etiez* (where is it that you are . . . was)"—I was making a little stab at French, and mixing up my past tense.

"O hell, let's talk English," Guy said.

No argument from me. "Where were you, Guy?"

"They got me up on the Somme. Before that, I was farther south, you know, *l'enfer* (the inferno)."

The French used the word *enfer*, to refer to Verdun—the biggest and bloodiest battle of the entire war for the French. In 1916, the Germans had attacked the French there, trying unsuccessfully to capture the fortress city of Verdun. The battle had turned into a war of attrition, both sides feeding millions of men (over a million casualties resulted) into an area measuring only about ten miles by ten miles.

I was back to being the wide-eyed novice, eager to hear war stories. Le Brun took a little prying, but he opened up after a while.

"After the first few weeks, which were just a blur, we settled into a kind of mad routine. We would march out of the line, those of us who could, and go to the support area. Reinforcements would come, from somewhere. They would make sure we were up to full strength, the right number of men, then we would march back into the line.

"In my company, say, there would be one hundred and fifteen men. Moving forward through the communication trenches, we'd get shelled, lose a few men. Up in the front line, the Boche shelled us all the time. We'd lose more men, every day. We might not even attack, might not even be attacked, might not see a single Boche the whole time we were there."

The story was fascinating, I couldn't get enough of it. The English could care less. They played bridge and ignored us.

Le Brun went on with his story, "After a few days, my company has 70 men, then 50, then 30. And never a shot fired. Just occupy the trench, get blown up. Once we were down to 20 men or so, they'd march us out again. As we came out, a new company would replace us.

"We'd get more replacements, go back in, and do it all over again. We were losing men *all* the time, and weren't even *fighting*, just occupying land. I suppose a similar number of Boche were sitting over in *their* trenches getting shelled by *our* side. So we both sat there, German and Frenchman, serving no other function other than being a target. Many of them died, and many of us died."

He made a motion like scales being weighed, "measuring" the number of dead on each side. "I guess some accountant kept track of who was winning."

When the people of Le Cateau heard there were Allied prisoners in town, they responded most generously, sending us some of their food. Nearly every afternoon, nuns from a nearby convent sent us a little pot of rice from their ration. When the sisters heard a Frenchman was a prisoner with us, they began to include some homemade cookies. Cookies! Mannah from heaven! Wait 'til Sister Marie Francis heard this.

All the French people I had met so far—soldiers, civilians, both on our side of the line, and here behind the German lines—were extremely compassionate and grateful to the Allies. One got the impression these people truly appreciated what we were trying to do. This stood in stark contrast to the English attitude.

So far, I had not received any gesture in the way of thanks from the English. Yes, it was fine an American had joined their army, but they regarded me with a coolness, almost to the point of disdain. They made me feel I was more of an aggravation than I was worth. Braver men than the English I never saw, but I could not bring myself to like them.

On April 27, the five of us were taken from the "luxurious digs" of officers' quarters to the factory where the enlisted men were held. The place was infested with fleas, and these fleas were bigger, could jump farther, and bite harder than any fleas I had ever seen, even in Minnesota. Their bites hurt so bad, that you couldn't feel the lice burrowing under your skin. It was a sort of counter-irritation principle, similar to getting rid of a headache by dropping a rock on your foot.

The factory itself was a big rectangular empty box. Smudgy windows stood high up on the walls, but there was no clue as to what had been made in the factory, for all the equipment had been taken out. There were some cots, a few benches, a latrine in two of the corners, and hundreds of bored prisoners, milling around.

A man sitting next to me on a bench swatted his ankle.

"God damn!" he shouted. A spot of blood appeared on his ankle. Some flea had just eaten dinner.

His accent was American, and he had on a medical uniform.

"Was that 'God damn' (I pronounced it in American fashion) as opposed to 'God damn' (I pronounced with an exaggerated English accent)?"

He jumped up and started pumping my hand like a man possessed.

"You're God damn right it's God damn! Here, come over here." He ushered me over to a non-latrine corner of the factory, away from prying ears.

"Chuck Maxson, Medical Corps. Baltimore. Handcuffed volunteer with the English. Got snapped up near some town I couldn't pronounce if my life depended on it," he said, the words coming fast and furious.

"Ben Gallagher, Medical Corps, too. Minnesota."

His eyes lit up like the Fourth of July.

"Damn, damn, damn but it's good to see another guy from the good ol' US of A. I swear to God on a stack of Bibles I've had it up to here with these English. Had it up to here!" He held his hand above his head.

"Me, too!" I made a downward gesture with my hands and put my finger to my mouth, "just don't say it too loud."

"Oh yeah, sorry." He looked guilty like he'd been caught talking in school.

"Boy, an American. You sure are a sight for sore eyes, my friend, a sight for sore eyes," Maxson said.

He was a sight for sore eyes, too. Tall and skinny, Maxson was a beanpole, but an *American* beanpole, one of the home team.

"You know what, Chuck?" I looked around to make sure no one was listening. "I don't know about you, but the next time I meet an Englishman, I hope we're on opposite ends of a machine gun. I don't even care if he's on the *trigger* end. If he's English, I hope he'll *pull* the trigger, and put me out of my misery." Lord, it was nice to let my hair down and tell someone what I was thinking.

"Better that than drink their God-damned tea," Maxson said. What do you know? I wasn't the only one who'd had his fill of English tea.

Maxson held up an imaginary teacup, his pinkie pointing out. He put on his best English accent.

"Oh, I say. Rather. Quite. Jolly good show."

"Ssshh!" I said. We were attracting attention.

"Ooh, terribly sorry. Hate to be such a *raffish* colonial," Maxson said, putting special emphasis on the English pronunciation of the letter "r".

We laughed. We laughed and laughed. Tears ran down my eyes. Maxson laughed so hard, he started to snort each time he breathed in. That made us both laugh even harder, and he snorted even more. By now, we were rolling on the ground, grabbing our stomachs. Fleas jumped on us and bit us. French and British soldiers stared at us. German guards stared at us. And we kept laughing. Laughing and snorting. Laughing and crying. Laughing and rolling. Laughing and laughing. It felt good. It felt so good it hurt.

One morning, all 400 officers and men, English and French alike, were told to line up outside. The French mayor of Le Cateau and a committee of townspeople promptly distributed to each and every man two army hardtack biscuits. These biscuits had originated from American Aid packages, but we all appreciated the gesture. The French civilians no doubt could have used those biscuits themselves.

Then another wagon came out.

This time the French officers and men were singled out. In the wagon were a number of boxes marked "American Committee for French Relief." Inside the boxes were cans of meat, fish, baked beans, jam—all stamped with a large U.S.A. mark. Maxson and I stood, holding our two miserable hardtack biscuits, as the French soldiers got can after can of U.S.A. goods. We, the only Americans there, got none. We could not help but see the humor of the situation, knowing that our own folks had perhaps contributed to these very relief packages.

As we walked back to the factory, I felt someone tug at my elbow. It was the French priest, the stretcher bearer, the one who'd heard my confession. He handed me a can of jam.

"Bon appetít, mon fils! (Bon appetit, my son!)"

Chapter 13

TEN MILLION MEN

May 1–21, 1918

Maxson and I shared the jam the next day on a long train trip into Germany. On our earlier trip, the Germans had packed us into boxcars. This time, we were in regular passenger cars, a *great* improvement. With the exception of our armed guards, we could have been on a train going to Chicago. German trains looked more "American" than British trains. We crossed the Rhine River at the city of Rastatt. High wooded bluffs rose on either bank here, looking very much like Minneapolis. We detrained in Rastatt, where shower baths and facilities for delousing were present.

I experienced my first real bath and change of clothes in six weeks. Our clothes were totally infested with vermin, and most of us were pretty well covered with scabs and sores from scratching. Now I realized, as never before, the wonderful healing value of warm water. We had no soap, but they gave us a kind of pumice stone. A whole cake of it would not make a spoonful of lather. Yet the warm water alone did the trick. The sense of well being one felt after that bath, and donning of clean clothes cannot be adequately described. I stepped out of there a new man. My skin tingled and glowed. My shirt felt crisp and starchy. I had gone through a metamorphosis: had molted my old skin, and come out, a butterfly. A caged butterfly.

Rastatt had an old fortress at the edge of town that served as our temporary prison. The food was hearty, (much better than the "nettle stew" at the Feldlazarett), and the bunks were clean, so we had little to complain about. The Germans ran a kind of canteen, but I had no money, nor did Maxson, so we couldn't buy anything.

Mid-May I was finally allowed to send a letter home. No doubt my parents had been worried.

May 15, 1918

Dear Mom and Dad,

The good news is, I don't have to eat *English* cooking anymore. The bad news is, it looks like I'll be eating *German* cooking for a while. I was captured March 28th. I am unhurt, well fed, and warm. Please let Sister Marie Francis know that the Germans have more Catholic priests than the English, so my soul is being well cared for.

Love,
Ben

After a few days, some officers and I were sent to another town, Karlsruhe. My friend, Maxson, from Baltimore, stayed behind. He was a jolly fellow, who saw the silver lining in everything. I was sorry to say good-bye and hoped to see him again.

Everyone knew the German Intelligence Service interrogated prisoners in Karlsruhe. We had also heard they hid microphones in the rooms so we were all a little nervous. I was confined in a third floor hotel room with three English officers. The windows were glazed, locked with padlocks, and screened with iron bars. It was suffocating. No one talked much, knowing the Germans were listening. The least mention of a town or unit might give the enemy something they wanted, so we kept quiet. To pass the time, we played bridge, which I hated. The game bored me to tears, plus my lack of skill no doubt bored the poor Englishmen even more. The pack of cards may have had been given to us as a form of torture.

The Germans finally let us open one window, allowing in a little fresh air, and we could also view the village below. Several times an air raid alarm sounded. I had seen the English and French suffer air raids, now it was the Germans' turn. I was leaning against the window sill, looking out. Three stories below, mothers were pushing baby carriages, or holding young 'uns by the hand. Even from this height, you could see how thin, how terribly thin both the mothers and children were. The blockade was starving *everyone* in Germany.

No aeroplane engines were audible, but a siren started up, indicating an air raid. One young mother on the sidewalk caught my attention, I would see her face until the day I died.

She had a faded scarf on, covering her hair. At the sound of the siren, her face lifted up to look at the sky, bringing her into full view from my window. Her dark eyes were sunk in deep sockets. She had lost so much weight her face resembled a skeleton. Cheekbones jutted out, ready to tear open the skin they looked so sharp. Her arms were like sticks coming out of her threadbare jacket. (It was May, but chilly still.) She held the hand of a child of three years or so. In her other arm she held a baby. The look on her face broke my heart.

She was terrified, and not just for herself. 'What will happen to my child? What will happen to my baby?' All that, she said, in one look. Then she swung the three-year-old up in her arm, clutched the baby closer to her, and ran down the street. As she ran, a loaf of bread fell out from the inside of her coat. In her haste, she didn't notice it.

Other people were running around. One small boy, about ten years old, saw the loaf on the ground and scooped it up at a run.

The young mother had turned the corner, but then came back running—apparently she had noticed her missing loaf of bread. She ran up and down the street, frantically looking everywhere, on the sidewalk, in the gutter, up and down the street she ran.

Aeroplane engines started overhead. RRRRRR!

Whoomp! WHOOOMP! Whoomp! RRRRR! . . . Whoomp! WHOOMP! The mother looked up again, her mouth now wide open, crying, tears streaming out of her sunken eyes. RRRRR! Whoomp, WHOOMP! She sat on the curb, sat the child next to her, hung her head down, and convulsed with sobs. The bread was gone. Who cares if a bomb lands on me?

What was the *matter* with us men? We were supposed to *protect* mothers and children, not terrorize them. If we brave men had differences, we were supposed to settle them man-to-man, but what were we doing? We were dragging innocents into *our* fight. We were dropping bombs on them, forcing them to leave their homes and flee down dangerous roads. With submarines and blockades we were starving children, old people, mothers. We were stealing the last loaf of bread from this woman on the street. And *all* of us were doing it. *All* of us. We brave men of England, France, Germany, and now America, had all declared war against those who could not harm us. We were bullies, overgrown, brutal bullies. And the children suffered.

Karlsruhe was an interrogation center for prisoners, so it was only a matter of time before they called on me. On the afternoon of May 21 my turn came.

They brought me into a bright, cheery office. Big windows looked out over the Rhine River and the wooded bluffs on the other side. There was one desk, two chairs, and one German officer in the room.

"Sit down, Lieutenant Gallagher," the interrogating officer said with a smile, "pull up a chair, I believe they say in America, do they not?"

I sat down. He sat on the edge of his desk. Smooth, this character was, smooth and oily. His uniform was just a little bit rumpled, just the tiniest bit. He probably knew that Americans resented the crisp, Prussian look. He wanted to get on my "good side."

"I am Captain Gruber. Cigarette?" He pulled one out of his pocket and handed it to me. I didn't light it.

"One of yours. From Virginia, I think. You grow a lot of tobacco in Virginia, don't you?" Off the desk he came, wandering around the room, turning his back to me and looking out the windows. "Beautiful place, Virginia. I went to school by Charlottesville, the University of Virginia." He shook his head a little. "In the autumn, when the leaves changed . . . those Blue Ridge Mountains," he said, then turned back toward me, "beautiful. Ever been there? Is that where you are from? Where *are* you from, Herr Gallagher, if you don't mind me asking?"

I wasn't saying anything, wasn't saying "uh, huh," or letting myself fall into breezy conversation with him. This was a wolf in sheep's clothing.

"Surely, Herr Gallagher, America is not going to lose the war if you simply tell me where you're from, will it? Look around you," he gestured, "this is no torture chamber. This isn't the Spanish Inquisition. I'm not going to stretch you on the rack or poke your eyes out," he laughed at his little joke. Some joke! I'm his prisoner and he's joking about poking my eyes out. He kept on talking, trying to loosen me up.

Nothing.

"As a matter of fact, I have some cousins in Milwaukee who work at a brewery." He made a great expansive gesture with his arms. "They make *ten* times what I make in the army. They are *rich*. They live like *kings*. Have their own house, their own automobile, a telephone. To tell you the truth," he lowered his voice to a conspiratorial whisper, "I'd like to go to America when this war is over. Maybe you could help me out a little." His index finger pointed at me then back at him, as if we were real chums now. "It never hurts to have friends." Oh, he was good, he was so good. It would have been the easiest thing in the world to start chatting away with him.

Nothing.

"No? Not friends? Can't help each other out?" he asked, hurt that I should be so "impolite." How could I suspect anything from old Captain Gruber? Why, we were pals!

He lit another cigarette.

"OK, we're done," he said. That *did* throw me off track. I thought they would have worked on me a *little* longer. I started to lower my guard a little. This interrogation hadn't been half bad. "Oh, wait, just a few formalities before we go. Paperwork, you know. Doesn't every army have its paperwork?" Another big smile and a nod from Gruber. His gestures, his expressions—he really seemed like another American, with just a trace of an accent.

Gruber pushed a sheet of paper in front of me and handed me a fountain pen.

"Please fill this out completely, it will help us expedite your transfer to your permanent location. I'll be back in just a few minutes," he said. Oh, well, paperwork. Gruber was right about *that*. Every army had a mountain of paperwork. It was almost a relief to see the Germans had it, too.

He left the office, I picked up the pen.

The sheet of paper started innocently enough, and he must have figured I'd just fill in every space, the same way I had filled out every other form I'd ever seen in my life.

> Name—
> Date of Birth—
> Unit—
> Date of Entry into Service—
> Date of Departure from United States—
> Transport Ship—
> Route of Passage—
> Defensive Measures Taken en Route—
> Arrival Point in France—
> Numbers of Tanks in Your Sector—

Almost by reflex, I started filling in the blanks. I had gotten past name and date of birth when I saw the ruse. That Gruber was one clever son-of-a-bitch.

Gruber came back in ten minutes and picked up the paper.

"Herr Gallagher, you've spilled ink all over this form. I can't read anything you've written!" he said, irritated as hell. Some of the ink dripped down onto his trouser leg, making a stain, a *permanent* stain, on his uniform.

"I'm sorry, Captain Gruber, it must have leaked. Germany can't seem to make a pen that can write," I said, all innocence.

He dropped the paper in the wastebasket, turned around once, then put both hands on the desk and leaned towards me. *My* ruse had worked, he didn't look like an American anymore. He looked like a hopping-mad German, like the enemy.

"Very funny. Very funny, Herr Gallagher. I recall you Americans are big on jokes," he said, suddenly distancing himself from "you Americans."

"You'll soon find out," I said.

Gruber pushed himself up off the desk, turned around to face the windows, and put his hands behind his back. I could hear him counting to himself, trying to regain his composure, "*Eins, zwei, drei* . . . (one, two, three . . .)"

It didn't work, he whirled around and *slammed* his hands on the desk. When he spoke this time, he was furious, red in the face. Spit came out while he was talking.

"Just why are you in this fight, anyway? What's an American . . . wait . . . Gallagher. That's an Irish name, isn't it? Why is an American, with Irish blood, no less, fighting to maintain the British Empire? You heard about the Easter Rebellion, didn't you? British soldiers, British gunboats firing on your very own Irishmen!" Divide and conquer, that's what Gruber was trying now. Get me to forget my American roots, and concentrate on the Irish. No sir!

"I am at war with Germany because my country, America, is at war with Germany. Your submarine attacks, and . . . " I said, in a slow, measured cadence. At long last, I found out what it was like to be a louse, burrowing under someone's skin, driving them mad.

"Oh nonsense! You went to war for money, pure and simple. America loaned England money and wanted to make sure it collected on those loans," his words and spit were firing at me like a machine gun.

"That's funny, the British told me we stayed *out* of the war because of money. I guess it all depends on your point of view, doesn't it?" I said, with the biggest, friendliest smile that ever came out of America's heartland.

Gruber had gone from red to purple now. What had happened to that chummy Virginia graduate I had just met fifteen minutes ago?

He waved a hand dismissively. "Not that it really *matters* why you entered the war. Our U-boats won't let anything across the Atlantic. Do you hear me? *Nothing* will get across the Atlantic!"

I reached into my front pocket and pulled out the cigarette he'd given me.

"Then how did *this* get here?" I asked, with genuine puzzlement on my angelic face.

Now it was his turn to say nothing.

He sat down at the desk, trying to regain his composure. Opening a drawer, he pulled out a fresh sheet of paper. The color on his face returned to near normal. But now his questions were all business, nothing chummy about them at all.

"All right, Herr Gallagher, how about one last question. Nothing loaded about this question, nothing to debate. Fair enough?" Was that a note of pleading I heard?

I ran the cigarette under my nose and took a deep breath in.

He ignored my smart aleck maneuver with the cigarette. "How many Americans are in France?" he asked.

"Captain Gruber," I said, his pen at the ready, "you can write this down. I think it's about a million, but if it takes *ten* million to beat you, that's what we'll send, *ten million*. And Captain Gruber?" I wanted to make sure he was looking at me, not at the piece of paper.

He stopped writing and looked up.

"Yes?" he said.

"You can write one more thing on that piece of paper. We *will* crush you!"

I put the cigarette in my mouth.

"*Haben Sie Feuer?* (Have you got a light?)"

Chapter 14

PRISONER IN THE BLACK FOREST

May 22 – September, 1918

He didn't light it.

I don't think Captain Gruber liked me. The next day, two other Americans, named Phipps and Quigley, and I were hustled aboard a train by two of the grumpiest guards I ever encountered. On our long trip they didn't give us *any* food. The whole time the guards ate like kings, right in front of us. Captain Gruber put them up to it, I'm sure. That man just didn't appreciate my style.

Our destination was the town of Villingen, in the southern part of Germany, near Switzerland. Villingen was in the middle of the Black Forest. The Black Forest-images of Hansel and Gretel, skipping through the woods, came to mind. And images of ogres, trolls hiding under the bridges, and wicked witches appeared, too. We were not going to the Black Forest for rest, or vacation—we were going there to be imprisoned—jailed—warehoused until something, some event beyond our control, set us free. We would not be characters in a fairy tale—we would be prisoners in the Black Forest.

One of the guards told us—with his mouth full and ours empty—that Villingen was originally set up to house Russian prisoners.

"*Alte Feinde* (old enemies)," the guard said, mopping out his bowl of soup with a piece of rye bread, "*Und jetzt, neue Feinde, die Amis* (and now, new enemies, the Americans)," he laughed, opening his mouth wide, showing us his partially chewed up food. Up until this point, I had never "surrendered my heart to hatred" regarding the Germans. But that heckling guard, with his haughty "kick 'em while they're down" attitude, just pushed me over the edge.

Yes, the Germans had their Major Landenburgs, their kindly Rhinelander fellows, their fearless machine gun officers. They could and did show kindness, but the Germans also had a darker side—worse than the dark side the Britishers sometimes showed, much worse than the carefree French. The Germans were merciless when they were winning.

When their star was shining, when the war was going their way—as it was now—then the German demands kept going up and up. They wanted the British fleet, the French ports, the coal-bearing areas of eastern France, land in Russia. More and more and more. And once they had all this, supreme imperial power, then what? More land. More ports. More and more. There was no end to it.

And what kind of treatment would people get who came under German rule? For that answer, we only had to look in the open, laughing, food-filled mouth of our German guard. All for him. None for us.

God help us if Germany won this war.

The train chugged along, curving through steadily rising hills. Trees started to close in, so closely packed that the forest looked black, hence the name Black Forest. Hunger made my bones feel hollow, as if I were cannibalizing my own bone marrow to stay alive. Our bastard guards gave us water, but that only teased our stomachs. Our innards churned with each swallow, turning the water over and over, saying "Where's the food, where's the nutrition?"

Despair came from two directions. First, the war was not going well for us. Though the Germans did seem to have slowed (from what I could see at the

Feldlazarett), they certainly had a lot of fight left in them. They could *still* win the war before many Americans arrived. Second, the duration of our imprisonment was unknown. Would the war end in 1918? 1919? 1920? Would a new stalemate occur? Would new trench lines form that held and held and held, while we waited and waited and waited? And while these thoughts assailed me, the Black Forest got thicker and thicker—walls of wood, miles deep, imprisoning us.

We arrived at Villingen and marched right through the center of the medieval-looking walled town. Huge, thick watchtowers poked above the walls, as if Villingen had always guarded prisoners. The stones in the wall were black and gray, with green steaks running down from copper drain pipes. The walls seemed to be crying for the prisoners. No one in the town cried for us, though, or even turned their heads as we went by. On a hill outside town stood a rectangular camp with barbed wire around it. Surrounding the camp, in all directions, was the Black Forest. There was a kind of relief to be at the end of our long journey, but no joy in seeing our own prisoner-of-war camp. The despair and desperation I felt on that walk up to Villingen I cannot describe; my comrades, Captain Phipps and Lieutenant Quigley, felt the same.

I had a personal reason for dreading this internment, too. For six months, my growth as a doctor had been tremendous: first, Maxwell's tutelage at Chichester; then, my front-line work. Even in the German Feldlazarett, with its terrible conditions, I had done *some* "doctoring." In this prisoner-of-war camp, my skills were sure to rust. There would be some kind of sick call, probably, and I would be able to help there, but it wouldn't be the same as manning a Battalion Aid Post.

All hope was not lost, though, for there were some rumors doctors were to be exchanged.

"*Achtung! Herr Oberst Leutnant Ehrt!* (Attention, Lieutenant Colonel Ehrt!)"

A fat, blustery Prussian with a humorless scowl and a chest full of medals strutted out in front of us. Next to him was a slighter fellow who translated for him.

"Welcome to Villingen prisoner-of-war camp. You will be fairly treated here if you follow the rules." The translator's voice was flat and heavily accented. He regarded us as one might regard a handful of rats, entrusted to one's care.

A long list of do's and don'ts—mostly don'ts—followed. I was so hungry I could hardly pay attention.

"From 9:30 to 11:30 every morning, you will be allowed to walk outside the camp for fresh air and exercise. You will sign a parole card promising you will not try to escape during your walk. If you break your parole and try to escape, you will be shot." For the first time, the translator put some inflection in his voice, emphasizing the word "shot." He looked like he would *love* it if we made a break for it, probably shooting us himself.

"One last thing. Notice over there," he pointed to his left, to the middle of the camp. There was a square area with lines around it and a low net in the middle. In my fog of depression and hunger, I thought I was seeing a mirage. A mirage of a tennis court!

"If you hit the tennis ball over the fence," he pointed to the barbed wire fence surrounding the camp, "Please ask a guard to get it for you. *Achtung!*" That *was* a tennis court. What was a tennis court doing in a prisoner-of-war camp?

Our commandant returned to his office, his translator following. The guards marched us into the main enclosure. A bunch of prisoners mobbed us, their accents from all corners of the United States. I couldn't hardly put a face to the accent, though; they were all talking at once.

"Hey, where'd they get you?"—a Northeastern, maybe New England accent asked.

"Lux told us Americans would be in this batch!"—Southern.

"Hungry? We've gotten some Red Cross stuff!"—Southern, possibly Texas.

"We could tell you were Yanks, you can see it"—Midwestern, but not Minnesota.

"Any news? How's the war going?"—New York, no doubt.

"Don't you worry about Ehrt, he's all fuss and feathers"—bland and neutral, hard to tell.

"How'd you like that crack about the tennis ball? It's the only joke he knows. He tells it to all the new prisoners."—the Northeastern accent again, Boston?

"Yeah, there's not enough rubber in all of Germany to make a damned tennis ball."—Midwest, Chicago.

"What's the news from the Front?"—Southern.

"Any more Americans coming?"—deep, deep Southern.

"Are the Germans running out of steam?"—neutral, unidentifiable.

"When did they get you?"—New York again.

"You hurt?"—too hard to say.

"You got a tennis racquet?" Everyone laughed at that last line.

I had to hold up my hands. It was a welcome sight, but a little too much at one time. Phipps and Quigley, too, looked overwhelmed. One fellow stepped forward.

"Bill Tenney, Vermont, nice to meet you." He was the one with the New England accent. Tenney turned to the bunch of eager Yanks, waving them off.

"OK, OK. Been a long trip. Let's get you fellows a little grub and get you bunked down." He led us toward the barracks."I know there's places you'd rather be, fellas, but for now, this is home."

There sure as hell *were* other places I'd rather be, but at least I was among friends, and they were Americans. As I stepped into the barracks, I looked around the camp. Guard towers stood at all four corners, an electric wire ran above the barbed wire fence, feeding big electric lights, guards with rifles marched outside the camp. Whitewashed rectangular barracks stood near the barbed wire. In the center of camp, there were some other buildings (Kitchen? Showers?) and that damned tennis court. For now, and for God knows how long, this would be my home.

Oflag (Officer's Camp) Villingen was originally set up as a Russian officers' prison camp, and still held about 200 Russians, mostly men taken early in the war. Cement barracks, good beds, and a pleasant climate made the living comfortable. Our food was drab, but it was fleshed out with rations from Red Cross parcels.

The whole notion of a prisoner-of-war camp struck me as odd. At the Front, every diabolical means of killing or maiming the enemy was considered "fair." Poison gas to smother the lungs, flaming oil to roast the flesh, explosives to break the body; all this was acceptable. When technical means failed, men would batter each other's brains in with wooden clubs, little changed since ancient history. But once you held your hands up; said "I surrender," then you became a kind of "guest" of the enemy country.

In the prisoner-of-war camp, all your needs were met. Food, medical care, sleeping quarters. Granted, the food was none too delicious, and the sleeping quarters were none too luxurious, but they sufficed. As prisoners, we did no useful or productive work, merely used up food and resources that Germany could have used. Of course, in England and France, there were large numbers of German prisoners doing the same thing we were—lolling around, doing nothing. That, I believe, is the whole reason for the decent treatment of prisoners—"You take care of our men, we will take care of your men." All reasonable and rational.

But in the setting of a war? Where all reason and rational thought were so out of place? If we took "good care" of each other's men in the prisoner-of-war camps, then why didn't we take "good care" of each other at the Front, too? Why didn't we all climb out of these muddy, cold trenches and all "agree" to above-ground barracks in the war zone? Neither side would have an advantage, and we'd all sleep better.

But you can't do that. It wouldn't be "right."

If we can agree on rules of "decency" for the captured, why not rules of "decency" for the uncaptured? Why not declare all fighting to occur on Tuesdays, or between noon and four P.M.? But such a proposal would invite laughter and ridicule. Fight only on Tuesdays? That's insane! It's more sane to fight year-round, day and night. It's more sane to drop bombs out of the sky, fire huge artillery shells at a point on a map, sweep machine gun bullets into masses of men, sink ships in mid-ocean, leaving their crews to die of thirst in their lifeboats.

Fight only between noon and four P.M.? What madman would propose that? Sane men, modern men, felt it better to release poison gas in the middle of the night, hoping to catch the enemy napping, choking him to death as he just wakes up. Sane men, modern men, felt dawn was the *best* time for an attack, and a moonless midnight the *best* time for a raid. Round-the-clock death—that was good and proper and sane.

But now that we were behind their prison camp wire, under the scrutiny of their guards, now we were safe from poison gas, from bullets, shells, and clubs. Two months ago, the German in the guard tower would have strangled me with his own hands if he had seen me on the battlefield. In a trench, he'd have shot me in the gut then stove my face in with his rifle butt as he passed by. But now, in this civilized setting of the prisoner-of-war camp, this same guard served me soup, helped me delouse my clothes, and told me about his uncle in Chicago.

Madness. This whole conflict was madness. We killed each other in one place. We took care of each other in another place. But we were enemies in both places. And once the war ended, we would shake hands and make up, as if the whole thing were a misunderstanding. Somehow, the insanity of the situation had never struck me so clearly as it had here, in Villingen. Maybe this happened because I had so much free time, too much free time, to think about such things.

But the mind cannot occupy itself with such big questions at all times. The workaday routine of camp life set in, and soon I was more preoccupied with fighting boredom than answering great philosophical questions.

The morning walks were a good way to fight off boredom and get some exercise. We signed a parole card, promising not to run away. That struck me as another odd aspect of imprisonment (we killed Germans in battle but wouldn't think it proper to lie to them), such was the order of the day.

A few of us would go out at a time, with an unarmed German along—more a chaperone than a guard. During these walks, the Black Forest lost some of the gloom and foreboding of my first day in Villingen. It *was* black, and the woods *were* thick, to be sure, but there were clearings, here and there, with some meadows. Wild flowers and thick grass filled these meadows, quite a contrast to the ravaged fields near the Front.

In one of these meadows, there was a small mound—five feet high, about twenty feet long by ten feet wide—called the "*Keltengraben* (Celt's grave)" by the Germans. No one seemed to know its exact contents or the original date of construction. As we passed it nearly every day on our walks, we adopted it as a local landmark (of possible utility as a rendezvous point if we ever tried a legitimate "escape"). To tweak our noses at our captors, we renamed it "The Old Hun's Grave." But the Germans either didn't understand the joke (calling them Huns right to their face) or else didn't care, for we could never get a rise out of them.

Out on the morning walk, we swapped "capture" stories.

"I was on a freighter in the Indian Ocean," one old sea captain told me, "when the German raider *Wolfe* took us. The most gentlemanly pirate you ever saw. Made sure we all got off safe, then sank my ship with three shots below the waterline."

An infantry lieutenant, John Walker from Cleveland, had an all too common capture story—he got lost. "We were on a night raid. Up goes a flare. I jump into a shell hole. When the flare goes out, I look around. Where'd everybody go? I lift my head up, everything looks the same. Did I come from this way, that way? Pretty soon I crawl through a break in the wire and jump into the cleanest, neatest trench you ever saw. Funny, I think to myself, our trench was all full of mud. Well, guess where I was?" (The Germans tended to have better maintained trenches.) "How about you?" he asked me.

"Got overrun back near Amiens. I don't think they ever got Amiens, but they got me. That's about it. Not much of a story there, I'm afraid." I turned to our other walking companion, an aviator. "How'd they get you, Major Brown?"

He just shook his head.

Later, at dinner, I asked about the aviator's story. (He wasn't at our table.) A few knowing grins went around.

"It's no wonder Major Brown didn't want to tell you," someone said, "he made quite a gaffe."

"Oh?" I asked. We were sitting down to thin barley soup and black bread. Some canned meat from our Red Cross parcels fleshed out the meal pretty well. The barracks' walls had a few signs on them, instructing us where to put our dishes, our cups, our silverware. Another sign gave the menu for the week. Pretty depressing reading, all of it. I wish they'd put a few pictures up.

"Seems he was leading an entire squadron on patrol, spots his aerodrome through the fog, and brings the whole lot of them down for a perfect landing. Hops out of his plane, his men follow, and the German commander of the German aerodrome walks right up to him and shakes his hand. How do you like that?" Tenney, the man from Vermont, said. He was grinning. You couldn't *help* but grin, it *was* a pretty good story. Boy, that would be embarrassing.

"He landed at a German aerodrome?" I bit into a hunk of gristle. No one said the Red Cross parcels were gourmet fare. "No wonder he doesn't want to talk about it," I said.

Tenney finished the story, "That very afternoon, a Hun flyer goes over the American aerodrome and drops a message, thanking them for the timely delivery of some fine machines. They asked if they could send the squadron leader back, so he could deliver some more."

Inside the camp we did what we could to pass the time. We converted the tennis court into a kind of baseball diamond. Our bats were pretty crude, and forever breaking, but the games were fun, nonetheless. We got hold of some books and set up a little lending library. Sometimes a fellow would recite a long poem, providing a little entertainment at night after lights out. I even won a few kudos for my rendition of "The Cremation of Sam McGee" by Robert Service. It's too bad Mike Cahill (the Oxford Battalion's Medical Officer, the fellow who had memorized so much Shakespeare) wasn't in our camp, he could have entertained us for hours. (I had learned he was alive and well, but was at some other camp.) That rounded out our home-grown amusement.

The Germans showed us moving picture shows a few times a week, but they were awful. (Why they couldn't capture a Charlie Chaplin movie was beyond me.) All the flickers had the same plot (a love triangle); all had the same few actors and actresses (Germany was running short of everything, including motion picture actors); and there was no organist to provide the all-important background music. The best part of these shows was the smart aleck comments the other fellows would make.

"Go on, kiss her Fritz!!"

"What are you waiting for, Gretchen? Better make hay while the sun shines!"

"You don't want to die a virgin, do you, honey?"

Our guards would sometimes get angry at our "supplementary dialogue," and threaten to stop the movie projector, but we just kept on shouting.

The Germans had a canteen, operated by a civilian named Lux. Cahill would have used a Shakespearean phrase to describe him—"a lean and hungry man." Lux wore dark clothes, dark shoes, and a dark expression. Lux's forehead was quite high, his ears overly large, his mustache neatly trimmed, and his heart black as coal, for Lux was a terrible crook.

Through some arrangement between the German government and the Allies, we received some pay while imprisoned (another example of the "civility within barbarism" that was the war). As fast as we got our pay, Lux did his best to part us from it.

"Good coffee, fellows. Real coffee. What are you saying to that?" Lux asked, every inch the snake oil salesman. The canteen was next to the mess hall, no more than a counter at the end of a room. Lux guarded his wares there like a cat over a mouse. He would lure us in with his latest offerings, though the quality of the goods was always suspect. Lux's English was good, and he tried hard to pick up our slang expressions, but he was forever mixing things up. "What do you say to that?" became "What are you saying to that?" Not exactly wrong, but not exactly right.

"I am having one little chocolate, too, today. Come by me and you are having it right good, hmm?" He asked, in garbled English. He stood by the canteen counter, all hospitality and thievery. If there was such a thing as reincarnation (as some eastern religions believed), then Lux had been a Mississippi riverboat gambler, a pickpocket, and a highwayman in his past lives.

Lux's first loyalty was to Lux, and we suspected that most of the canteen's profits filled *his* pockets, rather than the German Treasury. It was said that "any man has his price." In Lux's case, that was especially true.

One surprise search of the camp turned up a number of illegitimate articles (compasses, files, and the like). Scuttlebutt had it that Lux had provided them to the prisoners, but no one dared turn him in, as we might need such articles in the future.

A good enough bribe to Lux could probably have gotten us: the key to the front gate, a taxi to Switzerland, and diplomatic immunity to cross the border. For a bigger bribe, Lux would serve us the Kaiser's head on a silver platter. But none of us had the asking price, so we settled for coffee, sugar, chocolates, and other little amenities, all at tremendously inflated prices. Some of the goods looked suspiciously similar to what came out of our Red Cross parcels. Lux denied that, of course.

There were Russian prisoners in our camp, so we arranged some activities with them, too. None were any good at baseball, nor could any of them appreciate my rendition of "The Cremation of Sam McGee," so we had to find another avenue of entertainment. We organized language classes. Trying to teach the Russians English was a terrible job. First of all, for *me* to teach *them*, I had to learn a little Russian myself. Russian used a different alphabet, and its grammar was fantastically complicated. Each verb had two different forms, depending on whether an action was done once or done repeatedly. And each adjective and noun could have a dozen different endings, depending on how it "functioned" in the sentence. So I made little progress in learning Russian. That, of course, handicapped my ability to teach a classroom full of Russian speakers.

Usually, in a class, the teacher knew both the language to be taught (in this case, English) and the language of the students (here, Russian), so the teacher could explain confusing points to the students in their own language. Since I knew damned little Russian, I could never "explain" the hard points at all, I just kept blundering along in English. It was a case of the blind leading the blind. If they learned anything at all, it was a miracle. One had to admire their patience and doggedness.

Lunch was quite an event when I was with them. Listening to 200 Russians slurping up their soup at the same time was something.

Poor fellows, though. Once members of the Russian aristocracy, they were now in a bad way. They had no Red Cross to send them packages, and no communication from home. A revolution had broken out in their country toppling the Tzar and the Bolsheviks were now in control. They had no way of knowing what awaited them when they returned. A lot of them expressed an interest in coming to America.

The Germans let us put together a little Fourth of July bash. Lux sold us a lot of wine and whisky. It was watered down, but we just drank more of it. We toasted, sang, toasted, feasted on Red Cross parcels, toasted, and, just for good measure, raised a few more toasts to good old America, the land of the free, and the home of the brave.

That night, we irritated the Germans by singing a song *"Ach du lieber Augustin"* that ended with a rousing, *"Deutschland kaputt!"* The Germans couldn't see the humor in it, but we sure did, and kept on singing it, even after lights out, when we were supposed to be quiet.

But we finally got tired and did quiet down. Then one of the sailors, who had never talked much before, started telling us a story. The whisky must have loosened his tongue.

"I never told anyone this before, fellows. I killed a man once."

The barracks were quiet, but no one was sleeping.

The sailor told us he had been first mate on a sailing vessel and a part of the crew had mutinied. As first mate, it was his job to whip the crew into submission and in the effort he had killed a man.

"They acquitted me," the sailor said. "The court's opinion was 'an officer must use whatever force is necessary to restore order in a mutiny.' They didn't have to tell *me* that. *I* know what an officer has to do. But I didn't have to kill that man. I could have just crowned him one, but I didn't. I killed him because I *wanted* to kill him, not because I had to. I was guilty. Guilty as sin. They should have hanged me."

He never spoke about it again. Neither did we.

One day we heard some aeroplane engines, and were surprised to look up high over our heads and see nine Allied bombers, flying in a "V" formation, high over our camp. They dropped bombs on Offenburg, about ten miles to the north of us. On their way back, they flew right over us, very high again. Still, we jumped, cheered, and waved our arms. Our actions angered the Germans to no end—they kept yelling at us to get inside our barracks. The Germans crawled low to the ground the whole time, afraid of being seen and bombed, but we had no fear. These were *our* planes, a full *seventy miles* east of the Rhine! We *must* be doing well, we *must* be advancing, to be able to launch planes this deep into Germany. It was a beautiful sight, that "V" formation. We had been starved for news, couldn't decipher much from the heavily censored German papers, but these planes told the story, in no uncertain terms. We knew that Paris must not have fallen, that the Germans had to be losing. *Die Allies vorwärts, die Deutschen rennen jetzt* (The Allies are going forward, the Germans are running now), I thought to myself, reversing the words of that rotten German doctor in the Feldlazarett. With any luck, he was seeing some of these "V" formations himself. Maybe that bastard guard on the train had seen a few, too. Ha! Then I remembered the woman on the sidewalk, holding her children, looking for the lost bread, crying.

Maybe she had seen that "V" formation, too.

July 20, a new prisoner, Lieutenant Isaacs, joined us. It turned out he was raised in Cresco, Iowa just south of Waseca. What's more, Isaacs' brother had come up to Waseca many times to play baseball against us. I thought the name sounded familiar. About ten years before I had pitched a game against his brother, and he got three home runs off me.

Isaacs and I were walking around the compound. Isaacs was a very intense man, and hated the Germans. They had beaten the hell out of him earlier, when he tried to escape off a train by diving through a window.

"Tell me something, Gallagher. How would someone from Iowa go about getting out of this place?" He was studying the wire, the guard towers. He wanted out.

"Lieutenant Isaacs, we have pondered that question long and hard, and we have come up with three ways to get away from Villingen," I said.

"Enlighten me," he said, no humor in his voice. This man was all business.

"One—the war ends," I said.

"No way of knowing when that will be," said Isaacs.

"Two—exchange of prisoners. The other doctors in here, me included, are hoping the Red Cross swaps us for some German doctors. They say it could happen any time," I said.

"I'm not medical," Isaacs said. "I'm Annapolis, and I have information on the German Navy that the Allies could use. I was taken aboard one of their submarines when my ship was sunk. I saw the map of their sea routes. We could use that information to sink those U-boat bastards. You medical guys can sit on your asses here all you want. I'm looking for 'live wires' who . . . "

"That brings us to number three," I interrupted him, making no attempt to be polite. "Do you know what number three is?"

He pointed to the barbed wire and made an arch-like motion, mimicking a jump over the wire.

"Escape," I said.

For the first time, Isaacs smiled at me.

Chapter 15

ESCAPE

Chess was a game pitting two equal opponents across an 8 inch x 8 inch square "battlefield." Skill and skill alone determined the victor, for there was no "lucky throw of the dice" or "lucky draw from the deck." A knight moved the same for the white as for the black. There was no "cheating," no hidden moves. The battle was all out in the open, fair and square. We prisoners had a chess game going on with our German captors.

At first blush, the match seemed uneven. They, after all, had guns, guard towers, barbed wire, lights, and the dense Black Forest to keep us penned in. The Swiss border, twenty miles away, was guarded at all crossing points. Even if one were to get all the way to the border, the icy-cold, fast-flowing Rhine River added yet another barrier to freedom. We could get no maps, of course, or compasses through official channels. And our daily walks revealed that the Black Forest was cut by innumerable ravines and gullies, making any attempt to walk "cross-country" almost impossible. So this chess match—the Germans wanting to keep us imprisoned, we wanting to escape—seemed no match at all. They had all the advantages.

Almost.

We had "the prisoner's advantage." Every prisoner, from war captive, to armed robber in the state penitentiary, had time. Time to think. Time to think of escape. Time was "the prisoner's advantage." A guard, no matter how dedicated, had only one shift to think about his work. His shift might last 8 hours, or 12 hours, or even 24 hours. But at the end of that shift, he returned to his "other life." That "other life" might not be far away (our guards stayed at a barracks nearby) but it was something *other* than guard life. The prisoner had no "other life," for he was always a prisoner. So a guard might think about stopping escape attempts for several hours at a stretch, but a prisoner *never* stopped thinking of escape.

It never occurred to us the Germans might actually *shoot* us if we tried to escape. Shoot us during a battle, yes, that we understood. In combat, the chess match was even—they had guns, we had guns, they had artillery, we had artillery, they had trenches, we had trenches. Ready, set, start shooting. Combat was a big, murderous version of capture-the-flag, with live ammunition. But to shoot us for trying to escape? When they had guns and we didn't? Unfair.

You couldn't shoot a man who had used his wits to outfox you. Bad form. Just bad form.

So, with the knowledge the Germans *could* shoot us if we tried to escape, but a belief they *wouldn't* if push came to shove, we set up escape plans. We would beat them at this chess game, even if they had the guns.

And each escape attempt would be a new game.

Game 1 — The Parole Card Gambit

Ivan Fodorovitch strolled out of Villingen POW camp one fine morning. He had just handed over his parole card. Only it wasn't *his* parole card, it was his brother's, Gregor Fodorovitch. Technically, Ivan had NOT given his word to not escape.

Russian bishop threatens German queen.

Once outside the camp, Ivan bolted through the woods. He *was* within the letter of the law in performing this escape. It was a clever move, switching the parole cards like that, kind of like the game of three card monte, with the ace forever showing up in the wrong place.

Russian bishop takes German queen.

The Black Forest defeated clever Ivan, though, for he soon tired of cutting through ravines and cold streams, and returned to a road, where he was soon captured.

Russian bishop captured, Russian king trapped. Checkmate.

The Germans, never long in the humor department, didn't see Ivan's move as clever, and threatened to shoot him. But they didn't.

New game.

Game 2 — Under the Bottom

Another Russian officer, who'd been languishing in this prison since 1914, made a bold and simple escape attempt. One area of the fence lay in shadow, so he simply ran out to it one night, scraped the dirt away at the bottom of the barbed wire enclosure, and wriggled under it.

Russian rook takes a German knight.

The brutal simplicity of his plan drew our admiration, and we all marveled at the shallow "scrape" he'd managed to wiggle through.
He stayed out longer than Ivan Fodorovitch had, apparently learning from his comrade's mistake.

Russian rook takes second German knight. Check.

But hunger drove him to a farmhouse, where he was caught trying to steal some eggs. He, too, was dragged in a few days later, dejected by his recapture.

German queen captures bothersome Russian rook. Checkmate. New game.

Game 3 — Sneak Attack

In a true chess match, there was no cheating. Not so in this one.

One day in September, the Germans called a surprise *Appell* (roll call). They went right into our barracks and uncovered hidden items such as compasses, wire cutters, and primitive shovels.

German knight jumps American pawns. German bishop provides coverage. Checkmate in five moves.

Someone had informed on us, we suspected the Russkies. The Germans would "pay" them extra food in exchange for information about escape attempts. We made it a point to keep our plans to ourselves from then on.

New game.

Game 4 — Over the Top. The All-American Gambit.

Joe Durso and I plastered ourselves against the wall of the barracks, in the shadows. It was night, and the escape attempt was on. Joe and I were two of the "light men" in the escape, our role was to knock out the lights and plunge the camp into darkness so two other groups of men could escape. Lieutenant Willis, the escape committee chairman, had gone over the plan with us a half dozen times that very afternoon.

"The 'light men' went to the four corners of the camp, staying in the shadows. At 10:40 they threw their weighted wires up and over the electric lines which provided power to the camp lights."

Knocking out the camp lights was the key to the entire escape. The two groups of escapers needed pitch blackness to make their moves. We had studied the lights for a long time, looking for their "Achilles heel."

All the camp lights had electrical wires running to them, and these electrical wires looked vulnerable. If we could somehow pull the electrical wires down, they might short-circuit, and the lights would go out.

One of our prisoners had spent some time in Argentina, and had seen the gauchos down there using "boleros," which are two balls connected by a rope. When thrown around a cow's legs, the rope wrapped around and tripped the cow. He wondered whether we could fashion a kind of "bolero" and throw it around the electrical wires that went to the lights.

We had gotten some lengths of wire and attached rocks at each end, creating a kind of "bolero." The idea was to throw these weighted wires up and over the electrical lines. With any luck, the "bolero" would wrap around the electrical line, pull it down, short-circuit the lights, and darken the camp. Whether this plan would work we did not know.

Willis explained the rest of the escape plan, "Once the lights are out, we'll put together the ladders, push out the screens from the barracks windows, lay the ladders on the wire, crawl out, and send you a letter from Switzerland." Willis was nothing if not confident.

We had filed away at the window screens on our barracks, so that the screens could be easily pushed out. The process had been laborious; we had no files, and we had to hide our intentions from the guards. We used spoon handles to grind away at the screens. Day after day, night after night, different men would gnaw at those damned screens. Our fingers got bloody raw after a few days of this. Meanwhile, our bed slats had been transformed into cleverly concealed ladders. Obviously, we couldn't keep a ladder sitting around in the barracks, so we disassembled them, scattered the component parts, and practiced putting them together, over and over again, until the ladders could be built in 20 seconds. The "ladder men" would be the first group of escapers. The "guard men" would be the second group of escapers.

Willis continued, detailing the plans for the "guard men." "Once the lights are out, everyone make noise, throw cans, blow whistles. Anything to distract the guards. When the real guards come running out, the "guard men" will mix in with them and try to go out the gate." We had fashioned some of our coats and caps to look German—at least in silhouette—and had carved some wooden rifles. In the dark and confusion, the false uniforms and rifles might work. The "guard men" might go right out the front gate, unnoticed in all the confusion.

Willis looked over the three different groups of men—first, the "light men," second, the "ladder men," third, the "guard men." "This plan is not foolproof, or guaranteed, or safe. The lights may not go out. The ladders may break. The Germans might shoot any of us, and stray bullets could go right through the barracks windows, hitting people who hadn't even joined in the escape." He let that sink in. It was a lot to think about. The prison camp was basically safe. If you towed the line, you would not get shot. But if you tried to escape, well, you might very well *get* shot. All of us had been off the battleground, out of danger, for a long time. We were, in effect, "volunteering" to go back into the battleground, when it was perfectly honorable to remain a prisoner, and play it safe. I knew *I* had a few second thoughts.

"Say the word and we call it off," Willis said, looking over everyone.

No one said a thing.

Isaacs was going out over the wire, he was a "ladder man," but he had one problem—his boots were worn out. He would need good ones to tramp through the Black Forest and get to Switzerland. I gave him mine; they fit him perfectly. I would not escape, (the "light men" were only to knock out the lights), but my boots might.

American pawn moves forward two spaces.

Durso looked down at his watch.

"10:38, we'd better get over to that corner," he said.

There was one stretch of about ten feet that was bathed in light, then it was dark again in the corner.

"I thought it was shadow all the way over there," I whispered.

"Me too. Think we should run through it?" Durso asked.

"As opposed to, what? We can't exactly walk through it," I said, not so much irritated at Joe, as I was scared of running through that patch of light.

"10:39, Ben, we'd better run."

We pushed off from the barracks and took off running.

Durso had been a pilot. He had the makings of a hero, but bad luck prevented him from performing any heroic deeds.

"The first time my squadron went into combat, we brought down three Hun planes. Fighters. Three fighters!" Durso said.

"Did you get one of them?" I asked.

"No, like I said, my *squadron* was in action. *I* was in the infirmary, with measles."

Later, Joe did get into combat; he told me about his first dogfight.

"This triplane, a Fokker, I think, was on my tail, but I pulled a hard left turn, he passes me, I kick back right, and I've got him."

"You brought him down?" I asked.

"No, I missed." He shrugged his shoulders and held his hands, palms up.

"You missed?"

"I missed. Have you ever tried to *fly* a plane, *cock* a gun, *aim* the gun, and *hit* another plane? Mind you, the other fellow isn't puttering along a ruler-straight country lane at 20 miles per hour, either. He's twisting and turning every which way trying very hard *not* to get shot. I fired at him all right, but I didn't hit him. All my shots flew past him. I hit some innocent little cloud."

"I don't think they count a cloud as a kill, Joe," I observed.

"No they don't. It's a shame. I'd have been an ace if they did. I shot a lot of clouds, Ben, but I never shot a German," Joe admitted.

Later, Joe was flying over Chateau Thierry, one of America's first big battles in the Great War.

"No one around. No Germans. No Americans. Nobody. Not even any *clouds* to add to my tally. All of a sudden, I see black. I figure I've been shot dead. I reach up. It's oil. Oil all over my goggles. Sprung an oil leak somehow. No anti-aircraft fire, no Red Baron shooting at me, just a mechanical problem. Well, Ben, an aeroplane is just a flying engine, and an engine can't run without oil, so I have to go land, but quick," Joe said.

"Ended up behind the Germans, did you?" I asked, then felt myself a fool. What kind of question was that? Of course he ended up behind the Germans! How else would he have ended up in this prisoner-of-war camp?

"Not only did I land behind the German lines. I came down next to a detachment of their Uhlans," Joe said.

"Their cavalry?" I asked. For some reason, the Germans called their cavalry Uhlans. It sounded vaguely Mongolian, perhaps they thought themselves modern day Genghis Khans.

"Yes. Their cavalry. I came bumping to a stop next to a bunch of fellows riding horses. And these fellows are holding spears. Spears, Ben! They come riding up to me pointing their spears at my plane. It was like being taken prisoner by Sir Lancelot."

Durso and I dashed across the lit area to the darkened corner. We made it! It was my deepest and most sincere desire not to get shot dead right then and there. Nothing happened, the guards had not seen us.

Durso grabbed his rock-wire-rock "bolero" and I grabbed mine. He looked down at his watch.

"10:40, Ben."

We heaved the "boleros." They went up, wrapped around the electrical lines, and pulled them down, just as we had hoped. To our great surprise and joy, the lights flickered for an instant, then went out. It worked! We started running back to our barracks, through the middle of the pitch-black camp.

American pawn takes German bishop.

We were in the middle of the compound, the exact center of the yard, when all the lights came back on. Joe and I froze, squinting in the brilliant light.

"I hope their aim is as bad as mine," Joe said.

Bang! Bang! Bang!

They shot me? Everything went completely black. I saw nothing. Someone grabbed my arm. An angel? St. Peter?

"Ben, get moving! Those are the lights exploding. Let's go!" Joe shouted.

My eyes adjusted to the dark. I could make out outlines of the barracks. There was a crash as the barracks' screens fell out. You could hear the ladders scraping as they were laid on the fence. The "ladder men" were making their escape. Guards started shooting and blowing whistles. The "guard men" would be mixing in with the real guards now, trying to escape out the front gate. So far, the whole plan was working.

"Ben, come on!" Joe shouted again.

American rook threatens German king.

The Germans tried to line us up and count us, to see how many had gotten away, but we played sleepy, making it harder for them to line us up just right for an accurate count. And we mixed up our roll call, too. When they called for Isaacs, for example, I must have thought they said Gallagher, because I said, "Here!" An honest mistake.

At dawn, we discovered some terrible vandalism in our barracks. Someone had stolen our bed slats and someone else had cut our window screens out.

"Who put this ladder here?" the captain of the guards asked.

It was a mystery to us.

"Who knocked down these electrical wires?"

We looked at each other, shrugging our shoulders.

"You think this is a game? Is that what you think? Well, you will find out how much fun it is to play games with us," the guard said, fire in his eyes.

Two weeks later, Durso and I were again leaning against the barracks. But this time it was daytime and we were just killing time, not planning an escape.

Three guys were still loose as far as we knew—Isaacs, Willis, and another fellow named Puryear.

"They really let us have it, Ben. Let us have it good, the Heinie bastards," Joe said, joking.

"Yes, they did. No more morning walks. No more buying stuff at the canteen. In to bed an hour earlier," I said, playing along with Durso's mock horror. The Germans had acted like spoilsports after the escape, taking away a few petty privileges and giving us long lectures about the foolishness of trying to escape. Hey, we were prisoners, it's war time, it's our *duty* to try to escape. They didn't see it that way.

"War is hell, huh Ben?" Durso shook his head, dug his toe into the dirt, and twisted it around, then he kicked a rock.

"Yes, war is hell, Joe. Maybe I'll be able to save a little money up, now that we can't buy from Lux for awhile," I said.

Joe summarized the escape, "Well, five got out. Four got over the wire, one out the front gate. Not bad. The Fritzies recaptured two of them, but that still leaves three." Joe was digging his toe in the dirt again, starting a tunnel, maybe?

"Did you hear what Willis said, when he was crawling out on the ladder?"

"No," Joe said.

"I guess a guard looked right up at him. Shouted for him to come down. So you know what Willis said?" I asked.

"What?"

"Don't shoot. I'm looking for my tennis ball!" I said.

"No!" Joe couldn't believe it. I couldn't either, the first time I heard it, but a man holding the ladder steady inside the barracks swore it was true. That Willis had some nerve. What would Abe Haskell call it? Chutzpah—that was it—chutzpah.

"Yes! I guess that threw the guard just long enough. Willis jumped down, played hide-and-seek behind a tree with the guard. Then took off running in a hail of bullets," I said.

American bishop takes German queen.

A Red Cross inspector came to the camp a week later. He was a short, efficient man, as precise as a Swiss watch, perhaps because he was from Switzerland.

As he was going around the camp, he looked at the numbers of the barracks. He seemed to be looking for a specific number. When he got to ours, he knocked on the door. No one was inside, we were all milling around in the yard.

"Can I help you with something, Inspector?" I asked.

He looked a little flummoxed. "Your embassy in Zurich asked me to deliver a package to this specific barracks. It is *highly* unusual. I am an *inspector*, not a postman, you know." He looked at his watch. "I do *not* have a lot of time to waste." He may not have, but we sure did.

Durso was standing next to the Swiss inspector by now, "Well, let's have it, the package, come on." He held out his hand. Diplomacy was not Joe Durso's middle name.

The Swiss fellow handed off the package, pulled his hat down and left in a big huff.

We went into the barracks. No return address on the package. Durso tore it open. Out came tennis balls, one, two, three.

Checkmate. German king is taken.

What had happened? We had no way of knowing at the time, but after the war I found out what happened to Puryear, Isaacs, and Willis, the three "tennis balls."

Puryear did everything wrong, walking right down main roads, once walking through a town full of German soldiers. He carried himself with complete confidence, rather than skulking around like a thief in the night. His rumpled old jacket might have struck the Germans as belonging to one of their own allies (Bulgarian perhaps?). When some of the soldiers eyed Puryear a little too closely, he shouted *"Achtung!"* and got them to snap to attention and even salute him!

On October 11, at 5 A.M., Puryear went off the road, came to the Rhine River, shed his clothes, and swam across to freedom.

Isaacs and Willis traveled together, cutting across the difficult terrain of the Black Forest. They had close calls with passing civilians, some woodcutters, as well as some German soldiers. Both worried they were getting lost in the confused tangle of woods, when they came upon the Rhine River. A thick fog enveloped the area.

Blackening their faces with mud, Isaacs and Willis crept up to the river. At one point, Willis snapped a dry twig, alarming a German sentry posted just 20 feet away. The sentry switched on a light and pointed it directly at Willis, but the thick fog hid him. Off went the light, but the alert sentry did not go away, forcing Willis and Isaacs to painfully, painfully creep away, watching their every step.

To approach the river itself, the two men immersed themselves in a small tributary stream and crawled over sharp rocks on the stream bed. One rock slipped so loudly that another German light was turned on, this one, a powerful spotlight. Again, the fog saved them, as they froze in place (by this time, they were freezing both literally and figuratively). For two hours, they crept along this stream, only their heads above the water.

The Rhine at this point was a swirling mountain stream, with whirlpools, sharp boulders, and a strong current. Now only yards from freedom, with only a river separating them from neutral Switzerland, Isaacs confessed to Willis that he wasn't a good swimmer.

Willis, showing a bravado few men possessed, told Isaacs, "I'm a good swimmer, but I expect to drown, too."

The two pushed off into the Rhine, fighting the current's tendency to push them back to the German side. Both suffered cramps from the cold, exhaustion, and hunger. In a moment of despair, Isaacs rolled on his back, closed his eyes, and commended his soul to God. Then his feet hit a sandy bottom, the soil of Switzerland.

By now, the men were widely separated, each fearing the other may have drowned. Isaacs followed some railroad tracks until he came to a customs house. And Willis? He walked inland until he saw a building on the edge of a town. He stumbled in the door, freezing, dripping, half-dead. Where was he? A tavern.

Now that's an escape!

Chapter 16

HOME FREE

October 1918 – The End

There was an interesting paradox to seeing new prisoners arrive at Villingen. We were actually *happy* to see them! Why should we be happy to see Americans taken prisoner? More American *prisoners* meant there were more *fighting men* at the Front. Our growing presence was obvious, as prisoners came in from many different divisions. These men, though dejected by their capture, spoke with pride about the role America was now playing in the war.

The British were *still* treating us with coolness and indifference; the French were welcoming us; and the Germans, more and more, were coming to respect the fighting quality of *die Amis* (the Americans).

"*Teufelhunde* (devil dogs) they called the Americans. There was a lot of talk about some place called Belleau Wood. Apparently the Germans and Americans were going at it hammer and tongs there. According to one of the guards, the Germans were surprised at the tenacity of the American *Teufelhunde*; the Germans had been told the Americans were soft, and didn't like to fight.

"*Mein Bruder war in Belleau Wald* (My brother was in Belleau Wood)," the guard said. "*Die Amis können kämpfen, genau* (The Americans can fight all right)."

News filtered in through these new prisoners, and through an increasingly open and dissatisfied German press. On August 10 we read of the great British attack east of Amiens. Marcelcave, the town where I was captured, was again in the hands of the Allies. If only such an attack could have come during my terrible days and nights in the cellar with those wounded men. It seemed the "turning of the tide" had finally happened.

About this time, I received a letter from the Waseca Commercial Club through the American Express Company. In it was a check for five dollars and a funny letter, exhorting me to "Get the Kaiser" if I had a chance. The German censor must have been napping. Or maybe the censor didn't like the Kaiser much himself anymore.

We had a big map of France nailed up on the wall in one of the barracks. The German papers printed the official German war report, signed by Ludendorff. Much to our surprise, they also published the official Allied reports. The German report would be rather indefinite when the Germans were retreating, but the pins on the map told the story. The pins kept moving farther and farther east—the Boche were on the run at last.

I thought of those blistered Tommies as we were retreating. "We always win the last battle," one Tommy had said. I hoped he was still alive.

One of the new prisoners told me a million Americans had actually landed in France. Seems I had told the interrogator Gruber the *truth* when I said a million! And here I had just been trying to impress him with a big lie.

The German attitude had changed dramatically. In March, when they were calling the shots, they were demanding all kinds of things—the British fleet, Belgian and French coastal areas, huge reparations. But now that they were on the run, they were singing a different tune. They were eating humble pie, and starting to make peace overtures. What was the attitude now of that cocky German doctor who had taunted me, or that guard who had withheld food from us? I'll bet they were currying favor with any and all Americans, bowing and scraping before them. More than anything else, the attitude of the Germans galled the hell out of me.

On October 11, the Germans transferred the Russian prisoners to other camps. Some of these Russians were very fine fellows, and I was sad to see them go. One of them, a Lt. Serge Savelief, whose home was in Astrakhan on the Black Sea, was quite a character. He spoke French well, and was one of the few Russians able to pick up much English (just as we had a hard time learning their convoluted language, they had a hard time with ours). Serge tried to teach Lieutenant Tenney and me a little French. We weren't very good pupils, though. He spent more time and effort trying to teach us than we ever did trying to learn it. In the course of our lessons, we grew to like him. Savelief worried about his wife and daughter back home in Russia, not knowing what effect the Bolshevik Revolution would have on them, or on him when he returned. He hoped sometime to come to America to live. It was a sad *Dosvedanya* to Serge.

Another Russian, a Captain Trubnikoff from St. Petersburg, gave me a wonderful gift just before he was transferred—two paintings of the woods near the camp. Each painting in size was 12 inches by 12 inches, and showed dark green trees, gray rocks, and a reflective stream. The pictures captured the dark, shadowy presence that was the Black Forest. Beautiful work, and Trubnikoff had done it with only crude paints and canvas. It was a real gift from the heart.

"For your helpink me English to speakink," he said.

I was touched, and treasured those two paintings. No matter what, they would grace a wall in my home some day.

Once the Russians left, only the Americans remained, about 125 of us.

John Walker, the infantry lieutenant who jumped into the German trench by mistake, was standing around one day, doing nothing in particular. It was November 10. I joined him.

"John, a penny for your thoughts," I said.

"Look at them, the guards. All chummy with us now. Now that they're losing, the war," Walker said.

He was right.

Walker went on, "They laughed us off, we Americans. Now *we're* the only thing between them and the vengeful British and French. See that one, that one over there?"

He pointed to a tall, bearded guard.

"He tells me what great friendship there is between Germany and America. Great friendship!"

"Tell that to the children on the *Lusitania*," I said, picturing the sinking in my mind. Cold water, filling up the corridors, the cabins; everyone trying to get out, trying to get to the upper deck, the water closing fast around them. Closing around the mothers, holding their children, the mothers trying to reassure their frightened babies as death swallowed them up. The Germans who did this wanted to be our friends?

"Amen," Walker said. "Amen."

German newspapers now trumpeted revolution, especially the *Frankfurter Zeitung* which had been closed down by the government several times during the war for its independent and "socialist" editorials.

The political situation in Germany was becoming more and more chaotic.

- Kaiser Wilhelm II had been "in charge" of Germany during the war, though everyone knew the Prussian military leaders called the shots. Defeated, the Kaiser abdicated (stepped down) and went to Holland.

- Germany was not a democracy, so an orderly "succession" of power was not in place. (In America, if the president died, the vice-president took over, after him, the Speaker of the House of Representatives, and so on. Germany had no such system.)

- General Ludendorff, whose plans and leadership had *almost* brought the Germans victory, had resigned. That left a lot of other high-ranking German generals in charge of the armed forces. Would these generals follow the instructions of the civilian government, or would they continue on with plans of their own?

- A headline proclaimed Germany was now a republic! What did that mean? Could you create a republican form of government by simply "proclaiming" it?

- Germany had a new prime minister, a Prince Max of Baden. He was some blood relation of the Kaiser, but the Berlin government considered him a "Red" (Communist). Baden was asking for peace terms from President Wilson, but no one was sure if Baden really "spoke for" Germany. Just who was running the country?

- Pockets of revolution were popping up all over Germany. Local "committees," patterned on the Bolsheviks in Russia, were taking over local government functions. Would these "committees" follow directives from Berlin, or would they break off into little "Russia's"?

The specter of anarchy hung over the whole country. Germany's army was falling back; Germany's leadership had flown the coop; and Germany's people were starving to death after years of blockade.

And there we were, prisoners, helpless behind barbed wire, in a country going to wrack and ruin. What would happen to us?

At lunch that day—the usual soup and bread—Walker and I picked up the conversation.

"Ben, they say some revolutionary committee is coming to take over the camp tomorrow, the Soldiers' and Sailors' Council," Walker said.

"What's it mean to us?" More and more, our food was coming from Red Cross parcels. If some "revolutionary council" took the packages from us, we might starve.

"That's the big question. I understand they shot the base commandant in Karlsruhe. He didn't take down the imperial insignia fast enough, so they let him have it," Walker said.

"He didn't fit into the new scheme of things, huh?" I asked, wondering what, exactly, the new scheme of things actually *was*.

"That's right. I hope we do," Walker said.

"They wouldn't shoot prisoners, would they?" I asked.

Walker shrugged, "How should I know? I've never been in the middle of a revolution before."

That night at 9 P.M., we were just getting ready for lights out. The door to our barracks slammed open. In walked a fellow we'd never seen before, he had no insignia on his shoulders. He was short, with no hint of a smile on his face. On his hip was the fattest pistol I'd ever seen. On closer inspection, it was a flare gun! Why would he carry a flare gun with him? Was he looking for a symbol, *any* symbol of "officerhood"? Or was he going to fire it into our barracks and burn us alive? The concerns that came to mind seemed silly, but in the unpredictable new world of "revolution," anything seemed possible.

"*Achtung!* Germany has agreed to an armistice. Tomorrow at 11 A.M. there will be a cease fire. The war is over," he said, sounding official and important. He started out the door, then came back in. "Oh yes, one more thing, Col. Ehrt has been asked to leave. His services are no longer needed. That is all." The door banged shut.

Services "no longer needed"? Col. Ehrt may have been hanging from a tree or slumped against a wall at that very minute.

No one shouted, cheered, or stamped his feet. One of the sailors spoke.

"They nearly won it, the sons of bitches. I sure hope to hell they never try again."

Amen.

Our train was pulling into Berne, Switzerland. The previous few weeks had been a maddening waiting game but we finally were released from Germany. Our guards had wanted to repatriate us, all right, but the confusion resulting from the "revolution," and the end of the war had caused endless delays. At long last they finally sprung us. Walker was sitting next to me on the train. A few hours earlier, we had cheered ourselves hoarse when the train passed the German-Swiss border.

"Ben, take a look down there, at the far end of the platform." Walker's eyes were as wide as saucers.

I wriggled past him, took the window seat, and stuck my head out for a look. The train was still creeping forward, coming slowly to a stop at the Berne station platform.

"You mean those girls at the end of the platform?" I asked. The station itself was the cleanest thing I had ever seen. But the "brightest" spot was a bunch of pretty girls wearing dresses ending only halfway down their calves. There were a *lot* of well-turned ankles on that platform. They were real close now, and were waving something. I pulled my head back in and looked Walker in the eyes. He was ready to bust his buttons.

"Those are . . . ," I started to say.

The train came to a stop exactly beside the girls; they were waving American flags. One of them stuck her head in our window, and planted a huge kiss right on my lips.

"Hey you guys, welcome back," she said in a clipped Chicago accent, "how about a little chocolate?" She threw a handful of Hershey bars into our laps. "You British?"

"No," I said.

She cocked her head a little to one side. Escaping steam had drowned out what I said.

"Aussies?" Her face was creamy white and she had the cutest little button nose. She was smiling so wide you could see the gums above her teeth.

"Nope," I repeated. No steam that time, she could hear my accent. She grinned, with her right hand she reached back and started waving her friends forward.

"You're not, by chance, Canadians, are you?" she asked. Minnesotans and Canadians sounded a lot alike.

"No, sister. You are looking at two dyed-in-the-wool, A-1, real McCoy, American boys. There are 200 of us on this here train," I said, so proud of being an American I could have died.

Walker chimed in, "Born in the United States, ma'am, each of us, and raised on apple pie."

By now, four heads were poking through the window, each one prettier than the next. They all had on hats which were getting squished in the window frame. And they all talked at once.

"You guys Americans, are ya?"

"Y'all Yanks?"

"Where ya from?"

"Want some sandwiches?"

"Don't tell anyone, we got a couple of beers in this basket here. Promise you won't tell, huh? The Red Cross'd kill us if they found out." A girl with strawberry blonde hair produced two beers from a picnic basket. She looked all around before she handed them to us.

Our laps filled up with goodies. They kept handing us things with one hand, while trying to hold their hats on with the other.

"Give me a big hug, you lug," the girl with jet-black hair said. It sounded like an order to me, so like a good soldier, I obeyed.

"Yeah, me too. What's the matter, never seen a girl before? We won't bite," the strawberry blonde said.

They didn't bite. Boy, could they kiss! We had orders to stay on the train, and stay we did. But an open train window and a bunch of American girls made for a grand time. You'd have thought Walker and I had won the war single-handedly. Of course, we did nothing to dispel that myth.

Walker was in the midst of describing how he had had his hands around the Kaiser's throat when the train started pulling away from the station.

"'Mercy, mercy,' he was beggin' me." Walker's hands were choking an imaginary Kaiser.

Toot, tooooot! Hsssss! Ker-chug, woof, foof, foof, foof. The train started moving. The girl with jet-black hair was riveted by Walker's account; the other girls had a healthy dose of skepticism for my friend's fantastic yarns.

"Really? He said, 'Mercy, mercy'?" she asked. By now, she was walking alongside the moving train.

Walker said, "Those were his *exact* words. Come to Cleveland some time, I'll tell ya the rest of the story!"

The train was picking up speed.

"Wow!" She was enthralled.

She and the other girls walked alongside the train as long as they could, then we pulled away. They waved to us, getting smaller and smaller. The girl with the jet-black hair stood there, her mouth hanging down, her eyes wide open. What a story she had for her Mom and Pop! She met the man who made the Kaiser beg for mercy. Golly!

We sat back in our seats, no room for our legs with all of the goodies. Walker fished out the beers and worked the caps off.

"Mercy, mercy?" I asked.

Walker took a long pull on the beer.

"I'll admit, I may have stretched the truth a bit with that one." He was nodding, beer foam on his lip.

The Swiss countryside was rolling past the windows. It was late November, and the meadows low in the valleys had a dusting of snow. Fat black and white cows pushed the snow aside looking for grass. Big bells hung from their necks.

The beers tasted good. So good. I looked at the label. German!

"Ben, that platform back there. That little slice of America. Now that was rich." Walker was pointing backward with his thumb. His head was back against the seat, his eyes closed. Reverie.

"That is a fact," I agreed. The girls' smell was still in the air. Perfume. Powder. Clean clothes. Soap, Something. Something distinctly feminine was floating around. I closed my eyes, too, drinking in their smell.

"Ain't no girls in the world could grace a platform like that, like our American girls did," Walker said.

"They think like us, they talk like us, they know how to joke around. Nothing like 'em in the whole world, John. Here's to American girls!" I toasted. We clinked beer bottles. American girls. Nothing like 'em in the whole world.

CLICK-CLICK, click-click. CLICK-CLICK, click-click. On through Switzerland we travelled witnessing a fantastic sequence of tunnels and valleys. One minute—complete darkness, the next—bright sunshine and a snowy wonderland. We rode high along the walls of the valleys, one side of the train looked at a solid rock face, the other down a sickening cliff. These Swiss engineers knew what they were doing.

Our initial burst of enthusiasm after we crossed into Switzerland, and the second burst of energy when we saw the American girls, had worn us out. The 200 Americans on the front part of the train had quieted down, a lot of them dozing. In the rear half of the train were 300 or so British soldiers, also enjoying their first taste of freedom.

A porter came around with some envelopes, and started handing them to a few of the men. He had one for me. In it was a telegram, from the American Expeditionary Forces.

> To: 1ST LT BJ GALLAGHER
> FROM: AEF HDQRS
>
> EFFECTIVE IMMDLY: YOU ARE RELIEVED OF SERVICE IN BRITISH EXPEDITIONARY FORCES. REPORT TO ALLEREY, FRANCE FOR REASSIGNMENT TO AMERICAN EXPEDITIONARY FORCES. WELCOME BACK.

CLICK-CLICK, click-click. CLICK-CLICK, click,-click. Tunnel, valley. Tunnel, valley. CLICK-CLICK, click-click. CLICK-CLICK, click-click. Tunnel, valley.

My service with the British Army was over. I was under American command now.

CLICK-CLICK, click-click.

The English were brave and loyal soldiers, to a man. They had taken all the Germans could dish out, and they had held. I would fight alongside them anytime. Bravo and kudos to the English-fighting man.

Tunnel, valley. Tunnel, valley.

BUT I LIKE AMERICANS! I like American speech, American coffee, American humor, American cooking. The English have tradition, history, and a mountain of culture to their credit. But Americans have AMERICA going for them, and that's enough for me. No tears did I shed when I read the telegram.

Once inside France, the train stopped at some railroad yard. The rear half of the train, holding the British soldiers, was uncoupled and reattached to another locomotive. Our American train went one way, the British train went another. I did not cheer, out of respect to the Englishmen, but I was happy to see them go.

Our All-American train chugged into the town of Allerey, about twenty miles south of Dijon. There were four or five base hospitals here, including the Minnesota Hospital Unit. Imagine my surprise when I got assigned to No. 26 (the Minnesota Unit), and before long I ran into people I knew. Teachers, classmates, nurses, and friends were there from Minneapolis City and University Hospital. It was like coming out of a dark tunnel into the bright sunlight, and for a while I was almost dazed. I took time to write Mother.

Allerey, France, Sunday, Dec. 1, 1918

Dear Mother and All:

I hardly know how to begin or how to finish this letter for I am so happy to be free and among friends again. And fate has favored me this time, for by mere chance our trainload of interned prisoners was sent here where there are several hospital units, and amongst them the

University of Minnesota Base Hospital so that I fell in with friends from the very first. Doctors and Nurses from the Twin Cities and Rochester largely. And who did I meet a few minutes ago but Captain Rudolf of Waseca, Minnesota, U.S.A. Doc arrived a few days ago attached to some hospital unit here. He says he saw you people at home in September, and it is great to get news direct from someone who has been there so recently.

I am tired now after two days and nights on the train across Switzerland and France. My thoughts are so confused by the sunlight of freedom and friends that it is impossible to write much today. I am perfectly well as are all of us, but we are sort of quarantined here for a few days so we do not carry in contagious disease. After that I do not know what will happen—whether we go home soon or not for some time. In any case I will write again and tell you something of where I have been, etc., during the last twelve months. Sufficient to say now that we had a nice trip across Switzerland on Friday from Constance through Zurich, Berne, and Geneva to Belgrade in France, where we were transferred from the Swiss military train to an American hospital train and brought here, arriving this morning. I immediately met legions of friends and feel I have awakened from an awful nightmare. It was a very bitter experience of course though in letters home I did not for the most part mention the unpleasant things because in the first place the German censor would have scratched it out and in the second place you would be no happier for knowing. That is one reason, but only a minor one, why I was sorry that any of my letters were published in the papers.

I hardly know how to tell you to address mail; perhaps until you get further directions it will be best to send it in care of American Express Company, Paris.

Probably this letter will reach you before some I wrote a few days ago, and surely before Christmas with good luck. Love and best wishes to all and remember that the joy of being here now partly compensates for the bitter months that are gone. After all, the great result has been accomplished, the Germans are licked to a frazzle and know it and it should be the happiest Christmas America has ever known for the war is over and right has won because America stepped in at the right time and stepped in hard and I am sure that victory is due as much to the spirit of the people at home as to anything else.

Love to Joe and Grandma and all the kiddies.

Lovingly,
Ben

The world was my oyster. We had won, HAD WON the Great War, the War to End All Wars. Mighty Germany, threat to all the world, had been tamed, and *I* had been part of it. And here, among friends, I seemed to walk on air.

Then I got sick.

It hit me when I was doing a little sightseeing in Dijon. Chills started running up and down my back, my forehead felt hot, so I checked into a hotel to rest. Two days passed, I got worse, pretty soon I could hardly get out of bed. Movement of any kind set off a throbbing pain in both temples. Each limb ached as if the muscles had been pummeled with an iron rod. Food did not interest me. My throat was on fire. This was no regular cold. If I stayed in my hotel room, alone, I'd probably die. God help me if I had "the Spanish sickness," as they were calling the Spanish influenza. Near delirium, I dragged myself into a nearby American Base Hospital.

A medical captain gave me a good going over. He checked off my physical findings, my complaints. The diagnosis was clear to me even if it weren't to him.

"Lieutenant Gallagher, you have the Spanish influenza. We'll put you in our officers' ward and see if we can't set you to rights again." The captain had the automatic smile, the necessary optimism of a good clinician. His "bedside manner," as we called it, was professional and friendly. All this was to his credit, but I wondered whether all that "bedside manner" would do me a lick of good. Dead was dead, no matter how "nice" your doctor.

"What's my temperature?" I asked. It had to be sky-high.

"104.5," he said, flatly. God Almighty. Another degree or two and my kidneys would shut down, then my brain, my heart . . .

It's said, "a little knowledge is a bad thing." That certainly applied to me. We had buried people at Villingen, young, strong people, who had succumbed to Spanish flu. And I was not particularly strong. The poison gas in March had damaged my lungs; the trench fever must have weakened me some, and many months of a prison diet had thinned me. And there was no specific *treatment* for the Spanish flu. You sweated it out, recovered, or you died. That was it. You lived, or you died. At the time, the Spanish flu was raging across Europe, people were dying by the thousands. Some compared it to the Black Death of the Middle Ages. Religious zealots were calling it the will of Divine Providence, punishing a world that slaughtered its young men in a senseless war. I called it a bad viral infection, striking down an undernourished, weakened population. And I was both undernourished and weak.

In my internship at Minneapolis, in Chichester, and at the Front, I had treated many people with high fevers. Oftentimes these patients would get "delirious," thrashing around in bed, calling out to people, hallucinating. I had often wondered what "delirium" actually was. As I lay in that bed, soaking in sweat, aching all over, I wondered if I, too, would become delirious.

It didn't happen, I slept a lot. Hallucinations never came to me, a lot of thoughts raced through my head. My "mind's eye" saw a lot of things, but I never for a minute thought they were real. I knew I was in a hospital bed in Dijon, France. The thoughts came in no particular order.

—A woman crying on a sidewalk, lost bread, hungry children, falling bombs.

—Oswald Bradley holding down a man as I wrapped a gashed thigh wound. "Steady, lad, steady," Bradley says.

—Lieutenant Enbanks snoring above me, the bunk sagging.

—Major Jones congratulating us on joining the British Army.

—Ka-pow! The man with subcutaneous emphysema blowing his head off with a rifle in the mouth.

—Durso and I throwing our "boleros" over the electrical wires.

—"Vive La France!" I say, and a Parisian café erupts.

—Tat-tat-tat-tat! The man in front of me falls, I pick him up.

—RRRRRrrr RRRRRrrr! I look over my shoulder, a German plan swoops in to get me.

—*"Ich bin ein Rheinländer, ein guter Mann,"* a big white-haired German carrying my men with tender, loving care.

—A German guard on the train laughing, his mouth full of food.

—George Cave's breathing stops.

—George Cave's breathing stops.

—George Cave's breathing stops.

That thought got stuck, like a grammaphone record skipping over the same spot.

—George Cave's breathing stops.

—George Cave's breathing stops.

I closed my eyes extra hard, tried to think of something else, something pleasant—that night in Paris, the American girls on the platform. No luck. After a while, I must have fallen asleep again, for it seemed like hours had passed—the angle of the sun coming in the windows had changed. The recurrent thought about George Cave ended, and I was once again able to think more clearly.

Would George Cave haunt me the rest of my life?

They injected me with a lot of medicines, including some quinine. That may or may not have helped, but it felt good to know they were trying. Probably what saved me was my nurse, a nice girl from Philadelphia, who kept lifting my head and spooning broth into me. She prevented me from getting dehydrated.

After the fever subsided, I was completely sapped of energy, more tired than I'd ever been. Twenty-three hours a day I slept, getting up only to relieve my bladder. The hospital threw some gala Christmas party, I slept through it.

"Lieutenant Gallagher, you can return to duty," the kindly Captain told me. I'd been in the hospital for eight days. I was still weak as a newborn kitten, but I was glad to be getting out. The Captain still showed me his best doctor manners, but something was bothering him; he couldn't meet my eyes. His own eyes looked puffy. Was he getting sick?

"Oh Captain, one thing before I go. I wanted to thank that nurse, sorry, I forgot her name, the one from Philadelphia. I *swear* she kept me alive. She kept spooning the broth into me. What was her name? *Annie?* That was it. *Annie,"* I said.

The Captain looked down at his clipboard, still avoiding my look.

I couldn't read his meaning, so I went on jabbering, "She's not on duty today? Well, could you at least thank her for me. You know I'm in the Medical Corps myself, I've seen a few nurses in my day, but Annie went above and beyond the call of duty. She saved me." It felt so good to be able to talk without the pain in my throat.

"I'm sorry, Lieutenant Gallagher," the Captain said.

"Sorry?" I asked. He looked up now, his bedside cool and professionalism gone. Tears were falling down his cheeks. Sniffing, he wiped his face with his hands.

"She's dead. Annie Abeyta was your nurse. She herself contracted the Spanish flu three days ago. She developed overwhelming pneumonia. We buried her this morning." He sniffed again, then fumbled in his pocket and pulled out a handkerchief. Without saying another word he turned and went down the hospital corridor, holding his clipboard under his arm, and blowing his nose. His bedside manner had not saved Annie.

God Almighty, Annie was dead. And *she* had been caring for *me!* Why had God taken her and spared me?

The war was still killing people, good people.

The Minnesota Unit had me on light-duty for a couple weeks (swabbing a few sore throats, changing some dressings, nothing too difficult). Gone was the initial thrill of being among one's own countrymen. It was time to go *home*, *everyone* had it on their mind. But the wheels of transport that work so fast when going *forward*, did not move so fast in reverse.

America and the Allies had thrown together all their shipping might to get us over to Europe. More ships, more trains, a *war* was going on! The enemy was at the gates of Paris! Damn the torpedoes, full speed ahead! Now, the situation was the opposite.

The war was won. Over. There were a million or so men who wanted to get back to Chicago, Biloxi, Dallas, and Baltimore. Loved ones were waiting in Minnesota, Nebraska, and California. No matter how painful our separation from our families, there was just not the *impetus*, the *need*, to move us fast enough back to America. A painful waiting game began.

Fortune smiled on me, I got across the Channel to England. But once there I was becalmed, waiting in London for some word, *any* word, on how I could get home.

My billet was a small hotel not far from the British Museum. Two beds were in my room. They told me another American was coming soon, but weren't sure who it would be.

I had no medical duties, and had regained most of my energy. Bored, one day I decided to take in the sights of the British Museum. Most interesting to me was the Rosetta Stone, a large block with three different languages on it, including Egyptian hieroglyphics. Some clever French fellow compared the different languages and somehow "cracked" the code of the hieroglyphics.

When I returned to the hotel room, I noted that my new companion had arrived. The bed looked rumpled, the pillow had a dent in it, as if someone had taken a nap. A bag of clothes was on the floor, with the initials A.H. on it. Whoever A.H. was, he was nowhere to be found. I went to the American Expeditionary Force Repatriation Office, to see if I could find a way home.

A.H., A.H., Andrew Harrigan, Anthony Hilldebrand, Alex Houston. I toyed with various names that would fit "A.H." as I rode a double-decker bus to the Repatriation Office. With any luck "A.H." would be a nice fellow, someone I would like. After all we might be stuck in that hotel room a long time, waiting for transport home.

London itself was busy, traffic humming, busses and taxis going everywhere. It was winter now, gloomy and rainy, but at least the gloom of war was gone. Men in uniform were still in abundance, many, poor lads, getting around on crutches. Blind men and amputees were begging on street corners. They all had on the khaki uniform of the British Army.

The Repatriation Office was cavernous, with sheets of paper hanging on the walls. Lists of dead, lists of wounded, lists of missing hung down all the way to the floor. Announcements to various units, orders, equipment lists—everything imaginable that had to do with a million-man contingent was up on those walls. But one list and one list alone interested me—ship assignments. Ship assignments home.

Amidst the bustle, another fellow was also focusing his attention on that very same list. He was about fifty feet away when I first saw him. Dark hair, dark eyes, he was standing on tiptoe, trying to read something. He had the look of a vaudeville singer, the kind of look that made girls swoon. His uniform hung a little slack, the English cooking hadn't agreed with *him* either. I wanted to shout at him, but, no, better to surprise him with a joke. A.H. wouldn't have it any other way.

"I say old chap, you don't need a ship to take you back to the colonies, you could always swim." My English accent was pretty good now, if I did say so myself.

"Ben!" Same old Abe, big smile. Haskell threw his arms around me and gave me a big bear hug. Here he was in the flesh, alive and kicking. No German had killed him, nor had any jealous husband. It was a miracle.

"Abe! I thought sure you'd have become Belgian royalty by now. Maybe even had a few little princes of your own." In Abe's letter, so many months before, he'd mentioned that he was stationed near some castle—home to a Belgian princess or something.

"Oh that," he waved his hand away, "never did meet up with that Belgian countess. Too bad, too. I could have gotten used to living in a castle."

Boy it was good to see him. Boy oh boy. I felt like a kid in a candy store.

"Don't tell me you wangled your way into my room at the hotel, Abe," I said. A.H. The initials. It took no Sherlock Holmes now to solve "the mystery of the initials."

Abe grinned that big, winning grin of his. "There are ways, Ben, there are always ways."

Clever man, Abe Haskell. It's good he was on our side.

"How'd you like it up in Belgium, Abe?" I only wrote him the one letter, I should have written him more.

"Oh, not too bad. Not as bad as it was for a lot of folks. We were right next to a Belgian unit. Tough bunch, too. With all this hoopla about us Americans, and the French with their Verdun, the British with the Somme, a lot of people forget the plucky Belgians up there, keeping the Hun at bay. Didn't matter that the Germans had 95 percent of his country occupied, King Albert of Belgium never gave up. Unsung hero, he was," Abe said.

"You know, Ben, at the start of the war, they hardly had any army at all," Abe continued. "But they slowed the Germans just enough, in 1914, to save Paris. And they paid for it, too. In nearly every Belgian town, Ben, there are long rows of graves marked *'Fusillés par les Allemands'* (shot by the Germans). The Germans shot hostages, anytime they were fired on. Fifty hostages shot for each German killed. FIFTY! Men, women, children—didn't matter to the Germans, as long as the number added up to 50."

We stood there for a while. Just stood there, thinking about all those slaughtered Belgians. All around us, a beehive of American soldiers jostled past, looking at the lists on the walls, going in and out of offices.

"Why aren't you back in America by now?" I asked, changing the subject.

"Not enough ships for all of us. I'm just hanging around, like you, and about a million other guys." It seemed there were a million in this building alone.

With nothing better to do, we strolled around London.

"I heard you got captured, Ben," Abe said.

I filled him in.

"How about you, Abe, tell me more about your time in Belgium."

He filled me in. Damned if he didn't *get* a medal! Just like he had wanted to when we started out way back in Minneapolis.

"You're going to impress them with that medal, Abe."

"It was less heroic that you might imagine, Ben. They must have had a surplus of medals or something. But we don't have to tell Brenda or Ruth that, do we?" Always with the girls, that Abe, always with the girls. Abe had tried to minimize his heroics, but even in his toned-down version, it sounded like Abe had kept his cool under some pretty intense fire. Details I couldn't extract from him, and I didn't push him. He no more relished combat memories than I did.

"So what's next?" I asked.

"We're never going to get home unless we get to Liverpool first. All the ships leave from there. Let me see what I can do," Abe said, a glint in his eye. If anyone could work the "system" and get us home, Abe could.

"What about after we get home?" Abe asked.

"I don't know, I feel so rusty after being stuck in that damn prison camp for so long doing nothing. Maybe I'll try for a surgery fellowship at the Mayo Clinic. How about you, Abe?"

"I don't know. Plenty of time to decide. Now let me get to work on our tickets home," Abe said.

Two weeks later, Abe and I checked into a Liverpool hotel.

"So far, so good, Abe. I owe you." He *had* worked a miracle. We were one step closer to the Promised Land, home.

"Fear not, Ben, I will not let the moss grow under us here, either. One quick trip to the transportation office should get us on the next ship out. How much money do you have?" he asked.

"Oh, I don't know. I drew a little back pay . . . " My pitiful treasury was about to get raided.

"Do you want to go home?" Abe asked, seeing my hesitation. The implication was obvious. Abe would need to grease some palms if we were to get home anytime soon.

"Yes," I dug out my wallet, "is this all on the up and up, Abe?" I asked, trying to hang on to a shred of decency and honesty.

"Ben Gallagher! You accuse me of bribery." Abe had a stricken look on his face. "You accuse me of using influence and gifts to gain an unfair advantage! I am shocked and appalled." No Shakespearean actor, not even Cahill, had ever put on such a performance.

I forked out everything I could afford.

"You are wise beyond your years, Ben Gallagher. The room is yours to do with what you will. This may take me all day," Abe said.

He walked out the door.

There was nothing, but nothing to do. Liverpool was just as gloomy and cheerless as the first time I saw it. I opened up my field journal, to make an entry for the day. A small chit of paper fluttered out and landed on the floor.

Mrs. George Cave
Rock Ferry
Cheshire, England

I put my hand to my forehead. How had I forgotten to write George Cave's mother? I sat right down at the desk and wrote.

Dear Mrs. Cave,

I am an American Medical officer who was attached to the 2/5 Gloster Battalion in the 61st Division, and as I was with your son George after he was wounded and captured, I am taking the liberty now of writing to you. I too was captured that day at Marcelcave, March 28th, and was moved back with the wounded men, including George, to a German Field Hospital where there were many other British wounded.

No doubt you have long ago received information through official channels, but on the day before he died, George gave me your address and asked me, when I returned from Germany, to write to you. He seemed to suffer very little from his wounds during those days he lived, and his attitude at all times marked him as the truest kind of soldier who, knowing that he had made the supreme sacrifice for his country, dies happy in the consciousness that he had given all a man could give.

He was buried, with services by a priest, in the little war graveyard along the old Roman road, about 10 or 12 miles east of Amiens. With a map perhaps I could locate the place more exactly. I expect to sail from here in a few days for America, where my home address is Waseca, Minnesota, and if there is any further information I can give you, I shall be very glad to do so.

> Sincerely,
> (signed)
> B.J. Gallagher
> 1st Lt. Med. Corps. U.S. Army

I went down to the desk and posted the letter immediately.

In the afternoon, there was a light tap on my door. In the hall stood a gentleman of about 50 in a tweed jacket. Next to him was a young girl of thirteen or so. Her eyes were puffy and red, she kept sniffing.

"Dr. Gallagher?" the man asked.

"Yes, I'm Dr. Gallagher. Please, come in." The room had only two small beds, one chair, and a desk. Everyone stood, though I invited them to sit.

"Pardon the intrusion, sir. I'm George Cave," the man said.

My mind reeled, was this some kind of a joke! The George Cave I knew was dead.

"Senior," he added, seeing my reaction. Of course, it was George Cave's father.

"Mr. Cave, I . . ." hadn't I just sent the letter this morning?

"Rock Ferry is just up the railway a bit, just a few steps away from here. The hotel clerk knew George, they went to school together, you see. When he saw the letter, he sent it to us straight away. That's how we got here so quick," Mr. Cave explained.

The man continued, "And this is Sally, George's . . . my son's sister." She nodded her head toward me, and sniffed.

Everyone in the room relaxed a little and sat down, I on the chair, the man and girl on the bed. For the life of me, I couldn't think of what to do next. There was nothing in the room to offer them in the way of refreshment or food. Then, I remembered a chocolate bar I had put in my coat pocket. I offered it to Sally.

"Oh, I do so love chocolate. Daddy, do you think it would be too awful if I had a little taste?" Sally asked. He nodded his assent.

While Sally nibbled—taking small bites, trying to make it last a long time, her father spoke. "Dr. Gallagher, your letter to us about George came rather like a thunderbolt out of the clear sky."

"You hadn't heard? Surely, the Red Cross . . .," I was stammering.

"No. No word came from them. No word came from anybody. All we got was a 'Missing in Action' telegram. That's it. 'Missing in Action.' No further word," Mr. Cave said.

"Letters we sent. Telegrams. Everything. Wrote to the Army, the Red Cross, everybody. And the months, they passed. Come November, the war ends, and our fellows start coming back. First the chaps from the Front—no word from them—then the prisoners come back. We thought surely some prisoner from his unit might have seen him." Mr. Cave paused.

I should have written before, why had I forgotten?

"Closest we came," he went on, "was a fellow from the Bucks. He recalled seeing George, lying on a stretcher outside the town of Marcelcave in France. The fellow thought George looked dead."

"What day was that?" I asked.

"March 28th." The day of my capture. The start of my purgatory in the cellar.

"Your son got good treatment, Mr. Cave. The Germans treated their prisoners fairly, never sparing morphine when a man needed it," I said.

"He needed it? A lot of it, Georgie did?" This from Sally. "Did he hurt much?"

"Yes, some. But I was right there with him. He was comfortable. He was never alone," I said.

Sally began to cry, full out, no holding back. Tears were streaming down her face, onto her dress, onto the chocolate bar. Her nose stuffed up. I offered a handkerchief. Chocolate was starting to smear her dress.

"The missus," Mr. Cave spoke, "has taken terrible sick with this, Dr. Gallagher. After the telegram came, the 'Missing in Action' telegram, she just hasn't been herself. No sleep can she get, no rest. Wanders the house at night. And never a bite to eat. Dr. Gallagher, I wonder if you might see fit to looking her over. Maybe she needs some heart medicines, or maybe, maybe she just needs to hear from you, hear how it was with her George." Mr. Cave's eyes were puffy and bloodshot. He, too, had not been sleeping much.

"I'll be happy to see her."

The train took us to Rock Ferry, past row houses, and a few farms amidst a bleak, midwinter landscape. Sally tried to get the chocolate stain out of her dress. After regaining her composure, she told me about her schoolwork. Mr. Cave sat with his thoughts.

It was a small affair—the Cave home—a one-story brick, with a nondescript yard and hedge. Lace hung in the windows. The weather was cloudy and misty. This was an English working-class neighborhood.

Mr. Cave ushered me through the front door of his home, before disappearing to a back room. Sally went into the kitchen to brew up tea. A picture of George, in military uniform, was on the mantelpiece. He had long, thin fingers. In the corner of the living room stood the largest piece of furniture, a piano.

Sally reentered the room, carrying a tea serving.

"Tea? I'd offer you sugar, but, I'm afraid we're a bit short still."

She set up my cup. "George was quite the piano player." Wiggling her fingers in mock play, she said, "He loved the American tunes so much, the ones the Negroes play. Ragtime, isn't it? Maple Leaf Rag, he liked so much, by a Mr. Joplin."

She sipped her tea. "Would you like to see his room?"

That caught me off guard. I didn't really want to, but could think of no reason to refuse, so I found myself accompanying her down a hallway to the last bedroom on the end. There, I entered George Cave's world.

A quilt lay at the foot of his bed. Adventure stories lined a small cutout bookcase at the head of the bed—Jules Verne, Robinson Crusoe, Ivanhoe, the Knights of the Round Table. Two trophies sat on his dresser, one for best orator, another for best debater. A certificate on the wall commended him for best essay—"How the British Empire Helped the Heathens." A closet door stood ajar. Out the window I could see a whitewashed fence, covered with weathered vine. This was George's view.

Sally stood, holding her cup and saucer. "I suppose we'll need to give his clothes to the church or something. I imagine there are a lot of closets like this," she opened the door completely. "A lot of closets, full of clothes looking for their rightful owners."

Suddenly, I imagined George Cave's clothes springing to life, going out in search of the body that used to fill the sleeves, the legs, the chest. His clothes flying across the Channel, to France, to find him. And all the clothes of all the young men who died springing to life, too. Closets in Paris, Berlin, London, New York; dressers in Kansas City, Lyon, Nuremberg and Glasgow, opening up and sending out a ghostly army of clothes, looking for their owners. Some of the clothes would sink into the ocean, some into the chalky soil of the Somme, or the mud of Flanders. And George Cave's clothes would wander to a Field Hospital graveyard, along the old Roman road east of Amiens. There, his clothes would melt into the ground, disappearing forever.

We left his room and closed the door.

Mr. Cave, waiting in the hallway, led me to his wife. She was lying on their bed, propped up by pillows, here eyes as puffy red as Sally's. In an instant, I knew the diagnosis—grief—the grief of a mother who's lost her child. Her only son.

"Thank you, Dr. Gallagher. It was so kind of you to write us about George." She dabbed at her eyes, and blew her nose.

I sat on the bed.

"George gave me your address the night before he died, asking me to write to you. But I forgot, pure and simple," I confessed.

"You can't imagine how we have worried after George. I kept thinking that he might be lost somewhere, unable to tell people where he lived," Mrs. Cave said.

I took her hand.

"Your son was in a hospital, getting treatment, getting medicine to keep him comfortable. He did not suffer, Mrs. Cave. When the end came, I was there. He closed his eyes, and went to sleep. He was not afraid. His last thoughts were of you."

We sat in silence for several minutes. There was nothing more to say. Mrs. Cave needed no more medicine. She knew her son was at rest, his sufferings over.

"Dr. Gallagher, thank you."

It was raining. George Cave *would* haunt me the rest of my life.

Abe and I were standing at the stern of the returning troopship *Regina*.

"Just a few more hours, Ben. A few more hours and we steam right into New York harbor."

Abe had spent every dime of my money, and had committed us to a responsibility for thousands of dollars worth of medical supplies going on board the *Regina*, in order to get us on the homeward journey.

"You know, Abe, if any of those medical supplies are missing, we have to pay. You know that don't you?" I said. The equipment was worth a fortune, more than I could earn in a year, in TEN years. It had been blackmail, making us take responsibility for it, but it was the only way we could get on that ship.

"True." Abe was nodding, in complete agreement with me, his face deadly serious, but the teeniest little smile had slipped onto his face. He had something up his sleeve.

"And you know about the problems with the keys, right Abe?" I asked, fighting off panic at the thought of working my WHOLE LIFE, just to pay for that equipment.

We had signed for two large chests of medical equipment. One was *locked* and had *no key*, the other was *unlocked* and had *no key*. Each presented a curious dilemma.

"Yes, Ben, I am aware of the interesting problem. Is it better to have a locked chest with no key, or an unlocked chest with no key?" He held his left hand out to represent the locked chest, the right hand out to represent the unlocked chest. He knitted his brow like a Talmudic scholar, wrestling with this difficult question.

"If *anything* is missing, we'll be paying for that stuff for the rest of our lives," I said, working myself into a tizzy. Maybe we should have waited for another ship.

"Mostly true, Ben." Abe held up one finger, as if he, the great savant, had solved this most unsolvable of riddles. Beneath us, the great propellers of the ship churned the water and threw out a great wake.

"*Mostly true?*" I asked.

"Well, Ben, you see. YOU signed that list. So, YOU will be paying for that stuff for the rest of your life." The upraised finger had come down, and was pointing right at me.

"You dog," I said. Months before, when we were crossing the Channel and I had made Abe throw up, he had promised to get me back, and he had just done it. Touché, Abe.

It was pitch black over the ocean, but the *Regina* itself was all lit up. No need for a blackout now. No submarines. No zigzagging.

"I'll tell you what, though, Abe. I'd have signed my own death certificate to get on board this ship." It was cool on deck, but the ship threw off a warmth, possibly the boilers were somewhere nearby.

"That was my next trick, Ben," he winked at me. "Well, I'm turning in. You coming, Ben?"

"No, thanks, Abe. I'm going to stay out here for a while. Night!"

I leaned against the rail and looked down at the wake. Churn, churn, churn. The black water of the North Atlantic turned white and foamy, then seemed to glow as it floated away, all phosphorescence. Overhead, Orion the Hunter, *the* constellation of winter, sank into the west. No clouds obstructed the brilliant, starlit night.

The Great War, my war, was over.

A terrible thought came to me, standing on that deck, looking at the water, the ship's wake, the stars. This war, the events of the last year or so, probably represented the high point of my life, or certainly the most significant point in my life. A medical career awaited me at home, to be sure, and there was nothing wrong with that. Some day, I might be a husband, a father. And those events would all have their challenges, their triumphs, and tragedies. But nothing would have the dimension, the depth of purpose, that this war had for me. It was, in every sense, a crusade to save the world from barbarism. And *I* had been in that crusade. What, in the remainder of my life, would compare to it?

Parts of the war had exhilarated me! I never tired of hearing the song, "Over There." Each time it nearly brought tears to my eyes.

"'Cause the Yanks are Coming, the Yanks are Coming!'"

That's right, the Yanks Are coming, and I'm ONE OF THOSE YANKS! The power in those words!

And the *friendships* I forged in the war. Could any relationship in the civilian world compare with the bond I made with Captain Craig in that awful dugout near La Vacquerie? The British officers may have been standoffish, but we were in that frozen tin shelter together, as close in spirit as people could be. When we were running across that open field and the man ahead of me was shot and fell, I picked him up by the good arm without a second thought, for he was my comrade, my friend, my brother at that moment. If I passed him now, in the street, and he asked me for a dime, I probably would ignore him, so different are the bonds in civilian and army life. On the battlefield, I would have died for him. On Main Street, I probably wouldn't have given him money for a cup of coffee.

The war itself had seemed like a game at times, from Abe Haskell shouting to me, "We're in!" to General White saying, "Well boys, the Boche are going to attack here in the morning, and I hope he does, for he will get an awful drubbing." It sounded like a kid's game—choose sides and see who wins. See who's better at killing. See who could deal death the fastest.

Before the war, death had a logic to it. An old man would die at home, or a TB patient would die in the hospital. Old people, frail people died.

No one at the Front was old and frail. They were young men, robust men. And they died. A batch on the road to La Vacquerie, one blown to bits in front of me, some falling near Cressy, a lot in Marcelcave. By ones, and twos, and dozens, they died. Sometimes they died fast, in an instant. Sometimes they took longer, like George Cave. And always, they were young.

The sun was coming up over the ocean. It lined up perfectly with the ship's wake. The "dawn's early light," as it said in our national anthem.

My own concerns seemed selfish, insipid. The Great War had been a crusade, and now I had no crusade. The Great War had forged close relationships, and now I wouldn't have such close relationships. The price for this crusade, for my relationships? Death. Mutilation. Blindness. Hunger. The destruction of farms, villages, a whole generation of men. Who was I to mourn the passing of the war?

And it wasn't just the soldiers at the Front who suffered. The tragedy did not end when a man disappeared in a shell burst, or collapsed with a bullet through his brain, or stiffened with tetanus and stopped breathing.

Death in the trenches, in No Man's Land, in the field hospital, was expected. Men assumed they would die there, and they did. The *real* tragedy was at home. Mrs. Cave did not want a hero for a son, a medal for the mantelpiece, or a footnote in some history book. She sought no fame, no glory, no riches. A crusade meant little to her. New friendships meant little to her. The rise and fall of great empires meant little to her. She wanted to see her son, to hold him. But she could not, for George was dead, and buried on the road to Amiens.

Mrs. Cave would grow old, and die someday, as would I. But not so George Cave. George Cave would not grow old, would not bounce a grandchild on his knee and tell a tale of long ago, for George would be forever young. Nineteen years old forever. And I would never forget him. I would tell my children about him, if I ever had children.

Whistles blew on factories, and boats by the hundreds greeted us in the harbor, as our ship passed the Statue of Liberty. Sister Marie Francis' prayer must have worked, for Lady Liberty had kept the torch lit for the world, and she kept it lit for me.

It was Lincoln's Birthday, a gala day. And all New York, all America was in celebration. Myself, I was glad to be back, but could not rejoice, after all I had seen.

EPILOGUE

Ben Gallagher received the Military Medal from the government of Great Britain for meritorious duty during the Great War.

It took the largest offensive in history to capture Dr. Ben Gallagher. Margaret Manahan captured him, and never fired a shot. She worked in the Medical Records Department of Mayo Clinic, where Ben was completing his training. Soon after meeting her, Ben Gallagher became much more diligent about signing all his records, and she found all sorts of reasons to visit him up on the wards. He married her on April 12, 1921. Five children blessed their union.

Ben continued his surgical training, then carried out a long practice in his hometown of Waseca. As a small town surgeon for over forty years, he did everything, from in-home deliveries, to an appendectomy on a farmer's kitchen table, to perforated ulcers, bowel obstructions, bad farm accidents.

Two paintings graced the wall of Ben Gallagher's guest room. They showed dark trees, gray rocks, and a reflecting stream.

In 1949, Ben suffered a stroke, recovered, and took up his practice once again. The people of Waseca County honored him with a Father of the Year award, as well as a citation for his "outstanding" career.

1960 brought recurrent bouts of shortness of breath, probably residual pulmonary damage from the poison gas attack of 1918. Saying, "When the ball game is over, you leave the field," he retired.

One October morning in 1962, he did not wake up. For four days people came to say good-bye. They came by the hundreds, each with a memory to share.

"He saved my daughter's life, here she is all grown up."

"He fixed my arm, see it? I thought I was going to lose it."

"He delivered my babies, all fifteen of them."

On the fifth day, Ben was buried in the Catholic cemetery on the Minnesota prairie south of Waseca, within sight of his birthplace.

The Story Behind the Story

My grandfather, Bernard J. Gallagher, M.D., wrote the original memoir you are reading. My father, William B. Gallagher, M.D., and late aunt Margaret Spoo (née Gallagher) rediscovered his journal, and edited it. Excerpts appeared in the June 1965 edition of *American Heritage* under the title "A Yank in the BEF." Excerpts of this journal also appeared in Lyn MacDonald's book, *Voices of the Great War 1914–1918*. Mary Malloy provided extensive editorial help on this final edited version of that journal.

Christopher J. Gallagher, M.D.

Memo from co-editor William B. Gallagher to his sister Margaret Spoo after her death in 1981:

Good night, Sis; working on this project with you was one of the sustained high points of my life. In it, we rediscovered our parents—and each other. You did a good job.

Say hello to them.

—